GERALD RONSON:
LEADING FROM THE FRONT

GERALD RONSON
LEADING FROM THE FRONT
My Story
WITH JEFFREY ROBINSON

MAINSTREAM
PUBLISHING

EDINBURGH AND LONDON

*All proceeds due to Gerald Ronson from this book
will be donated to the Gerald Ronson Foundation
for children's education*

First published in Great Britain in 2009 by
MAINSTREAM PUBLISHING COMPANY
(EDINBURGH) LTD
7 Albany Street
Edinburgh EH1 3UG

ISBN 9781845965099 (cased)
ISBN 9781845965303 (paperback)

A catalogue record for this book is available
from the British Library

Typeset in Century Gothic and Concorde

Printed in Great Britain by
Clays Ltd, St Ives plc

This book is dedicated to my family

ACKNOWLEDGEMENTS

There are several people I would like to thank for their help with this book. I begin with my wife Gail and our four daughters, Lisa, Amanda, Nicole and Hayley. Then there is my brother Laurence, my former deputy chief executive at Heron Alan Goldman and my current co-joint managing directors Peter Ferrari and Jonathan Goldstein. I would also like to thank my PA Kay Strulovitch, my secretary Emily Wright and my former secretary Paulene Clark. For their input, I say thank you to Lee Polisano, Cahit Atasoy, Antonio Eraso, Lord Greville Janner of Braunstone and Cyril Paskin. I am grateful to Jonny Geller at the agents Curtis Brown and everyone at Mainstream Publishing. Finally, thank you, as well, to Jeffrey Robinson.

Gerald Ronson, London, 2009

CONTENTS

PREFACE

I think of myself as a simple man. What you see is what you get. Although my wife Gail disagrees. She says I'm a complex character. She says what you see depends on what day of the week you're looking, what mood I'm in, how things have gone at the office, how things are going in our Community, how things are going for our daughters, Lisa, Amanda, Nicole and Hayley, and how things are going for their children. Gail knows me better than anybody because she's had to live with me for more than 40 years. But I'm not that way in my own mind.

She also says that I'm a creature of habit. My family and friends agree that I am the most predictable character they know. But that's OK with me, because I don't like change. Maybe other people need change all the time, which is why they have four houses, five cars and three ex-wives. Not me. Gail and I live in the same house where we have lived since the late 1960s. I work six and a half days a week, the way I have since the '50s. And even my office is pretty much the way it was when I first moved in there in the mid-'60s.

Call me old-fashioned if you like. And my family do. They say, 'How can you not want to use a computer?' But I'm not interested in computers. I don't need one. My pen works. I can write things down. My secretaries print out my emails and I dictate my responses. I don't have a BlackBerry, blueberry, or whatever those things are called, because I'm not interested in them either. My daughters are always asking me, 'How can you live without all this stuff?' I turn the question around and ask them, 'Why do I need it?' They tell me so I can keep in touch. But I can pick a phone up wherever I am and talk to whoever I want, and people can always ring me. I'm actually a very accessible person. As it happens, I do take a portable phone with me whenever I'm out of the country – Gail is forever correcting me, saying, 'You should call it a mobile' – but I only use it when I'm abroad. I never carry one around with me in England. In fact, they're banned in the office, at least when I'm about. Portable phones irritate me. It would take a very brave person to pull one out of their pocket in a meeting with me. I don't know which would be out the door faster, them or the phone. Maybe I'm just getting old.

The contraption I work with most is my dictation machine. Thoughts come into my head and I record them – Why haven't I heard from this person? Are those contracts in yet? How much is this thing going to cost? – so that I'll remember or one of my secretaries can send a note. But then, I do acknowledge that this is the twenty-first century and when I get into my car every morning, it actually says to me, 'Good morning, Mr Ronson.'

So I'm just an old-fashioned guy who is a creature of habit who works six and a half days a week. When I'm tired, Gail says to me, 'Take the day off. What are you going to do today that you couldn't do tomorrow?' And she is perfectly right. But it's discipline. That's how I am. Anyway, I don't do what I do because I have to. I go to work because I love what I do, even if it means 12- or 13-hour days. I sometimes think that for a fellow my age to be working this hard isn't too clever. But I haven't lost any zest for business. As long as I love doing what I'm doing – even if other people think I'm mad – then I'll keep doing it until I've had enough. Except that I can't see myself having enough, because in the back of my mind there's something driving me. Maybe it's a bit of insecurity and ego. It certainly isn't the money, because the more I make, the more I give away.

I inherited my work ethic from my father. He started at six in the morning and went through to eight or nine at night and only took off Sunday afternoon. I began working that way with him in the family's furniture factory when I was just 14½ years old, and being constantly at his side was the best business education in the world. He took me everywhere with him so that I could watch, listen and absorb. He believed in me and wanted me to be his clone, hopefully not with his bad points but with all his good ones. It would then be up to me to succeed or fail. If I had the ability, which he thought I did, and if I was willing to work hard, which I was, and if I shared his passion to succeed, which I still do, then I'd move the business forward, maybe even better than he did.

After a few years, when I was around 17, he started saying to me, 'You take care of it.' He'd send me somewhere on my own, like to one of our bank managers, to secure a couple of hundred thousand pounds for some development. That was an awful lot of money in 1957. And when I was just 17, old-time bank managers – who were pretty damn difficult to do business with anyway – were downright frightening. Dad knew each of them well because he was a drinking man and the way you did business in those days was over a boozy lunch or, later, in the pub. He would ring up the banker to say that he was sending me along and then add, 'Give Gerald a hard time.'

I'd sit there on the other side of the bank manager's big desk and he would be like a headmaster. I couldn't outsmart him and I couldn't be as worldly wise as him, so I out-homeworked him. I'd be up half the night before going over everything – what I was going to say, how I was going to say it, how I would answer if he asked me this, that or the other thing. I would never go without being 100 per cent prepared. I wasn't going to make an arse of myself. That's how Dad taught me to do business.

He'd been a champion boxer, my old man, fighting for the Jewish Lads' Brigade, and maybe that's how I learned to think that being successful in business is like being a boxer. The way you stay a champion is to go to the gym every day. Whether you're running or working out with weights, you have to keep training. When you're older, you have more experience – which is a great asset if you're fighting a novice – but even then you have to keep up your stamina, because the older you get, the tougher it is to go 15 rounds, and the longer you stay in the ring, the greater the chance you'll get hurt. You have to be good enough to deal with your opponent in four or five rounds. It's the same thing in business. You need experience to spot opportunities and to stay focused so you can analyse those opportunities and not waste your time running around in circles with things that can never really be a deal.

Also like a boxer, you have to understand that, at some point, you're going to get hit and when you get hit, it's going to hurt. You may even get knocked down. I've been up and I've been down, and, yes, sometimes the referee was starting to count me out, but I refused to stay down. I stood up, dusted myself off and kept on punching.

Staying in the ring hurts. Losing hurts even more. A few years ago, my managers lost me a substantial sum of money. When I was younger, I would have been very agitated, but at my age I can afford to be philosophical. Am I happy about it? No. But you have to accept the fact that if you're in business, you will make judgement calls, and sometimes you will make money and sometimes you will lose money. Managers can screw up or the market can screw up. The trick is to put it behind you and move forward. Make a mistake once, you learn. Make the same mistake twice, you need to analyse why you did it as stupidly as the first time. Make the same mistake a third time, then you are a schmuck.

Success is not a spectator sport. And real life is the toughest school of all.

In 1990, I went to prison for six months. Some people say I did what I did out of greed, but that's not right, because there was no personal gain. Maybe, sometimes, the excitement of the game drags you into things and you don't realise the people you're dealing with are dishonest. That's life.

Two years later, I lost approximately £500 million of my own money.

Those two very important moments in my life were unrelated. It was the Guinness affair show trial that sent me to prison, I say unfairly. And it was the Savings and Loan crash in the States that nearly cost me my company.

Either one of these setbacks might have destroyed me. Instead, I came out of both stronger. I don't recommend going to prison and I don't recommend nearly going broke, but sometimes you need things to happen to you in life that are a leveller. Sometimes when you're very successful, you think you walk on water. Life gets out of focus. You think you're more important than you are. You become selfish and a little arrogant. It's getting knocked down in the ring that puts things back into focus. You find out who you really are as a person, what you really believe in, what you want to do with your life and who your real friends are.

Disaster and tragedy steel you. You can't go through real life experiences like that and think they're not going to make a difference. Fortunately, they haven't scarred me externally, although there is no doubt they have left some internal scars. I know they have made me more aware. Have they made me more humble? Perhaps not, because I don't think I'm a humble person. But they have made me into what I am today, for better or worse.

As I said, what you see is what you get.

What could be simpler than that?

CHAPTER 1

....

I AM WHAT I AM

I am what I am, the grandson of Jewish immigrants who came to England around the turn of the last century from what was then the Pale of Settlement in Russia.

Anti-Semitism in the form of strict laws imposed on where Jews could live, how they could live and what they could do already existed in Russia in the eighteenth century, under Catherine the Great. Jews were taken out of villages and moved to land specifically set aside for them. It was a type of giant prison for nearly four million Jews who were forced to live under crowded and cramped conditions in an area stretching through what is today Lithuania, Belarus, Poland, Moldova, the Ukraine and western Russia. Jews could earn a living and support their families, but only in ways authorised by the state, and many professions were banned. Life was hard, borders were tightly controlled and attempting to leave the Pale was a criminal offence. But that didn't stop many people from hiring agents to smuggle them out. They went to ports like Hamburg and from there on to Britain or the United States.

By 1905, more than a million Jews had escaped Russia, about a tenth of them coming to Britain. Among them was my paternal grandfather, Maurice Aaronson, who was a cabinetmaker by trade.

A quiet, likeable, strictly Orthodox man, he might possibly have put up with conditions in the Pale had he not married an assertive woman called Betty – she must have had a Russian name but we never knew it – who decided that Russia was no place for them. Like so many others, she'd heard stories about 'paradise', which meant America and Britain, and that's where she wanted to be. But getting out together was difficult and dangerous, so Maurice left on his own in 1905 and headed for Britain. He landed at Tilbury and made his way to the East End of London because someone told him that the Jews lived there. My grandmother joined him a few months later.

Maurice had no difficulty finding work. His first job was on the bench in a furniture workshop, working all hours, though what he was paid for his work was pitiful. He and Betty had four sons. My father, Henry Aaronson, was the third. My grandfather was frequently in dire straits in his early years and his family was raised in real poverty, but my dad and his brothers learned a good deal about the furniture trade from their father. They set out to better themselves, scraped their pennies together and by the time they were young men had their own small factory at Old Ford, Bethnal Green. They made mainly chairs and tables, and dressing tables.

The Aaronsons lived in a tenement block at Old Nichol Street, Shoreditch. My father used to tell me what a treat it was in fine weather to sit in the local park, away from the heat and the smells of the tenement, and listen to the band that sometimes played music there. His friends were made at the local prayer house, where he was a faithful worshipper.

Half a mile away, the Raine family were living in similar circumstances. The families did not know each other, but the Raine family story was very much the same as the Aaronsons'.

Louis Raine was born Leib Shimelevich-Davidovich Rein, citizen of Davgeli in the Sventsiany District, Vil'no Province, in 1870. On his internal passport for the Russian Empire, which we have, his occupation is given as coachman, and in the space for his signature it says that he is illiterate.

Actually, he was a drosky driver, the equivalent of the horse-drawn cab driver in Britain. He married a rather timid woman named Khaia Genekhovna Stein, and they quickly had two sons. But when Louis was called up for military service in 1892 and assigned to the Home Guard, he worried that being a conscript in the Russian army could mean separation from his wife and young family for as many as 25 or 30 years, so he set about saving enough money to arrange for his own escape. His wife and boys would follow as soon as he got established somewhere.

He arrived in London, via Hamburg, in 1898. Louis' intention was to go on to the United States, but just as he was about to re-embark, the Spanish–American War broke out and he was told that if he went on to America, he could be conscripted into the US army. I don't know if that was true, and I doubt if my grandfather knew either, but he was taking no chances and decided to stay in Britain. As soon as he could, he brought his wife and sons over. Their first home was off Commercial Street in the East End.

This grandfather was a unique man. He was uneducated but streetwise and resourceful, not afraid of hard work and very strong. Family legend has it that he could bend nails in his teeth.

Because he had driven horses in Russia and knew a lot about them, he found a job tending to the horses at a local dairy in Whitechapel owned by a Mr Green. In those days, dairies, and breweries too, used horse-drawn carts for deliveries and were always looking to buy sturdy horses for as little money as possible. Prices in London were dear, but there were plenty of good carthorses for sale up north – that is, as long as a dairy or brewery owner was willing to make the trip and knew how to buy them. When Mr Green realised that my grandfather knew what he was doing, he started taking Louis with him to the sales up north. He quickly became confident enough in him to put my grandfather in charge of buying all his horses and bringing them back down to London.

This was a time when highwaymen lay in wait for people to rob, and horses were a big prize. But because my grandfather was so strong, nobody dared steal anything from him. So his ability to buy horses and then bring them safely back to London meant that he was in great demand. And before long, it wasn't just the dairy that was using his services. He was buying horses for local breweries too.

Now, Louis might never have heard the word entrepreneur – or if he did, he probably didn't understand what it meant – but he knew an opportunity when he saw one. As he brought more and more horses back from the North, he started thinking that the dairies and breweries needed some place to put them all, so he took what little money he had and bought mews properties to use as stables. That's how, from tending one horse at a dairy, he found himself in the property business.

By the time the First World War came along, my grandfather was considered such an authority on the quality and condition of horses that he was granted special permission as an alien to travel freely up and down the country visiting horse sales to make purchases. Along the way, he discovered what we would call today army surplus. The army needed horses for the war, but not every horse was suitable. Louis was clever enough to tap into a supply of rejects – horses ailing with sores and lice or just thought to be past their best – buy some, nurse them back to health, get them fit and sell them on. When he could, he earned additional money matching horses, like pairs of greys, for the breweries. And all this time, he kept buying properties to stable more horses.

When it occurred to him that he would be better off working for himself, he left Mr Green's dairy and opened his own. It seemed to him like a good idea at the time because one of the few things he'd brought with him from the old country was how to make *tvorog*. In Russia, poor Jews were given sour milk from dairies – the dairies were going to throw it out anyway – which they turned into a typical Russian cottage cheese. My grandfather now schlepped home heavy barrels of sour milk, made tvorog and sold his cheese to other Russian immigrants. That business was so good that Louis was soon known to everyone in the East End as 'Milky'.

What extra money he had from his cheese business he invested in more real estate, branching out from mews stables to small shops and business premises in Bethnal Green. He rented some sites and sold off others at a profit. Still, life for him and my grandmother was always a struggle. They had two more sons and three daughters, so there were a lot of mouths to feed. My mother, Sarah, was the youngest of the girls. To house his family, Milky moved to Bacon Street, Shoreditch. Their premises consisted of a shop – where he sold his cheese and some milk – a rear parlour and a living room with two floors above. The lower of these upper floors was divided into two rooms. Above it was one big room. All three girls slept in one of the lower rooms, and all four boys slept in the larger top room. Milky then spent what little extra money he had to bring his mother out of the Pale, along with two of his sisters, and they all lived above the shop, too.

Milky never learned to read or write English, and he suffered from diabetes, which in those days was a difficult illness to control. The day my mother got married, he was in hospital. He came out for the wedding and went straight back that same evening. His only recreation was to drink a bottle of Scotch a day. I never knew him, because he died in 1939, the year I was born, but everything I have been told about him makes me think that he lived exactly the way any man of spirit would choose to live – as his own master. He was a remarkable man with a gut instinct for a deal who made ends meet by working hard. And if entrepreneurship and hard work are passed along in the genes, then I know who I get them from. By the age of seven or eight, I was selling second-hand comics, swapping conkers, doing all sorts of little things to earn three and sixpence here, a shilling there. I was born with that. Thank you, Milky.

When his children counted up his assets in 1939, his real-estate holdings were worth something in the neighbourhood of £30,000. In today's money, that's around £7 million.

His youngest son, my uncle Tubby, followed in his footsteps and changed the family's situation forever. He looked at Milky's little dairy business and, through sheer determination, drive and ambition – it really must be a family trait – he turned it into Raine's Dairy Foods, suppliers to Marks & Spencer and Safeway and just about everyone else in the country who sold milk and cheese and dairy products. When the family sold the company a few years ago, Milky's tvorog business had become the biggest independent dairy and produce company in Britain.

* * *

The Aaronsons and the Raines were decent people who raised their children to live by the fundamental morals and principles of the Jewish faith. They were not essentially religious. There were no scholars among them. There were no aspirations to join the professional classes. Many teachers appealed to my grandparents to allow their children to continue their education, but on both sides of my family becoming a successful tradesman was considered the final achievement.

My mother and father were raised close enough to each other to know the same streets, but when they met it was miles away, in a coffee restaurant in central London. This was the mid-1930s, the days of the *thé dansant* and the *café dansant*, when it was perfectly respectable for young people to spend the afternoon or early evening dancing.

My mother was an unusually good-looking young lady. She was elegant, stylish and had lovely strawberry blonde hair that was her natural colour. One of my daughters describes her as being 'regal'. She was very fond of dancing and on this particular afternoon she and her sister were sitting in a café near the Palladium when a handsome young man – who also loved dancing – asked her if she would like to dance with him. Romance began with the opening bars of the music.

My father was well over six feet tall, broad-shouldered, strongly built and carried himself well. He was self-confident and exuberant. Nowadays, he might be called macho, especially because, as a lad, he had been a very good boxer. Unfortunately for my father's boxing career, his father disapproved of boxing. And the night my father was scheduled to box in the Jewish Lads' Brigade championship final, his father forbade him to go. So Dad did exactly what I would have expected him to. He crept out of the house when nobody was looking. His opponent was a much bigger boy and a harder puncher. He broke my father's nose. But my father somehow won the fight, and that made him champion. In his eyes, his future as a boxer was on the rise. But he didn't know what his father would think about the broken nose, so when he got home after the fight, he sneaked upstairs without anyone seeing him.

A little later, my grandfather called to him. My father scuttled under his bed. Receiving no answer, my grandfather went up to his son's room and ordered him to emerge. My father poked his head out and tried to explain that he'd just won a championship fight, but his nose told its own story. My grandfather berated my dad for fighting, grabbed a broom handle from the corner of the room and hit him with it. He opened up a cut that needed six stitches. This was the only time my dad remembered my grandfather losing his temper. And he never boxed again.

At the time that my father met my mother, he was the salesman for the furniture business he'd put together with his brothers. He travelled extensively up and down the country and enjoyed, comparatively speaking, a high standard of living. He dressed well – I remember him always immaculately turned out – enjoyed good food and drink, and had an MG sports car. He was a man's man and swept my mother off her feet. Maybe he reminded her of Milky – not in stature but in strength, drive and spirit. Maybe that's why she so quickly fell in love with him.

They were soon engaged, but neither set of my grandparents was entirely in favour of the marriage. The Aaronsons liked my mother very much, but they wondered if her personality was robust enough to cope with my dad's. The Raines did not like the idea of a younger daughter getting married before her older sisters, which, in those days, was a typical Jewish attitude. Milky even told my mother that though Henry would provide her with the material things in life, he might not be psychologically the ideal mate for her. In spite of their parents' reservations, the marriage came about among general rejoicing.

In the beginning, Henry and Sarah – now called Ronson, having dropped the two As from Aaronson to make the name more Anglicised – set up home in Wanstead. They chose it because, by then, my father had leased a large retail furniture shop and warehouse in High Street North, East Ham. By the time I was born, on 27 May 1939, they had moved to Amhurst Road, Clapton, N16.

When the Germans began to blitz London, they decided to move further out, to Whipps Cross, near Epping Forest. Even that turned out to be too near London for comfort, so we had a spell at Aldermaston with Uncle Tubby and his family, then moved even further away, to Cambridge. While we were there, a large bomb fell on the road we had lived in at Whipps Cross and demolished it. Obviously, the inconvenience of evacuation had been worthwhile.

In 1941, when the constant bombing of London eased off, we went back to the city, living in Amhurst Park. Soon after, my parents bought a house in Church Mount, Hampstead, which was where I grew up.

Apparently, I was a very tiresome child. During my first two years, according to my mother, I did nothing but cry very loudly. My mother would lay me down in my cot, fast asleep, and leave, only to have me start bellowing. Years later, Uncle Tubby told my wife, 'It was as if the boy had been given a signal. Within a second or two of Sarah tiptoeing out, he'd start to shriek – not just cry but shriek – and he wouldn't stop.' This went on for some months and got so bad that the doctors were afraid I would rupture myself. Some doctors told my mother that I was hyperactive and had excessive energy. It was only when I was three that someone realised I suffered from indigestion. My diet was changed, the crying stopped and I haven't cried since.

By turns, I was creative and destructive. When my father gave me a little toy car, I became the terror of the block. I used to drive it as fast as I could, chasing other children. Once, I took the car to the top of the hill and zoomed down, crashing into the brick wall at the bottom. I could have killed myself, but that didn't occur to me.

I think it was a case of having a lot of energy, not knowing what to do with it and not wanting to be bored. My behaviour apparently improved after I started school at Annemount, a kindergarten in Holne Chase, not far from where we lived then and only a few hundred yards from where I live now. The school was run by a wonderful woman named Miss Jamaica, who was still running it at the age of 91. In fact, among her pupils were my four daughters. She had a delightful, very gracious personality, and we all respected her. But it was clear from the start that I was not cut out for formal education.

I couldn't have been there more than a few days before Miss Jamaica telephoned my mother to say, 'I have never had anybody like him. He's too buoyant.' It seems workmen were making a path alongside the lawn and bits of dry clay were lying around, and some of the other five-year-olds and I started throwing these at each other. I was shipped home for the day and duly reprimanded. But that made a lasting impression on me, because for several weeks after that episode, whenever it came time to leave school for the day, I would go up to Miss Jamaica and assure her, 'I have been a good boy today.'

In her 90th year, Miss Jamaica told a friend of mine, 'Gerald was a very gentle boy, very considerate, and everybody liked him.' I'm not going to argue with her, but, in all honesty, I was a nuisance. School for me was boring, I didn't want to be bored, and I didn't know how not to be bored without making trouble. It was much like this for the rest of my school days. I wanted to get out of school as soon as I reached the legal age, probably much to the relief of everybody else too.

It wasn't that I was badly treated or that I resented the discipline of being taught. Far from it. I just didn't see the point of school. Then I learned that my father had left school as soon as he could to join the family business. He'd done well and I wondered why I shouldn't do the same.

* * *

Though my parents were very affectionate to me, and though at the age of nine I was presented with a younger brother, Laurence, my childhood was in its way a lonely one. My father had an enormous love for his family – he lived for us, and later for his grandchildren – and loved having all of us around him. But he was a workaholic. The pattern of his life throughout my childhood and into my youth was mostly the same, day in, day out, year after year. He would leave for the office at dawn, work all day and not come home until late in the evening. His lunch was usually in a pub. On the way home, he would have a few drinks with his business friends, discussing deals. He was either supervising the factory or looking for new business. Or he'd be off in Scotland selling furniture, or in the north of England buying new supplies of fabric, or in Paris buying veneers for his bedroom suites. It was not that he wanted to be away from home or that he disliked home. It was what he had to do.

He worked every day, which meant he would go into the factory on Sunday mornings, and he was very paternalistic towards the people he employed. If my father liked you and you had a problem, he'd take his wallet out – I saw him do it so many times – and while he was talking to you, he'd count out a few hundred pounds to help you out. He'd never ask for anything in return. That was the sort of man he was.

He did not know what a holiday was for and, at best, averaged only one every five years. The idea of spending a couple of weeks fishing or sitting on the beach somewhere was as incomprehensible to him as spending the day at school was to me. That was his culture, and that was the culture I was brought up in.

Understandably, his work routine did not go down well with my mother. Much as she loved my father, she gradually found it more and more oppressive. She was always beautifully turned out, communicative, fond of books and interested in people. But he wasn't there to share that. Our house was very nice and my mother furnished it elegantly, but my father had no desire to enjoy it. Apart from the bedrooms, we inhabited only about a quarter of the house. We rarely used the dining room or the drawing room.

Though I loved my father, even as a small child I could see that his way of life made my mother's life incomplete. I saw that she resented it, and that she was lonely. Her loneliness and mine became a bond between us. I wasn't conscious of it at the time, but, my mother told me, I showed much more consideration for her than most little boys showed for their mothers. If I wanted to go out for a ride on my bike in the evening when she was sitting at home on her own, I'd say, according to my mother, 'I'm going out for a quick ride round the block, but don't worry – I'll be back in ten minutes.' And I would be.

My mother, on the other hand, used to speak to me as if I were a grown-up when I was still quite small. She told me that there was more to life than making money. She warned that when I grew up and had a wife and children, I must find time for them. She said that if I didn't, they would be unhappy and unfulfilled. If that happened, she said, I would suffer too.

My father knew a lot of people, but they were business associates. He drank with them but didn't have many real friends. My mother had a few friends, but her friends didn't drink, so as a couple they did not have friends in common. It was a different time, a different generation, a different life.

Although my mother's name was Sarah, everyone called her Sadie. As she got older, however, she decided that she wanted to be called Sarah again. She died on 8 October 2005 at the age of 93. She never complained specifically to me about my father, but what she said must have sunk in, because when I married I did my best to join in my wife's interests and to involve her in mine. I tried to help create interests for her and make a point of being together as much as possible. I think I can honestly say that, given my wife's own interests and the fact that four daughters arrived in the first five years of our marriage, Gail has not had the problem of loneliness that my mother had.

When my brother Laurence was born in 1948, the situation improved for a while, because my mother had another person to share her life. He and I were, and are, very fond of each other, but our age gap did not make for a close relationship early on. When I was 21, Laurence was only 12. He would clean my car for me, and I would take him up to the Hampstead Pond and help him sail his powerboat. I'd let him borrow my airgun when my parents weren't looking, until he was big enough to have his own, and we'd go for walks together. When girls telephoned me at home, and Laurence answered the phone and my mother asked who it was, Laurence would say diplomatically, 'It was for Gerald – nothing important,' and pass the news to me when I got home. Laurence, in short, was a very good brother, and he is a very good man.

But by the time the 1960s came along and Laurence had reached his teens, life at home changed. I was already working with my father. I wore suits, lace-up shoes, white collar and tie, had my hair cut short with a parting and generally looked like the businessman I was. He had his hair halfway down his back, wore winklepickers and drape jackets, and walked around like a member of a pop group. My father could not compute what was going on with his second son. As Laurence remembers those years, he weighed only about 8½ stone because he never finished a meal. During dinner, there would be some sort of argument and he would storm out. Maybe his father didn't understand him, but, at that age, he didn't understand his father. It takes two to tango.

Undeservedly, Laurence got a rougher ride from Dad than I ever did. And I've wondered sometimes how things would have turned out if he'd been born in 1939 and I'd spent my youth in the '60s. That said, as childhoods go, mine was ordinary and uneventful. I was blessed with good health, comfort and security. But my life wasn't influenced by any great event, experience or revelation. I was a Jew, and conscious of being a Jew, but my childhood wasn't overshadowed by any cultural influence. It wasn't cursed by sadness or deprivation. All I wanted to do was work in my father's factory.

* * *

I knew the factory well, because I used to visit it with my father every Saturday morning. For me, those visits were the high point of the week.

When the time came for me to sit the 11-plus examination, as it was called then, I failed. It might have disappointed my parents, but it didn't dismay me, because I didn't really understand what the exam was about. It didn't seem to me to have any relevance. I was stuck in school and my parents wouldn't let me leave just because I'd failed, so they put me in Clark's College, Cricklewood, not very far from home. I was sent there because two courses were provided, one in general studies and the other in commercial subjects, which someone thought might be more congenial to me.

Except that I wasn't having it. Whatever subjects were taught, I was allergic to school. It didn't take long before my mother received a telephone call from the headmaster asking where I was. Guessing that I'd gone AWOL for the day, she loyally told the head that I wasn't well. As soon as I came home, she asked me where I'd been. I told her that I simply hadn't been able to stand the thought of going to school that day, but that I hadn't been mooning about and hadn't got into mischief. I said that I'd gone on my own humble way to educate myself. I'd gone to see the railway.

Ever since I was a little tot, I've always been very interested in things mechanical. Whenever I was given a mechanical toy, I would take it to pieces to see how it worked. On days when I played truant, I'd go to look at mechanical toys in Harrods or Selfridges, or I'd go to garages to look at cars. I loved garages best when the cars' bonnets were up and I could see their engines.

As far as I was concerned, school did nothing to satisfy my curiosity. My interests were ignored. I also resented being treated like a number instead of as a person. I found the discipline purposeless and irksome. And, as I wasn't interested in learning what they tried to teach me, they assumed I wasn't interested in learning anything. But I have always been interested in learning about lots of things, and in my time I have tried very hard to learn a lot.

Nowadays, schools, colleges and universities adjust themselves far better to what young people want to learn, as opposed to what they themselves decide young people should learn. I saw how my daughters' schools were very different from mine. Even now, when they talk to me about their education, I can't help but feel that if I had been treated the same way, I might have liked school as much as they did.

When, at the age of 12, I started to prepare for my bar mitzvah, there was no sign of truancy. I was tutored by Reverend Freilich at the Hampstead Garden Suburb United Synagogue, did all my homework and never missed Sunday school. But there was no question of him ever making a rabbi out of me.

I remember telling Uncle Tubby at my bar mitzvah dinner that as soon as I could I was going to leave school, go into my father's business, make £10 million before I was 30, then retire. It's the kind of thing kids say when they're a little insecure. But then I think you have to have a need to prove yourself to want to be successful.

If I was insecure then, possibly it had to do with being a second-generation Jewish immigrant. There's something inbred that drives certain people to make something better for themselves. Don't get me wrong, I wasn't so insecure that I thought I wasn't as good as anyone else. But I'd been an only child for so long, and all I wanted to do was get out there in the world to show my father that I was his son. Many people might think that's normal. But is it? A lot of sons don't want to be like their father, especially if their father is as demanding and as big a character as mine.

Dad was a tough individual, a big, powerful man – I'm not physically as strong as he was – and whilst he wouldn't pick a fight with anybody, if someone started on him, then he would send a message to be received at the other end. He was a good man. But in his eyes, unless you were prepared to work at least 12 hours a day you were 'a good-for-nothing'. That's what he'd say. And, in his uneducated way – not ignorant but uneducated – he was right. After all, how can you make something out of yourself if you don't want to be the first one through the door in the morning and the last one out the door at night? Dad was also a fearless man. People who didn't know him would be intimidated by him. I would like to think I am more polished than he was, and maybe more financially astute, but I regard myself as a chip off the old block.

The older I became, the less able my teachers were to handle me. I wanted to think for myself. I learned about things that interested me and wasn't interested in what the teachers wanted me to learn. For instance, I've always been good at mental arithmetic. I'm still good at it. You can throw numbers at me and I can analyse those numbers in my head and give you the percentages. If anyone at school ever thought I was clever, it was because I was clever at what I wanted to be clever at, like geography, sports and arithmetic.

I proved I could study other things by getting through my bar mitzvah preparation, but over the next couple of years, as I became more and more determined to leave school, I played truant more often. It came to the point that the authorities called in the school inspectors. My mother did her best to explain that all I wanted to do was go to work in my father's factory. Thankfully, the inspectors merely put the onus back on my parents to do something.

The first thing my mother did was suggest that I leave Clark's College. She decided that if Carmel College – a well-known Jewish boarding school in Oxfordshire – would have me, that's where I should be. But it sounded to me like I was being sent to a concentration camp and I warned her, 'I'll be home on the first train.' So she came up with a compromise. She said I could leave Clark's if I enrolled in a polytechnic college – there was one near my father's factory – to learn subjects like woodcarving and furniture making. That was a way to meet the requirements of the law and, at the same time, feed my desire to start work. But I didn't like the sound of this either. Legally, I could quit school at 14½. I told my mother that, rather than accept the alternatives, I would hang on at Clark's and not play truant, on the condition that when I was 14½ I would be allowed to leave and go into the furniture factory. My parents eventually agreed and, for the rest of my time at Clark's, I behaved.

Needless to say, the day I quit school was a day of rejoicing for me, a day of great relief for my mother and a day of great pride for my father. Not only was I going to work for him, but I was doing it with years of pent-up enthusiasm. I remember leaving that very first morning with my father for the factory.

I couldn't wait to start. We walked around together for a few minutes and then I asked, 'What do I do?'

He pointed to a workman's brown coat and said, 'Take off your jacket and put that on.' I did. Then he pointed to the corner of the room. 'See that broom over there? Start sweeping.'

CHAPTER 2

....

BECOMING MY FATHER'S SON

When war was declared in 1939, my father still had his store in High Street North, East Ham, but with the war came demand for skills in many industries, and my father was called to play his part. He was a highly skilled cabinetmaker, just like his own father, so they put him to work in a factory that produced parts for the Mosquito, a fast new bomber made almost entirely out of wood. Nicknamed 'the Timber Terror', it was lighter than aircraft made out of aluminium and could fly at speeds of up to 400 mph, twice as fast as any other bomber in the sky. They put my dad on the night shift, which meant that by day he was free to do whatever he liked. Because he never needed much sleep, an advantage that I inherited from him, he spent the days working for himself.

Because there wasn't enough wood coming onto the market for him to make new furniture to sell in the store – all of it was going to the war effort – he did the next best thing. He renovated old furniture, which he bought at various auctions around London. When the war ended and wood became readily available, he opened a small factory in Bethnal Green to make bedroom furniture. His thinking was that everyone needs something to sleep on. But, as a perceptive observer of markets and trends, he quickly came to the conclusion that the demand for bedroom furniture would fade, because an increasingly affluent population could afford to buy dining-room furniture. So he switched from bedroom suites to dining-room suites – a table, a sideboard and four chairs to match, all for £65. That was the point when he changed the name of the family business, amalgamating Henry and Ronson to come up with Heron.

In spite of his hard work, those first few years were an uphill struggle. But failure was never an option. He was not a man to waste time in self-pity and I never heard him complain. He was a nuts-and-bolts manager who believed that knowing every aspect of his business inside out was an essential element for success. He kept a hawk-like eye on sales, marketing and transport. I used to wonder if his workaholic ways dated from this period, but, thinking back, I realise now that he had always been a workaholic anyway.

Dad never hid in the office. He was everywhere, wearing a brown coat, looking like one of the employees. Some lorry driver would pull in and tell him, 'I have a load of timber and I've got to get away in five minutes, so I'm going to dump it here.'

My father would say, 'No, you've got to wait half an hour and someone will be here to help you unload. And would you mind moving your vehicle?'

He'd be polite. But if the driver said, 'I'm going to dump it here and you can fucking sort it out afterwards,' that was like a red rag to a bull. He didn't care if the man was six foot six, before you knew it, Dad would grab hold of him. And if Dad hit him, it wouldn't be just a slap on the face.

I saw that plenty of times and would say to him, 'Was that really necessary?'

He'd say, 'I'm not having people talk to me like that.'

He'd say, 'If people talk to you decently, no matter who or what they are, you have respect.' But the East End of London was a tough place. When someone took a liberty or insulted him – and in those days, the words 'Jew bastard' or 'fucking Jew' would come very quickly – then, bang, that was it. Today, everything is so politically correct. Today, people don't have the same passion, they don't have the same hunger, they don't have the same commitment. They also don't go around smacking people quite so frequently. It was a whole different world back then.

He was a character, my father, a tough man who never took nonsense from anybody. But he could also be as sweet as pie. He was a generous and kindly man. I remember that there was an impoverished old lady who appeared near our house every Sunday morning and my father never passed her without giving her something. He would contribute freely to various charities, but he could not be called public spirited because he didn't take enough interest in where his money was going.

Dad's willingness to face a challenge, to go all out to win, set an example for me that I have never forgotten and always tried to live up to. He would have given me the shirt off his back. As tough as he could be, he thought the moon and stars shone out of my backside. He'd never tell me to my face that I was clever, but he used to tell everyone else, 'My son Gerald is one of the smartest, cleverest blokes in the world.'

Actually, I'm not. But that's beside the point.

* * *

I loved that factory, the smell and the atmosphere of the place, and never minded sweeping up shavings, or tidying up varnish pots, or doing anything I could, as long as I was there. From that first day until my seventeenth birthday, I worked in one department after another, and through those varied experiences began to acquire the same fundamental expertise that my father had. It was a great way to learn. I particularly valued the feeling of working at a man's job in the real world instead of being in the child's world of school and lessons and books. I got on well with my father's employees, and found it much easier and more stimulating to talk and listen to them than to the teachers at school.

My pay was five pounds a week. I worked hard and earned every penny of it. While I was still in school, I was actually quite a good all-round sportsman. I played cricket and football, did some judo and boxed. But the sport I was best at, strangely enough, was tennis. Don't ask me why. When I started work, I gave it up. These days, I go to the gym twice a week, but don't bother with any sports. I don't even watch football. I used to go to some of the big prizefights, but not any more. I'd rather watch it on television.

When I turned 17, I figured I was going to get a raise, but my father thought otherwise. He bought me a second-hand Ford. Some fathers are in two minds about their children and cars. I was lucky in that my father encouraged my interest in driving and in motors. Getting my own car was fine with me, because, by that time, I had become hooked on cars. I hardly noticed that I was still earning a fiver a week.

Around this time, Dad began delegating jobs to me, and I accepted any and all of my new responsibilities. But I have to say it was with mixed feelings. My father was not in the habit of rewarding success with praise and could be relied upon to blast the roof off if I registered a failure. To be fair, he never harboured grievances. He never harped or recriminated. Once he exploded, it was over and he forgot about it. It's yet another example that I have tried to follow.

The most important new responsibility he gave me, which turned out to be one of the most significant experiences of my life, came when the number of people working for him had risen to nearly 500. We needed more space. I had a good eye for buildings and, thanks to my maths skills, I could read plans, so my father put me in charge of building a new factory.

It's a well-proven axiom in business, one that even the greatest entrepreneurs respect, that you never go into a business where you haven't already had some experience. It is a bold man who takes the risk of flying in the face of that advice. But my father was, if nothing else, bold, and he often flew head first in the face of conventional wisdom. People must have thought he was mad. He applied for planning permission to build on a site nearby in Southgate, but the local authority said they wanted that for council houses and offered him a site at Harold Hill, Romford, Essex, on the outskirts of Greater London. My father accepted.

'You've got plenty of time,' he said to me. 'There are seven days a week. So get organised and do it.'

At a time when some of my chums were still studying for their A-levels, I was building a factory.

Of course, my father was always nearby. Since I was still living at home, he could ask me how things were going and I could refer any serious problems to him. But he hardly ever intervened and I rarely consulted him. I think he was secretly proud of this arrangement and I was definitely proud of it. The thing is that I had some big shoulders to lean on – those of an Irishman called Martin McQuen. He was another very important person in my life and I owe him a great deal. Without him, the building of the Harold Hill factory would not have been possible and my life would have been very different. Martin was my university education in the construction industry.

Two problems confronted me from the start – money and labour. The more important was money. We were doing well with our furniture, but this was a time when the costs of materials and labour were on the increase. We weren't making as much profit as we would have liked, given that we wanted to keep trading competitively and simultaneously build a brand new factory. In these circumstances, before buying materials we had to look around for good deals. As a result, I bought a lot of second-hand bricks, as well as second-hand pipes for heating and plumbing. It's a good way to save money, but a dangerous game to play. There are lots of hazards. It was Martin McQuen who taught me what I needed to know and showed me how to manage this. We had to bring in our own sand and cement, because, in those days, there was no ready-mixed concrete. He and I bought second-hand trucks, including one old Ford lorry for £90. We also bought a second-hand bulldozer. The knowledge I picked up in those months with Martin stood me in good stead years later when I moved into the building industry. He taught me how to ask the right questions to get valid answers, and that showed the people I was dealing with that I knew what I was doing. There is no authority more valuable than knowing your business.

Labour came next, and keeping those costs down was not easy. This was the mid-1950s. The building industry was tough, the trade unions were aggressive and labour costs were rising rapidly everywhere. Also, there were many Trotskyists on the sites. Here too I had Martin on my side. He enabled me to bring in Irish construction workers, labourers and gangers who were willing to work on Saturdays and Sundays, uninhibited by the rules and practices of British unions.

Not that these crews were easy to get along with. Seeing that the operation was more or less in the hands of a boy, some of the lads thought they could take advantage. Now and again, after they came back from a boozy lunch, one or two would get offensive. I was big and strong for my age, and, like my father, I could use my fists. And that's what it sometimes took to set the record straight. One brief exchange of blows one day meant I did not have to use my fists again. But I had to learn how to lead from the front. Because the best way to get people to work well for you is to set an example. I arrived at the building site at seven every morning, long before anybody else, to make sure that all the materials were there for the day's work, and all the equipment was in order. Then I was always the last to leave at night.

We built the Harold Hill factory and brought it in at an economical cost. Looking back at it today, I wonder how my father had the nerve to embark on the project in the first place. He was a practical man who knew a great deal about a number of things, but he knew nothing about building. Yet he put the project in the hands of his 17-year-old son. And I knew even less. However, he understood that responsibility develops ability and self-respect. It is one of the most important things he did for me, and I will always be grateful to him for it. Here too I have tried to follow his example. As each of my daughters reached the age of 18, I gave them added responsibilities with the family's charities and good works.

Dad was always finding new challenges for me. I was just 18 when he decided he wanted a new car. He drove a Rover most of the time, then bought an American Packard. When he decided he wanted a brand-new Rolls-Royce, he asked me to handle the transaction. I don't know if he couldn't be bothered to do it himself or if he thought the experience would be good for me.

The leading Rolls-Royce dealer in London was, as now, H.R. Owen on Berkeley Square. So I rang them and spoke to the sales manager, Peter Reynolds, on the phone. I introduced myself, told him what I wanted, and the negotiations began. Peter later told Gail and our daughters, 'I'd had some fairly tough negotiations in my time, but this was to prove more difficult than anything before. In the end, it wasn't about selling a car, it was about doing that deal.'

I insisted Peter and I negotiate over the phone and that took ten days. First, the colour wasn't right. Then the trim wasn't to my liking. Then the delivery time was too slow. And all this had to get settled before we agreed on the discount. At that point, I insisted he do a part exchange on my dad's Packard. When we finally agreed the deal, he asked when I wanted to pick it up. I told him I wanted it delivered.

Years later, he confessed that he did not enjoy negotiating with me but was intrigued by my way of going about things. So much so that he asked the H.R. Owen directors not to send the car to us with a liveried chauffeur – which was the normal way they delivered a new Rolls – but to let him bring it to me himself. So Peter drove it to the factory, parked in front and was directed to an office where he found a young lad sitting behind a desk.

He said, 'I've come to deliver a Rolls-Royce for a Mr Ronson.'

I said, 'That's me.'

I'm not sure he believed me until I handed him a cheque and the keys of the Packard, then held out my hand for the keys of the Rolls.

He suggested, 'You might want to come outside and look at it.'

I said, 'I'm too busy and I'm sure it will be all right.'

He left, as he put it, 'feeling mystified'.

Some years later, Peter Reynolds became de-mystified. I bought H.R. Owen and, with it, his expert services. I stated then what I restate now, that Peter Reynolds was the first honest motor dealer in the world.

* * *

In my mind, the path of my life looked like it was laid out clearly in front of me. Then came a great irony, for me almost a tragedy, that was a huge turning point in my father's life and consequently in mine. Just as we were about to put the last touches to the new factory, out of the blue, a successful mail-order firm made an offer for it. They required warehouse space urgently and mentioned a sum far in excess of our costs. My father met with the would-be buyer's lawyers. One of the cards he had in his hand was that the factory had still to be finished and this company didn't want to do that. My dad calculated into the price of the deal our additional costs to complete. After a lot of talking and the consumption of considerable amounts of Scotch, he agreed to sell for £195,000, which was a lot of money in 1956. It gave him a profit of approaching £100,000.

When the would-be purchasers agreed the offer, my father shook hands with them and considered the deal done. But within hours of that handshake, another call came in, out of the blue. Someone representing the famous cosmetics firm Max Factor telephoned to say that they too were in urgent need of accommodation. This person must have known what the mail-order company had agreed to pay, because without beating about the bush, he made a much higher offer. No letter of agreement with the mail-order company had been signed and no contracts had changed hands. Most people would have sold to Max Factor for the higher price.

My dad turned them down.

When I asked why, he told me, 'I've shaken on it. Your word has to be your bond.'

I never forgot that. And whatever criticism can be made of me, here too I have followed in his footsteps. My word is my bond. Not everybody plays by that rule. I'm generalising here, but in the States, for example, your handshake is merely the first step towards armies of lawyers. You agree a deal, and nothing means anything until the lawyers get hold of it and change it. That's not how I operate. When I give my word, my reputation is at stake and, for me, reputation is all-important.

As proud as I was of my father's probity, I was sick about the sale of the factory. I knew the furniture business, identified with it, and was on very good terms with the men and women who worked there. I had slogged on at the old factory for three years, from morning till night, and had spent months, from morning till night, on site building the new place. I was looking forward to running the business one day. The new factory was my future. Now it was going to be sold.

That was bad enough, but worse was to follow. My father announced, to the amazement of my mother and me, that he'd decided to get out of furniture and go into property. We were apprehensive about this, but we couldn't have stopped him even if we'd tried.

He said to me, 'Why should we slog along in furniture? No more furniture. I'm going to sell the factory.' Then he tried to wind me up, 'Maybe I'm going to give up work.'

'To do what?' He couldn't have given up work if he'd wanted to.

'Property's the thing. Money for old rope.'

'OK.' I decided to play along with him and put on an expression that suggested I was quite prepared for him to retire and let me get on with this business on my own. 'I think I'll start buying sites in the Home Counties for building houses, and maybe go further afield.'

I'd called his bluff, so now he called mine. 'Right. From now on, we're partners, 50–50.'

Our switch from furniture to property showed that my dad was an excellent judge of the commercial world at the time. So much property in and around London had been destroyed by bombing but in 1947 the post-war Labour government had deliberately restricted the development of commercial property by bringing in the Town and Country Planning Act, which put a 100 per cent tax on land development and a surcharge, through the requirement of licences, on commercial property. They didn't care about offices. They wanted to use cheap-money policies to build new council houses for the working classes – their constituents – who'd been dispossessed by enemy action. In 1951, the Conservatives had come in with a mandate to remove many of the regulations that the Labour government had introduced. They got rid of the 100 per cent development charge and by 1953 there was a surge in the buying and developing of land. Then they got rid of the commercial licences. That transformed the property market. Values rose dramatically and the pace of property development sped up.

On the other hand, with the Conservatives in power, relations with the trade unions deteriorated, creating problems in many industries, including furniture manufacturing. The big groups who were buying were squeezing margins on the manufacturers. My father decided that we didn't need to go through all this pain just to work for pennies. He was right.

He reckoned that taking his money out of furniture and putting it in property would yield quick turnover at high profit. He was right there too. He saw people he'd grown up with in the East End – people he regarded as complete idiots – making a lot of money in property. I remember he used to say to me, 'Sam was a dress manufacturer and Benny was a tailor, and if they can make so much money in property, I can make more.'

This was the '50s, when it didn't matter what you bought, there was money to be made. All you needed was a bit of capital, a friendly bank manager and a lot of energy. It was a time when there were characters in the business. Unfortunately, they have all gone. Today, the business is institutionalised, run by people who don't have the passion but are financially capable. The new generation, together with too many lawyers, have made the business much more sophisticated in terms of planning, construction and financing. But they've squeezed out the old-style entrepreneurs. I'm talking about legends in property like Charles Clore, Jack Cotton, Harry Hyams, Archie Sherman, Isaac Wolfson and Harold Samuel.

I knew Charles Clore well, liked him very much, and he treated me like a second son. He was very smart, bought companies with real estate, sold off the real estate and kept the companies, making a fortune out of the properties and winding up with the British Shoe Corporation, Freeman, Hardy and Willis, Lilley & Skinner and Selfridges in central London. He then set up the Clore Foundation, which became a major contributor to the

Jewish community in Britain and Israel, and sponsored the Clore Gallery at the Tate to house the world's largest collection of Turner paintings. Gail and I are still very friendly with Charles's daughter Vivien Duffield, who combined his foundation with hers and, through the Clore Duffield Foundation, has donated millions of pounds to worthy causes. Charles should have taken her into his business. It was a mistake that he didn't, because she's a very capable lady.

Jack Cotton was a different sort of man. He came from Birmingham and was an estate agent before becoming a developer. He specialised in shopping centres rather than office buildings, but is still considered one of the major developers during those years.

Harry Hyams was the developer who, in the mid-1960s, built one of the most controversial buildings in London, Centre Point.

Archie Sherman was probably the most astute man in the business when it came to individual shop properties. He knew every single high street in the land and what the rents were per square foot. He spent five days a week going up and down the country buying properties. He also developed one or two schemes. People who didn't know Archie could be intimidated by him because he was gruff and difficult. He liked people to argue with him because he wanted to see who would stand up to him. Most people didn't. But the better I got to know him, the more I saw that he was family-orientated and very charitable.

Isaac Wolfson used to invite me round to have tea with him at his home in Portland Place. By nature, he was a trader, and very smart, and he understood the business and money and how to use credit. He had all the charm in the world and often used it to raise money for charity. He built up Great Universal Stores, but also had an eye for property and really understood the game. He borrowed cheap money to buy businesses with properties that he could buy for less than the properties were worth. It was heads you win, tails you win, and he made a vast fortune.

The most difficult of the bunch to know was Harold Samuel, because he was a shy, reclusive man who came across as a bit cold and distant. But he was a very decent man and a great lover of the arts. He was Jewish, but he didn't involve himself in the Community. He was a very competent developer and possibly the best of all these men when it came to being a visionary. He built up Land Securities, which became the largest property company in Europe.

Two other property men I knew to some extent and admired for various reasons were Barney Shine and Johnny Rubens. Barney created a property company that owned Berkeley Square House. Johnny was a very caring man who was committed to supporting many Jewish charities. I'd known him since my childhood, when his daughter Ruth and I rode bicycles around Hampstead Garden Suburb. We are still good friends with her and her husband, Michael Phillips, who, much like Ruth's father, is very supportive of activities within the Community.

Of course, I was much younger than any of these men and only came to know them towards the end of their careers. But I saw what hard work and passion can do, and if my father gave me my work ethic, these men set the bar that much higher and inspired me to succeed.

* * *

Immediately after the Harold Hill factory was sold, Dad decided to sell our factory at Arlington Avenue and assigned that task to me. I couldn't have done it without a lawyer named Ruben Gale, who taught me about property the same way Martin McQuen had taught me about building.

My grandfather Maurice had known the Gale family from his earliest days in London, when their name was Galinsky. His friend David Galinsky had two sons, Sam and Ruben, who emerged from the East End to become eminent property lawyers. One day, just after Dad decided to get out of furniture and into property, he went to see Sam Gale and, as always, took me with him. While he was in with Sam, I stayed in the reception area reading the paper. A door opened and a man stepped in. He looked at me, then asked who I was and what I was doing there. I told him. He smiled, put out his hand to shake mine and introduced himself. It was Ruben. He invited me into his own office where, with charm and style, he asked me a lot of questions. How old are you? What games do you like to play? What are your hobbies? What do you want to do with your life?

The conversation took a turn that was to have a profound influence on me, when he wanted to know, 'Where do you go to school?'

I told him, 'I've left school. I want to make my way in the world.'

'And how do you intend to do that?'

'Bricks and mortar,' I said, thinking of Dad's new business. 'I'm going to build and I'm going to sell.'

Ruben looked at me thoughtfully for a moment, then said, 'Only fools build. They build, while others take the profit. There's a much better way to make money out of property. Go to an estate agent, find out what he has on the books, buy it, then sell it again, at a profit.'

I decided then and there that was exactly what I would do. It was only later that I found out why Dad dealt with Sam and not Ruben. I don't know whether Dad ever realised it, but Ruben didn't like my father. It was a matter of personality. As a result of this first meeting, Ruben and I became friends. He also became my mentor in the property business and my lawyer. In property he was astute, in law shrewd and in friendship wise.

No one could know it at the time, but over the next four years, 1958–62, the value of property shares would increase eightfold. In these conditions, a great deal of money could be made legally and easily. So easily that it irritates me to hear some property dealers attribute the expansion of their fortunes to their own acumen and vision. They talk about their successes as though they were men of genius. Frankly, a blind man with one leg could have made money in property in the late '50s and early '60s.

Having decided to go into property, Dad really went at it. We bought and sold quite a lot in east London, which was being developed and rebuilt. For my father and the Gales, born and bred there, this was their old stamping-ground. Buying and selling was much speedier in the boom days of the '50s, but the money involved was far smaller than it would be in the boom days of the '60s, and the business was far less complicated than it would become in the '70s and '80s. You could borrow on easy terms from the bank manager, interest rates were low and inflation hadn't taken off. One of our very first purchases was the Rivoli Cinema in Whitechapel Road. Dad paid £10,000 for it and sold it in no time for £45,000. Somebody built an office block on it.

In the meantime, I embarked on this new phase of my working life and began to look around for housing sites. The first I found was at Cow Lane, Watford, and the second was at Darkes Lane, Potters Bar. I bought a site in Lancaster Gate, and I built Heron Court and London House in St John's Wood. I also bought a site around the corner from where I was living on Sheldon Avenue and built a block of flats. It's still there, and I'm rather proud of it.

When I say built, I mean built. If Dad thought of himself as a property developer, I thought of myself as a builder. I named my company Heron Construction Ltd. Martin McQuen came with me, and so did a number of the lads – bricklayers, electricians and cabinetmakers – who'd worked with me building Harold Hill. It was a great life. I was the property buyer, the developer, the general manager and the builder. I used to work out viabilities on the back of an envelope. I can still do them on the back of an envelope. And I honestly believe if you can't get your scheme down on the back of an envelope, you really need to ask yourself if you should be doing it at all.

My entire office staff consisted of two people – Monty Land, who looked after the accounts, and Paulene Clark, who was my secretary for 37 years. Dad enjoyed this new phase of our business and used to come in every day. He'd light up a cigar and walk around, then go for lunch. One of the men he did deals with was called Denis – I can't remember his last name – but Denis was a fellow who talked with a posh accent and always wore a pinstripe suit and a bowler hat. The two of them would see off two bottles of gin, one each, before they settled on anything and shook hands to seal it. Dad would come back after lunch with another deal, never showing any sign of having drunk that much, then go to Sam Gale's office to get the legal side of it sorted out.

These were wonderful days, mainly because there weren't so many restrictions as there are today, which meant there were more opportunities for dealing. Dad was a hard worker and I think he even had some genius, but his strongest points were his instinct and his energy. He did not philosophise about policy or organisation. I was interested in both and spent a lot of time creatively thinking about our business. I began to see that there were limits to expansion through building more houses. I began to think that we could better broaden our financial base by acquiring properties.

Shifting more attention to this meant developing our organisation, which meant that I needed more property expertise in our office. I thought about who I wanted to bring in and settled on an able and easy to get on with man named Tony Royle. I first met him when he worked for estate agents Healey & Baker. Tony was one of the junior employees and the reason I got to know him so well was because no one else there would see me. I'd go to the office expecting to see the top men, but because I was so young, the top men couldn't be bothered. I was directed to Tony. When he left there to start his own practice, he continued doing work for us. I asked him to join me at Heron and he refused. I asked him again and he refused again. After I asked him and he refused a third time, I took a different approach. He was engaged to a woman named Myra, so one Saturday morning I went round to see her. He showed up and found us having tea. I told him that Myra and I had decided he would be joining Heron on 1 April 1963. Tony decided to shut me up once and for all by saying, 'I'm earning £1,750 a year. If you really want me, you'll have to pay me £3,500 a year, plus £500 a year for my flat, plus give me a new 2.4-litre Jag.'

I didn't flinch. 'OK.'

So on 1 April 1963, Tony started working for Heron. I'm afraid, though, his first day was an eye-opener for him. Since he had such good terms of employment, he'd thought he was joining an up-and-running large-scale property company. But that first morning when he arrived at our office – which was then at Chiswell Street, EC1 – and asked for the property portfolio, he was handed a couple of files on buildings. The same buildings he'd already bought for us.

Tony went to see my father in his office. 'Where's the property portfolio?'

Dad said, 'You've only just got here. You haven't bought any yet.'

Tony kept asking himself, 'Is this a property company I've joined?' And he stayed for the next 25 years.

* * *

Theoretically, by the age of 25 I was already a millionaire. But my life was still much like it had always been. I lived at home, and in my spare time I did very much what I'd done before. The pattern of my existence hardly changed. Work dominated it, and as a result of my long hours – a stimulus not a hardship – time did not hang heavy on my hands. I paid myself a salary of £2,000 a year and spent only about half of it. I lived comfortably at home.

Dad and I were always well dressed and many people remarked on it. They assumed that we were interested in clothes. To tell the truth, we couldn't be bothered. It was my mother who bought our suits.

If I wasn't working at the weekend, I might go to the cinema or to a dance. In the summer, I sometimes went with a chum for a week to Margate or Bournemouth and lounged around the beach. I also liked to fish. I didn't sense it at the time, but my horizons were very limited.

Dating in those days was different from how it is today. You might meet a nice girl at the local youth club and make an impression by buying her juice or Coca-Cola for a shilling. I had some girlfriends, but I was not by nature gregarious. I was shy. My male chums were like me, sons of businessmen, accountants or lawyers, without any highfaluting ideas. Our formative years were spent in the era of war, followed by the era of austerity, so we were not born and bred with high expectations. I didn't see a great deal of the girls I'd meet because I was too busy with work. I didn't see much of my male chums either for the same reason.

I was spending more and more time on the road because the more I built, the further I went from London. I saw business to be done up and down the country, and drove thousands of miles a year, maybe as many as 1,500 miles a week, getting up at six and working seven days a week. These were busy years and, in some respects, the happiest years of my working life. My heart was in building. For the most part, we were working the middle or lower end of the market, selling houses in the £2,500–£5,000 range, but I was also into commercial accommodation and built our first town centre at Hoddesdon in Hertfordshire.

Did I know what I was doing when we started as house builders in the Home Counties? Not really. Of course, in those days, I don't suppose you could go too far wrong, because I'm not sure anyone else in the business knew any better. What we did that the others didn't was to do all the work ourselves. We were Heron Construction, which meant we were physically building everything, employing all those people that came over from the furniture factory. Dad was buying sites, I was buying sites and Ron Hanbury, the Barclays Bank manager in Shoreditch, was lending us the money to pay for them. It all seemed to work and we all made good money.

The harder I worked, the more I realised that luck always plays a role. Sometimes it was good, sometimes it went against us, but Lady Luck was often there, somewhere in the background. I was always glad to be lucky, but there are many people who mistake good fortune for skill. I guess that's human nature. It's when luck goes against you that you sort the men from the boys, because when you've been unlucky, it takes nerve and resources to come back and start again.

There was a deal once we wanted to do in Sunderland. A promising site was going to be auctioned there, and I said I'd go and Dad decided to come with me. One of the architects who did some work for us in those days, Ernie Boyer, lived in Hertfordshire, which was on our route, and he wanted to come along too. We planned to pick him up at 6.30 that morning outside the De Havilland building in Hatfield, now occupied by British Aerospace. Dad was driving the Rolls, and we were there on the dot (Dad was always punctual), but Ernie was 30 minutes late.

Dad was furious and for the next half-hour he went on bawling Ernie out, calling him every name under the sun. I'm sure the roof of the Rolls was going up and down. After four or five hours – there were no motorways in those days – we were just getting near Sunderland when Dad insisted that before we turned off for the town centre, we had to get to Scotch Corner. I can't remember why, but I do know that signposting in those days wasn't as good as it is today, and we wound up going well past Sunderland before we turned round. By the time we got to the auction, it was over. In Dad's view, this was entirely Ernie's fault, and he let him know that.

I needed to rest my ears, so I got out of the car to walk around a bit. Lady Luck was with me on my stroll, and I just happened to bump into the estate agent who was selling the parcel of land we'd come up to buy. I asked him how much he got and he told me that the property didn't sell because it had not reached its reserve price. Immediately, I went back to Dad to tell him.

He got out of the car and asked the agent, 'What do you want for it?'

The agent took a deep breath and answered, '125 grand.'

Dad was quiet for a moment, then he said, 'It's a deal.'

The agent was delighted. What he didn't know was that we were prepared to bid up to £150,000. All this because Ernie was late and we got lost. Needless to say, the journey home was a lot more pleasant than it had been coming up.

The episode left me with a warm feeling for Sunderland. It was a place where you had to drink plenty of beer – Scottish & Newcastle – with the local authorities to get things done, and I'm not a beer drinker, but the people there are hard-working, solid and dependable, and I have had many happy dealings with them throughout my life. Many years after the Ernie incident, I would come back to Sunderland to rebuild the entire town centre.

As we became more sophisticated in the early '60s, we moved on to small supermarkets and retail developments, and that's how, eventually, we developed commercial property in 52 towns throughout the country.

What I learned from those early experiences is that there is really nothing mysterious about property development. Every asset is a future income stream. When interests rates are low, say you can only get 3 per cent on deposit, if you have a property producing 8 per cent, then that's a valuable asset. If interest rates are at 10 per cent and your property is only producing 8 per cent, then the value of your asset is on the wrong side of the equation.

Now factor in borrowings. If you're doing a development that will yield 8 per cent, you'd be looking to borrow money at 6 per cent, which gives you a 2 per cent spread. Leverage that on a 3x1 basis – you put up 25 per cent and the bank puts up 75 per cent – then, when you've finished the project and are collecting the rents, you revalue it, refinance it and take all your equity out of the deal. You have your initial investment back, plus the rent creating the cash flow and also the growth on the asset. It's having your cake and eating it.

In 1964, we became a public company, Heron Holdings, with £3 million worth of property and £4 million in development, which was quite a lot in those days. Twenty years later, we would be the second-largest private company in the country.

Our offices had already become too small for us, even though the entire company was just my father, Monty Land, Tony Royle, Paulene Clark, another secretary, called Carol, and myself. We looked around for new premises and found them on the Marylebone Road, not far from Madame Tussaud's. The building was called College House and the bottom three floors were occupied by the Bible College. We acquired the lease a couple of years after we moved in, took over the whole building, changed its name to Heron House and have been there ever since.

That same year, 1964, the country took a nosedive into a full-blown economic crisis. The Labour Party came to power and Harold Wilson appointed George Brown Secretary of State for the newly created Department for Economic Affairs. The department did not last long, but it lasted long enough to do a great deal of damage. Among other things, Brown pushed his Control of Office Development Act through Parliament, which put a stop to new commercial development. The act gave Brown the right to create the Office Development Permit, which you needed if you were going to develop a commercial office property. Because he wanted to redirect development to the North, he simply refused to issue ODPs to people looking to build in the south of England.

Many people kept saying it was only a temporary condition, but I believed it was going to be with us for some time. The squeeze threatened our cash flow, and without cash you cannot sustain property development. I felt that I needed to look around for property-orientated activities – properties where goods or services generated enough cash to tide Heron over – which was when I discovered petrol stations.

CHAPTER 3

....

MR SELF-SERVICE CUT-PRICE PETROL

Petrol retailing is my 'fuck you' business.

If everything else goes wrong, I can always continue to live my lifestyle pumping petrol. It's a business I understand – I've been in it for more than 40 years – and I am not being immodest when I say that I most probably know more about petrol retailing than anybody in the country. Pump prices go up and down, but cash is pumping 24 hours a day, and I have never lost money retailing petrol. I have also always made money selling packages of sites to the major oil companies. The petrol business is my hobby. I enjoy it. And it has never let me down.

Ever since I was a young boy playing truant from school to visit garages, I have been keen on motor cars. I still am. Don't ask me why, because I don't know. Maybe it's the smell of oil and petrol. But back in the 1960s, it dawned on me that when you own a petrol station, you own a property where you can sell a product to finance the property – and whatever else you sell on the site is an added bonus to the business. At the same time, petrol is something the public can't do without. You don't have to manufacture anything. You don't need a highly trained staff. You don't have to display the goods in a window. When the customer buys, you don't have to wrap anything up and deliver it.

To my mind, petrol retailing combines my property expertise and my business expertise. Back then, the cash flow from service stations was better than just owning a property and leasing it for 6 per cent, because there were bigger margins on fuel. You could make a 20 per cent return. Today, margins are much tighter, so you're looking at 10 per cent, unleveraged, depending on how you structure the deal. Of course, today, the price of the land the petrol station sits on is, on average, the same as the cost of the installation and building.

Before I took the leap and went into the business, I wanted to learn everything I could about it. So I drove around the country looking at petrol stations, studying them. I also made a number of trips abroad. The place that taught me the most, where I picked up the best ideas, was the United States. There, the huge volume of cars had brought filling stations to a degree of efficiency unrivalled in Europe. I visited more than 50 garages in America and asked questions. What struck me was how American filling stations made ours look like dumps.

This was a time in Britain when you pulled into a petrol station and some grease monkey came out of a filthy garage and filled up your car for you. Maybe he smiled, most of the time he didn't. If there was a restroom, it was usually foul, and more often than not it was locked. Sometimes the grease monkey remembered to offer to clean your windscreen. Other times he couldn't be bothered. There was a tiny cluttered office where you went to pay, and the guy threw the money in the till. Maybe he sold you a can of oil and if you were lucky, you could buy a bar of chocolate. But that was all. There was no service. There were no shops. It was a pit stop.

In America, petrol stations were called 'service stations' because service was the name of the game. That's how they kept customers and attracted new ones. They had attendants in smart-looking uniforms who smiled and always cleaned your windscreen and always asked to check your oil, because that way they might be able to sell you a quart of oil or windscreen-wiper fluid. They offered to check your tyres, because that way they might also sell you tyres. Service stations did a substantial trade in soda and coffee and snacks, had automotive accessories for sale and a car wash. It all produced cash flow. So I decided to import the concept of the American service station to Britain. This was revolutionary. There was nothing like it anywhere in the country. And it would change the industry forever.

I'd seen in the States that some service stations were managed by independent small businessmen who rented their sites from the big oil companies. That meant they did things their own way. Some did them well, some did them badly, and that was one thing I didn't like, because it meant there was no consistency, there were no set standards. My business was going to be run from the centre. My idea was to design a working model where everything would be uniform. Every one of my petrol stations would operate on the same principles, provide the same top value for money, offer the same quality products, pride itself on service, and demonstrate the same exacting degree of efficiency, which would come from close staff supervision and discipline.

I called my brand Heron and each garage displayed the Heron crest, which was designed by the College of Arms, bearing the Heron motto – *'Finis coronat opus.'* For the benefit of people who, like me, don't understand Latin, it translates as, 'The end crowns the work.' What I was saying was that at a Heron filling station, 'The finishing touches are the makings of a work of art.'

My strategy was to sell the Heron brand on three things – service, quality and price. And service was our top priority. Before anyone took up their duties on my forecourt, they had to go through a training course. Then they were required to 'sign the pledge', a copy of which was prominently displayed for every customer to see. 'We pledge ourselves to clean the windscreen, to check the oil, to check the water and battery, and to provide all possible aid and information with the speed and courtesy that is the hallmark of Heron service.' I recruited people who had a background of discipline and initiative. In many instances, we employed ex-servicemen who, having left the army, found civvy street a bit of a let-down. These were people who could automatically respond to the pace and order that Heron expected of its employees.

Quality meant that each Heron garage had to be spacious, uncluttered and with easy access. There had to be generous room between the pumps. There had to be imposing, well-painted canopies in bright colours with plenty of bunting. Each Heron garage had to look cheerful, welcoming, airy and clean. Everything was to be spotless, particularly the toilet facilities – pink tiles for the Ladies, blue for the Gents. They also had to smell nice. My garages had to be infinitely more attractive than the grease monkey's down the road. I wanted customers to remember how comfortable they were when they pulled in and how well looked after they were while they were filling up. We were going to do everything we could to make certain that every customer came back. We took petrol retailing to a whole different level.

In the beginning, every Heron garage had an 'Auto-Market' selling tyres, batteries and other accessories at cut prices. Food and drinks were on sale from vending machines, including basics like bread. Later, as we developed a better understanding of the business, I made critical changes and created the concept of the petrol station as a convenience store. Until I did it, no one in the UK had figured out that a petrol station was the ideal place to sell more than just petrol.

As for price, I offered three grades of petrol and diesel, and sold them all for five old pence per gallon less than the recommended prices of the major oil companies. No one in the UK had figured out that petrol could be discounted. The majors pretty much had a corner on the market. The only way I could take business away from them was by combining American-style service, a shopping experience and cut prices. This was radical. And it would work better than anyone could imagine.

* * *

The first thing I needed to do was buy sites. I was friendly with a man who worked at ESSO named Peter Britton and because he knew the business better than I did, I brought Peter into the company and together we started acquiring properties.

Obviously, having a site isn't enough, you also need something to sell, so I went looking for a supplier. But my plan to undercut the big oil companies' prices meant that I couldn't buy a supply of branded petrol from them. They had no interest in letting me compete on price. Of course, I tried anyway and approached all of them, but every one of them slammed the door shut in my face, telling me, 'No thanks, goodbye.'

So I went to an old-time Texan oilman named Don Johnson, who was managing director of Phillips Petroleum. A big guy who sat in his office wearing a Stetson hat, he had a joint venture at the time with ICI and operated a refinery in Teesside. I told him I intended to build a chain of petrol stations and sell cut-price fuel. I admitted that all the majors had turned me down because they didn't want some young company undermining their market. Then I asked him, 'Will you supply us petrol?'

He looked at me like I was crazy, then said, 'I like your cheek.'

I asked, 'But will you sell to me?'

He nodded, 'Yeah, OK, I'll give you a fuel supply contract. But I'm going to deliver it in grey tankers.' That meant no brand.

I signed with him and opened my first Heron petrol station at 7 a.m. on 6 April 1966 at Marshalswick Lane, St Albans. We priced our petrol at 5p less per gallon than the majors and by mid-morning there were queues for half a mile waiting to fill up. We actually needed to call the police in to direct traffic. It was all such a phenomenal success – we pumped 45,000 gallons on the first day – that we even made the television news.

Our forecourt was four lanes, and eventually we expanded to six with passing lanes in between, which no one in the UK had ever seen before. Within a year, I opened 12 more sites, all with our reshaped forecourts, using my property expertise to organise 100 per cent financing through the ICI Pension Fund and the Electricity Nominee Pension Fund. We paid rent for each site on a 20-year flat lease at 6 per cent per annum, with no rent review, and that became a licence to print money. At least it was until June 1967, when the Six Day War broke out in the Middle East.

Israel and Egypt started shooting at each other, the neighbouring Arab countries joined in against Israel, and the Suez Canal was shut. I was deeply worried for Israel, but I didn't realise that I was more than just a concerned onlooker until I received a phone call from Phillips on the second day of the war. They told me straight off, 'We have a problem.' They were bringing product into England for us from the Gulf and had a tanker stuck in the Canal.

I saw my whole business going down the toilet. Everyone in Britain was trying to fill up their cars, there was panic buying and my sites were running out of petrol, fast. I begged them to do whatever they had to, and they promised to try. It took a week, but they somehow found alternative supplies for me and we stayed in business, although I don't suppose I slept too well until the tankers started delivering again, because you can't have a petrol station without petrol.

There were reports at the time that Heron's petrol came not from Phillips but from behind the Iron Curtain. This was the height of the Cold War, so any insinuation that we were dealing with Communist regimes was very damaging. It wasn't true. But there were a lot of people in the petrol business willing to do, or say, whatever they could to keep customers from driving onto our forecourts.

Anyway, thanks to aggressive marketing and hard work, Heron made great progress and we took a lot of customers away from the oil majors. Not that they suffered enough to feel real pain, because they were too big and too rich. But then, being too big and too rich was their Achilles heel. Their dominant interest was in drilling and refining crude oil. That's what produced their wealth. They lacked any real interest in selling at the pump and, consequently, were second rate at retailing. That left the field open for someone like me.

I saw petrol retailing as a double-edged business. There were the products I could sell, and there was property. And it was property that made the business unique, because there was no risk letting it. The day the petrol station opened, the property investment was making a return from the petrol. It was a clever scheme. What I could never figure out was how come no other so-called clever people in the property business saw it too. But I suppose that applies to lots of things in life. There were then about 12,000 petrol stations in the UK, which left plenty of room for other people to do the same thing.

* * *

After those first twelve sites were up and running and making good profits, I started looking at ways to cut costs. That's when I invented the UK's first self-service station.

Some journalists wrote at the time that I became interested in self-service stations as a result of seeing them on my trip to the States. This is not so. There were no self-service stations in America when I was there. I came across the idea when I saw supermarkets taking over from corner shops. Supermarkets are a self-service business and I figured if people were willing to buy their groceries that way, they would also be willing to buy petrol that way.

Because you can't just one day change from full service to self-service – the customer wouldn't know what to do – I had to make the stations customer friendly. I found a pump manufacturer called Yungmans in Sweden and bought pumps from them that were easy for customers to use. I then rebuilt our service station in Hillingdon, put in the new pumps, enlarged the forecourt and built a shop where customers could pay.

We opened to a great deal of fanfare. Self-service became such a phenomenal success straight away that I immediately started to convert as many sites as I could. People liked it because they weren't going to some grubby forecourt with a grease monkey serving them. There was a modern forecourt with a passing lane. You got in easily and served yourself. It was a novelty, and the petrol cost around 3p less than at a conventional service station. Do-it-yourself was quicker, more efficient, more convenient and cheaper.

By the end of 1969, we had 66 Heron stations, 35 of them self-service, with 15 self-service stations under construction.

It was at this point that the major oil companies started sitting up and taking notice. I might have been a flea on the back of an elephant, but I had become something of a minor annoyance to them. So Shell, BP and Chevron all came knocking on my door. The same people who wouldn't sell me petrol to get started now wanted to buy me out. Chevron was especially keen. The American company was just starting to drill oil out of the North Sea and saw me as an opportunity to get their brand up and running in the UK. They didn't seem particularly bothered about the sites themselves, it was the idea that I had a lot of sites that interested them, because that would give them instant impact. They offered me a good price for the business. Many people would have jumped at the chance to sell out, but because I knew from experience how cut-throat this market was, I decided that before I sold anything to them, I needed to speak to the competition.

I knew most of the players in the industry because I was out and about networking all the time and used to go to all the industry dinners. So I rang John Bradley, who was the marketing director at Shell-Mex/BP – they were much bigger then than they are today and controlled something like 40 per cent of the market – and also spoke with John Riddell-Webster, who was another director. When I told them I'd had this offer from Chevron, Riddell-Webster said right away, 'Don't go selling your business to them.'

Oil marketing people are not the most sophisticated people in the world – that's not a criticism, just an observation – and if Riddell-Webster's reaction wasn't an invitation to raise my price, I don't know what was. But before he and I started talking numbers, I wanted him to know, 'I don't actually have to sell the business to anybody.'

He didn't want me to walk away and said, 'We will buy it.'

I said, 'Why don't you make me an offer I can't refuse?'

He asked to see the financials and two weeks later doubled Chevron's offer. I might have been only 27 years old, but I'd been in business a dozen years, so I suggested, 'I'll sell you the business if you pay me a fee so that I can continue running the sites. Then you put up money for expansion and I'll expand the business.'

That's how Shell-Mex/BP bought our sites for £4 million. They agreed to give me 2p a gallon to pump petrol and put up another £4 million for 20 years, fixed at 5 per cent, so that we could expand. I took down the Heron signs and began selling branded Shell petrol. I also started buying and building one new site a week.

A year or so later, when I had 50 new sites, I went back to John Riddell-Webster and said, 'I want to sell my sites.' He paid £10 million for the second tranche. Eighteen months after that, we had another fifty sites ready to go. But this time when I went to see Riddell-Webster he said, 'It's a bit much,' and turned me down.

That surprised me. But in business no doesn't always mean no. So I came back with, 'If you're short of cash, I'll lease them to you.' He thought about that, liked the idea and we worked out a deal. We leased those 50 stations to Shell-Mex/BP for £750,000 per annum for 35 years, which valued the lease at £10 million to £12 million.

Fifteen months later, I was knocking on his door yet again. But the speed of all this was more than Shell-Mex/BP could take. Riddell-Webster even confessed to me, 'We're happy for you to run the sites, but this is embarrassing for us because we have an army of people on the payroll who are supposed to be out there doing what you're doing and they're not buying anything. I don't know what they're doing. You're buying all the best sites in the marketplace.' I decided if he didn't want them, I'd find someone else who did.

All the time that I was buying the best sites, I was also coming to understand that the most important word in marketing is 'FREE'. As a result, I offered Heron Gold Stamps to build customer loyalty. It was exactly like today's airline frequent flyer miles. With every purchase, we handed out Heron Stamps, which customers could exchange for wine glasses, steak knives, table mats and other goods. We weren't the first to do it – S&H Green Stamps were well established in the US and Green Shield was already in the UK – but we were the first petrol sellers to offer a rewards programme. Here I was, putting cut-price petrol into a larger package for the customer and offering extra goods and services on our premises for lower cost. As a result, our overheads increased by a small amount but our volume increased substantially. And volume is crucial in the petrol business. As volume goes up, so do profits.

In July 1970, I spent the unheard of sum of £1 million to open the UK's first 'new-style' petrol station. It was at Blackbird Hill, Wembley. As well as all the amenities we'd offered previously, we provided piped music and an auto-shop in which more than 3,000 different items were on sale. For me, the Blackbird Hill station was the prototype for the '70s.

Other people realised that too, because when John Riddell-Webster turned down those next 50 stations and I started looking for someone else to do business with, Texaco was right there.

The man I knew at Texaco was the managing director, Carl Lewis. He was looking to rebuild the group, so I said goodbye to Shell-Mex/BP, gave them their money back – we walked away with no hard feelings on either side – and went into business with Texaco. Over the next four years, we sold Texaco 175 sites.

When Texaco got indigestion because I was building these sites so fast, we did a 50-site deal with Conoco, which was Continental Oil. Then we did a 50-site deal with Mobil. We'd begun as Heron, become Shell and then we were Texaco. After that, we rebuilt the Heron chain, then sold 150 Heron sites to Elf, the French petrol company which is known today as Total. In all, I built 968 sites – more than any of the major oil companies built with their armies of staff – and sold over 900 of them back to the major oil companies. We also trained Shell and Texaco in how to run self-service stations. They weren't in that business until we came along. And now that's what they do.

If I had to guess, I'd say that I've probably made, in old money, over £120 million in the petrol business. That would be around £500 million in today's terms. If we still had those other 900 sites, the business would be worth today £1 billion plus.

* * *

Heron petrol stations no longer exist, but we still operate 74 sites. We own 45 and manage the rest for BP. We still do business with ESSO and Shell, and represent 10 per cent of BP's non-motorway, retail English business. Most of our stations operate under the Snax 24 brand.

To make the business work today, you need several elements. It starts with the size of a site. I want to know the traffic count so I can determine if the site is big enough to serve that volume of traffic. If it's too big relative to the flow of traffic, I have to make a judgement call as to whether the investment is worthwhile. Some of the big oil companies use computers to work out new site volume. I do it out in my head because, after all these years, I know what to look for.

But you can't have rigid rules, because opportunities can jump out at you. I was out in the Midlands one day looking at a garage that had suddenly come on the market when I spotted a plot of land of about three acres adjoining the site with a For Sale board. At the side of the road, there was a house and peering out of the window of the house was a couple, both of them clearly in their 80s. They were trying to figure out who we were, so I went over to them and found out they were the owners of the land for sale. I asked how much they wanted for it, and they said £130,000. Right away, I said yes, but only if they gave me an option for the property on the spot. The point of the option was that even if we only paid as little as one pound down, and even if the option was written out and signed on the back of a paper napkin, it tied up the deal. If we didn't get an option, somebody else could come along and make a bigger offer and they would be free to sell.

The old boy agreed because he'd only just put out the For Sale board that morning. It was one of the best deals I ever made. The forecourt alone was worth in excess of £200,000, and the land around it was enough for the construction of a motel and a restaurant. We obtained planning permission, then sold the site with the permission for £250,000 profit.

So a service station needs to be in the right place. In addition, it needs to have a big, clean well-lit forecourt in order to bring in volume. You also need a good car wash. That's important because you can sell a wash for £3 to £5 that only costs you 25p. A good car wash can take £1,500 a week for selling water and a bit of soap.

Finally, you need a shop. I pioneered the modern filling station by turning the petrol-station business into a retail convenience-store business.

In our model, each shop is basically identical, although a few might be slightly different in shape. They are all about the impulse buy. Retail is the detail side of it. When you go in the shop to pay for your petrol, we want to get you to buy something. People don't service their cars any more, so in terms of car accessories we don't stock anything more than top-up oil, a light bulb maybe, or a little thing to make your car smell nice inside. Instead, we stock fresh sandwiches, coffee, doughnuts, sweets and cold drinks.

We're trying to get people to change their habits so that, instead of going to a major supermarket in the week, they top up their shopping on the way home during the week in one of our shops. So we sell milk, eggs and bacon, and chilled meals like a pizza to microwave back home. We sell soap, cigarettes and toilet paper. We know we're good at it because the average convenience store margin is about 19 per cent and ours is 25 per cent. We also sell 50 per cent more per square foot than the average shop. That means that if we're taking £20,000 a week, operating on a 25 per cent margin, we're getting £5,000 profit out of that shop. Add it all up and, after operating costs, rent and labour, we're looking at a self-service petrol station bringing in £200,000-plus profit per year.

Again, the key to making it work is volume. The more you pump, the more you make, while your costs stay constant. If you're pumping 150,000 litres a week, you may be making £6,000 to £7,500. We look for 80 per cent of our target turnover in the first year, 90 per cent in the second and 100 per cent in the third. Those are projections, because sometimes it takes five years to achieve what we expect with the forecourt shop and car wash. A lot depends on developments that may be taking place in the area. Patterns of activity change, so we have to stay on top of it. This is a business that requires a lot of attention to detail. And a lot of business people simply aren't willing to put in the time and effort. But I have always believed that retail is detail, which is why I visit ten or twelve of my sites every week.

I call it my Saturday job. I hit the road before 7 a.m. because I want to see for myself that my petrol stations are living up to my standards. On a typical Saturday, I do 500 to 600 miles – these are 12- to 14-hour Saturdays – so that I can spend 30 minutes on each site.

At every site, I walk around the forecourt to see that it's clean, efficient and attractive. I want to see for myself that there are no broken pumps, the brushes in the car wash are good, the wash is clean, all the light bulbs in all the signs are working, the little windows in the pumps are clean so the customers can see how much petrol they're pumping, the advertising posters on the shop walls are up to date and uniform, the rubbish bins have been emptied, there's no damage to the forecourt, there's no litter anywhere, the shrubs are cut and everything is functioning.

Then I go into the shop to make sure that the pricing is right, the shelves are full and clean – which is important, because if the shelves aren't full, then we're missing a sale – and the cash register area is clean and clear, so that the customers have room to pay. I check all the point-of-sale displays, because everything must be well displayed. I want every label facing out so that the customer can see what's available immediately.

There are 5,000 items in every shop and everything needs to be where it should be. We've designed the shops to be a convenient and congenial showplace so that the customer likes the experience of shopping there. Nothing is left to chance. The local manager has a chart telling him exactly where everything must go, and he'd better follow it to the letter. Because I have been doing this so long, I can walk into one of our shops and if there are 60 sandwiches on a shelf, I will go straight to the one that's past its sell-by date. And when I spot something like that, believe me, I blow up.

I check to see that we're giving out Nectar promotion points. I want to see clean and properly stocked storerooms, and that the timed deliveries are arriving on time. I also want to see that the employees are arriving on time and leaving on time. I want to know how the business is going, to pat the manager on the back if everything looks good and to give him a bollocking if it is not.

It's detail, detail, detail.

I also want to talk to my customers. I ask them, 'Do you always use this site? Do you get good service?' I introduce them to my manager and say, 'If you don't get good service, he's the man to complain to.' I hand customers my card and tell them, 'If you have a problem, ring me at head office.' They walk away saying, I met Mr Ronson on a forecourt and he gave me his card. Customers appreciate that human touch.

My managing director, Bill Ahearn, may get the odd call from a customer complaining about a petrol station, but customers hardly ever ring me. I may get one letter a year where somebody will write to say that somebody was rude or that the car wash ate up his aerial, but we have 300,000 customers a week going through our stations, so one or two complaints a year isn't bad.

The reason I spend more than 40 Saturdays a year on the road is to show my people that I care. They see my involvement, they see my commitment, and they respond to it. I lead from the front. That means I have to see things for myself. When you hire someone to go around every day to check on the business, he visits a site, probably has a cup of coffee with the manager and somehow forgets to look into every nook and cranny. Either he doesn't look behind the cashiers to see that there's nothing there that shouldn't be there, or he doesn't spot products on the wrong shelf. You say to yourself, why can't he do the same thing that I do? You tell yourself, maybe he just needs a checklist. So you give him a checklist and hope he'll look at it because that's all he's got to do all day. But that doesn't work either. You have to break things down so that the people under you can manage. At the same time, you have to be on top of those people, because you can't expect them to have the same passion as you for what they have to do. If people don't have a boss who's on top of them, their focus slips away.

You'd think it would be relatively simple to teach employees to check that a place is clean, to check that the shelves are clean, to check that the toilets are clean, to check that everything is where it should be. But I'm afraid it's only when the business is in your blood that you can see right away if something's wrong.

I believe that every aspect of the business must be well organised – discipline rules – and I couldn't have survived in this business for 40 years if it wasn't. I know that when a customer comes into one of our filling station shops, he doesn't expect Aladdin's cave. A visit to a petrol station isn't necessarily a joyous experience. I know that customer wants to get in and out as quick as he can. He's paying for his petrol. But as long as he's there, I want to get some extra money out of his pocket. The art of retailing is to squeeze a few extra pounds out of every customer's visit. You do that not just by filling up shelves, but by ensuring that the right products are properly priced and in the right location. If you don't have the right product on the right shelf, properly priced, you won't sell it.

Around 90 per cent of our sites are run by commission operators. The owner-manager doesn't need a lot of capital to buy in – the deposit is about £25,000 – but he has to run his site our way. We treat our commission operators no different than if they were working for us. If he doesn't want to do it our way, he can go and work for somebody else.

Our managers are predominantly Asian, mainly Sri Lankan and Indian. Many of them run our petrol stations like a family business, with their wife coming in and working the till at weekends. We charge them rent. The fuel belongs to us, the layout of the shop and the shop product comes from our distributors, and we get a commission back from them. The commission operator has to buy from our supplier, and if he buys something from someone else, he's out. We pay him a penny a litre for pumping the fuel, but he's employing the staff. And stock losses are down to him.

The sites are open 24 hours a day, 7 days a week. They generally employ ten staff. Every shop has a manager and big sites have a full-time shop assistant. There are two cashiers during the day and one at night. Every site must also employ a cleaner. A supervisor visits twice a week to ensure that everything is being run the way it should be. We have subcontractors who handle maintenance of the pumps and the car wash. If something goes wrong, it's all set up so that the manager simply has to pick the phone up and ring for help.

* * *

Today, the petrol-station business isn't what it was when I first started, because you can't buy good sites any more. The alternate value of sites for residential or other uses is greater than the value of a petrol station, which is why we haven't built a new site for more than three years. Sites that come onto the market these days are second-line rubbish. Either they don't have a car wash or they don't have a big enough shop. Or, under the new EC regulations, you need to replace tanks that are over 15 years old with double-skin tanks. It's not that we don't want to build new sites, it's that the value of the land has shot past what you can afford to pay for a petrol station to see an acceptable return.

Another reason is that, in the old days, the local authority paid for the roads and roadworks coming in and out of the petrol station. Today, you have to pay for that. And you have to pay for bringing electricity in. That's putting high costs onto the site. Therefore, unless you have existing sites – and the oil companies already own the best of those and won't sell – it's just not viable. That is why there are less and less petrol stations. In London, you drive around and you can't find one. They do exist, but gone are the days of the small sites. They've disappeared.

A relatively new development also has to be factored into this – the hypermarkets. Retailing fuel has become such an important part of the superstore operation. At the moment, Tesco, Sainsbury's and others can buy large supplies of petrol from the major oil companies at favourable prices, which enables them to sell it at low prices that still make them a profit. In some cases, their petrol is actually a loss-leader simply to get customers into the supermarket. They almost give it away. That hits the trade of the nearby filling stations. And that's another reason why the major oil companies have not developed more stations.

When I started in 1966, there were about 38,000 filling stations in the UK. Today, I'd say, there are around 9,000. By 2015, the way things are shaping up, there may be 6,000 or 7,000. More petrol will be sold, but there will be no place for the small site.

Every now and then, somebody asks me, to what do you attribute your success in the petrol retailing industry? The honest answer is luck. I was lucky because the oil companies were so dumb. They weren't lacking in ability – they were run by able people – but the mentality that enabled men to build up large and powerful oil companies was not one suited to managing petrol stations.

It's the difference between the wholesaler mentality and the retailer mentality. The big oil companies think like wholesalers. They have always made their money – and built up their power – from extracting crude oil out of the ground and refining it. They run fleets of ships to move crude from one place in the world to another and fleets of trucks to move refined product up and down the country. They explore and they build pipelines. Some of the leaders of the oil industry were great engineers, industrialists and even international statesmen. Their large-scale, high-calibre activities appealed to global thinking and fostered global perspectives. That's a far cry from what you need to think about when someone pulls in to fill up and wants to buy a stick of gum.

Not that they were lackadaisical. It was that they weren't interested or, frankly, knowledgeable enough. They mostly rented sites to independents, who had to buy fuel from them. They couldn't work up enough enthusiasm to retail petrol at the pump, which is why they subcontracted the running of the service stations. But that meant the quality and range of service varied greatly from one station to another, as did standards of cleanliness and hygiene. The same went for the appearance of the forecourt. You could pull into one of their stations and find that the tyre air didn't work or that the water was turned off. The grease monkey running the place didn't care because the oil company didn't care. At headquarters, they were overstaffed without anyone willing to manage the detail. They went home at lunchtime on a Friday. But retailers do most of their business on a Friday, Saturday, Sunday. It's a different psyche. The service station business needs to be micromanaged.

That's why they never showed much interest in opening up petrol stations north of Watford. To listen to some of them, you'd have thought Newcastle-on-Tyne was on the Bering Strait. That was lucky for us. The site in the North was going to sell the same amount of petrol at the pump as the site in the South, and at the same price, but to more customers. So I started buying petrol stations up there, paying half what I was paying for similar sites in the South. Eventually, a few of the big companies did go back to the North, but by that time we had some of the best sites. We were getting the volume.

I saw an opportunity and took it. I did all the things that today are taken for granted but in 1966 were the exception rather than the rule. Today, some of the majors operate excellent self-service stations, but there are still some that can't maintain the standards of cleanliness and efficiency that we have. Maybe it's because they can't produce enough senior managers who are willing to work six days a week.

Unlike the major oil companies, I never expanded my business into Europe. The reason is simple. You cannot be hands on, the way I am, if you're 1,000 miles away. Unless I could clone ten Gerald Ronsons and post them all over Europe, there was no way I could maintain the control that a successful filling station regime requires. Selling petrol is not like selling Coca-Cola. You can set up a bottling plant to manufacture Coca-Cola under licence and do well out of it. But the petrol market is very competitive with small profit margins. To be successful in foreign countries, you need to create an international or global brand. The majors have done that, but then they can afford to. Their huge international infrastructure deals not in millions of pounds but in billions.

In many businesses, a little piece of a big apple is fine, but there are very few businesses in the world where the apples are this big. For me to compete with them outside our own back yard would take a monumental investment. I just don't see a good enough return for the money or, especially, for the effort. But then they can't really compete with us in our back yard.

What I saw in the business when I first started holds true today. People still need to fill up their cars with petrol. In bad economic times, when people spend less in the supermarket and do top-up shopping during the week, petrol stations do more business. They're recession proof. That's important, because when you've been through more than one trauma in life, the way I have, you need something that you can count on. In 1973, when the economic downturn slowed property development, we had a devaluation of the pound and we had interest rates going up to 14 per cent, what kept Heron alive – and actually bailed out my property business – were my petrol stations.

Today, it's a very compact, cash-rich business. There is no debt. We do north of £300 million annual turnover. That's a lot of money, but nobody takes any dividends out of it. The petrol stations are owned by the Ronson Family Trust and the money it generates accumulates.

Do I need to work so hard at my Saturday job, driving all over the country for 12 hours to visit service stations? No. But I enjoy it. I still have some of the same people working for me after 20 years, which gives me a lot of pleasure.

Most probably, maybe five years down the road, I will sell or merge the business, because some of my management will be getting to retirement age and it's not a business my daughters will wish to run. I could sell it easily, any time, because of the quality of the sites we operate. But that's not an issue for today. It's not even in my thought process.

CHAPTER 4

....

EXPANDING THE FRONTIERS

When Laurence finished school in 1965, Dad brought him into the business, starting him at the very bottom. No favours given. Dad's attitude was, the only way you're going to win any respect as the owner's son is to work your way up.

One day, the two of them got into Dad's car at 5 a.m. to drive to the West Country. We had a building site in Patchway, next to where they used to make Concorde. Laurence was sitting in the back of the car and it was barely light, pissing down with rain and the site was a mess. Dad and the site agent started arguing about something, and the site agent said, 'If you think you've got somebody who can do it better than me, then the choice is yours.'

Dad never needed two invitations to take a person up on something like that, so he fired the site agent and turned to Laurence. He said, 'Jump out, you can look after this.' Laurence didn't even have a coat. But he got out of the car and before he could remind Dad that he didn't have a clue what to do, Dad was back in the car and the car was gone.

Whereas in temperament I was like my father, Laurence was unlike us both. He was good at school and enjoyed learning. I'm sure he could have become a well-educated man. He had the brains, the sensitivity and the interests. But my parents did not share in that side of his life, and I didn't have sufficient interest in it either. Although Laurence had the character, ability and aptitude to make it in the business, it soon became clear that this wasn't for him.

I'd agreed with Dad that it would be good for Laurence to start at the bottom, so I sent him to work at a petrol station. I wanted him to meet customers, to see at first hand what the business was all about, to understand what high standards we set for ourselves. He got on well with people and wasn't afraid of long hours or hard work, but his way of going about things was different from mine. Obviously, different people have different ways of doing things, but little things got in the way. For instance, my desk was always clean while his was messy. Even today, his desk is cluttered. He tells me that if he needs to get access to some paper or folder, he doesn't trust anyone to file it. He prints every email and amasses piles of paperwork. He also tells me that he doesn't have as many cupboards in his office as I do in mine. I guess that those of us who were raised in post-war austerity don't always understand people who were raised in the 1960s and '70s.

I remember saying to him one day, 'How the hell can you work with your desk like that? I couldn't work on a desk like that.'

Laurence simply answered, 'I'm not asking you to. Do you want results from me, or do you want me to be a carbon copy of you?'

That shut me up.

From time to time we'd fight like cats and dogs, but never for very long, and not because we were brothers. It always came down to differing business views. Laurence was not me and not my father, and, in a sense, that made it two against one. He went through a semi-rebellious stage. If Dad said that trees are green, Laurence would say no, they're yellow. They had rows every 15 minutes. Also, Laurence was coming into a business that I had been running for so long. It wasn't easy for him. He wasn't as focused on the business as he should have been. He did what he had to do, but there were other things that attracted him, like girls and cars.

Even though the situation often irked him, he usually put a cheerful face on it. One of his frequent quips was, 'You'll have no difficulty in recognising me as Gerald's brother – we're completely different.'

* * *

In 1964, I went to the motor show at Earls Court and saw for the first time one of the most beautiful Italian sports cars ever, the Iso Grifo. It was on display at a booth run by a dealer named Peter Agg, and, even though I already had a Lamborghini Espada at the time, I was so struck that I bought the Iso Grifo on the spot. I didn't even wait for a test drive. At the time, Peter also owned the Suzuki concession for the UK, but soon after I bought my Iso Grifo, that side of his business hit a rough patch and he had to reorganise.

Having had a first impression of me as a man who could make up his mind quickly, he dropped me a line, reminded me of how we met and asked if Heron might like to acquire his Suzuki concessions. The Japanese were moving aggressively into European business, so Peter and I began talking and I agreed to buy it. The lawyers and accountants then got involved, but they worked too slowly for my liking and after three weeks I said to Peter, 'I've already given you my word that the deal is on, so let's send these guys away and complete at the end of the week.' He said fine, we saved ourselves a lot of time and legal fees, and that was the beginning of a very good relationship.

To secure the deal, we had to go to Japan and meet with the Suzuki masters. It was a 15- to 17-hour flight, which is a long time to be stuck on a plane. And in this case, it was going to feel even longer, because Peter insisted on travelling economy. Now, economy class for a couple of hours is one thing. I honestly don't mind. On trips in Europe, I often fly in the back of the plane. But from London to Japan? On the way over, I said to him, 'Either this deal has to be even better than I expect, or I've got to reorganise your company so you can afford to fly first class.'

When Peter briefed me on what I needed to know about doing business with the Japanese, I reminded him that my style has always been to deal with the boss directly, eyeball to eyeball. But he warned that that wasn't how things worked in Japan. I had to start with the men at the bottom of the pyramid, then work my way up, getting agreements layer by layer until just about everything was set. It was only at that point that I could expect to meet the man at the top. He said it was the custom and that it was called 'ringi-san'.

This didn't appeal to me at all, but Peter knew these people, so I went along with him. Our first meeting was with a dozen or so junior executives in a room with a blackboard. One of the young men outlined the deal in a very elementary way, drawing pictures and diagrams in chalk to illustrate everything, as if he was speaking to a ten year old. I'd never felt so bored in my life and began to wonder, at that rate, how long I'd have to stay in Japan. I took a box of Monte Cristos out of my briefcase and passed them around. Half a dozen of these young men took a cigar from me and lit up. I don't know what they expected, but in a couple of minutes they'd all turned green and left the room, never to return.

We met them again the next morning. I offered each one a cigar. They politely declined and got right to business. Because it seemed to me that things moved more quickly after that, I continued offering cigars to everyone I met. And the deal got done far sooner than I'd anticipated. Heron became sole concessionaire for Suzuki in the UK.

Since those days, I've done a good deal of business with the Japanese and am comfortable with the difference in their style from the Europeans or Americans. The idea many Westerners have that the Japanese are becoming Westernised is a delusion. And, knowing the Japanese as well as I do, I can say it's a delusion they want us to have. Young Japanese may like to wear Yves St Laurent shirts and carry Louis Vuitton luggage, but they remain thoroughly Japanese. Their way of thinking and working, their culture, their educational system and its values, and their religion make them profoundly different from Westerners. It's foolish for any businessman from the West to think that he can penetrate the Japanese mind, let alone fully understand it. It's a misapprehension that will, guaranteed, cost him money. That doesn't mean you shouldn't do business with them, just that they only do business with us when and how it suits them. I know from experience that you can develop loyalty with them, but also that it's not the same kind of loyalty you can develop with Europeans or Americans. In the West, business relationships are often personal. In Japan, they never are.

A year or so later, Peter and I went over there again. This time, while we were in the factory, someone mentioned that sales were very slow in America and that a Suzuki warehouse in California was overstocked. Peter smelled a deal and said to me, 'Why don't we go to California on the way back?'

It didn't cost us any time because you actually gain a day when you go that way round, so we flew to LA and checked into the Beverly Hills Hotel. To my surprise, I bumped into a couple of friends – well-known English property guys – who were also staying there. But they were even more surprised to see me, because both of them were married and they'd checked in with a couple of girls. To each his own. But that's not my style. I'm someone who doesn't even add a few extra days' holiday on to the end of a business trip. I like to get on with things and go home.

At the Suzuki warehouse, we couldn't believe what we saw. There must have been 250,000 motorbikes there. The company was 50 per cent overstocked, and especially long on 125cc bikes. In his perfect English gentleman style, Peter said to me, 'We should try and do a deal. That is, if you put the money up.'

Of course, it would be Heron that would have to put up the money, and we were talking about a lot of money. But the Californian sunshine or the jet lag, or both, had muddled my brain, and without any hesitation I said, 'Let's have a go.'

Peter did some fast calculations. We would have to make minor adjustments to each bike, such as sorting out the lights for the indicators. But we could do that ourselves in England and it probably wouldn't cost more than £5 per bike. So Peter and I negotiated what was then the largest single deal ever on a single model. We paid £10 million. We imported the bikes, knocked the price up to compete with the Yamaha model selling for £350 – it was nearly the same bike – took out full-page adverts in the motorcycle news and trade papers, and sold the lot. In fact, our bikes were going out of the warehouse quicker than we could deal with the indicator lights. And we doubled our money. What we did and how we did it became part of the folklore within the industry.

Not long after that, Peter started telling me that the American motorbike championships were about to take place at Daytona, Florida, and how the British racer Barry Sheene was going to ride for Suzuki. He suggested that Gail and I go with him to Florida, so we did. Barry had worked for Suzuki since he was a boy of 16, and by the time I came along he was winning races, as he did that week in Florida.

In 1970, at the age of 20, he won the British 125cc Championship. A year later he came in second in the 125cc World Championships. He broke his thigh, arm, collarbone and a couple of ribs at the 1975 Daytona 200, which nearly ended his career, but Barry wasn't the kind of man to go out like that and seven weeks later he was racing again. He won five 500cc Grand Prix races in 1976, which made him world champion, and kept his title in 1977 by winning six Grand Prix races.

He left Suzuki in 1979 to go with Yamaha, crashed again very seriously in 1982 and was forced to retire two years after that. We sponsored him during his Suzuki years in a deal that cost, total, around £1.25 million a year. Japan supplied the bikes, we put in £250,000 and Japan then gave us the rest towards the programme. If you look at pictures of Barry and the bikes in those days, you'll see I also got sponsorship from Shell and Texaco – my partners in the petrol retailing business – as well as Heron.

I knew Barry well and liked him a lot. When he was in London, he often came to Friday-night dinner with us. This was before he married Stephanie. After they married, they'd occasionally come away with us on our boat for a holiday. He liked my daughters, especially Lisa and Amanda, and taught them how to ride a bike. He also taught me how to ride, but I've never been a fan of motorbikes. I did have a small bike that I drove around on Sunday mornings when the sun was shining, but I'm too old for that today.

Barry was a very down-to-earth, semi-cockney, no bullshit kind of guy who knew his limitations and was sensible enough to know when it was time to quit. He'd made himself a few million pounds and decided he wanted to live in Australia. He liked the climate there – it was good for his bones, which were all pinned together. He created a second career for himself there as a television interviewer and sports presenter. He was a good, level-headed family man and I still communicate with Stephanie.

It was a terrible loss when Barry passed away. But he lived life in the fast lane and these things do catch up with you. Sadly, it caught up with him in 2003, when he died of cancer at just 52 years old.

* * *

If owning and riding motorbikes didn't thrill me, cars always have. The Iso Grifo was just one of the exotic motor cars I've had. I also once owned a 275 GTB Ferrari, which cost £5,600 at the time and today would most probably be worth a couple of million. And then there was my Facel Vega, a luxury sports car built in France during the 1950s with a huge American V-8 engine. Ava Gardner owned one, so did Dean Martin and so did Ringo Starr. I nearly got killed in mine in 1963 when I was coming down the motorway at 155 mph – there weren't any speed limits in those days – and three tyres burst on me.

Having owned all sorts of cars, I am, deep down, first and foremost, a Porsche enthusiast. I am currently on my eighth 997 twin turbo. It is probably the most perfected car on the road, because every advanced model is basically an improvement on the old 911. That's the same secret of success as Mercedes'. They keep building the same car but making it better each time.

The problem with exotic motors today is that roads are different, which makes it impossible to drive them properly. A few years ago, I test-drove a Ferrari 250LM because I was looking to buy one. But you wind up sitting on a wooden plank with no springs. They're not drivable cars. Put them on a track and you can have a bit of fun for an hour, but you get to an age in life when that doesn't really appeal any more. I've driven around Silverstone, Goodwood and Bedford Aerodrome, and, frankly, all you're doing is going round in circles. It's nice to know what a car can do, but I think you grow out of that after a while. Maybe I'm talking like an old man.

My interest in motor cars became much more than a hobby in 1970 when I bought the Swain Group from the entrepreneur James Hanson. It included the famous luxury car dealership H.R. Owen. I didn't pay much for the business – if I remember, it was about £650,000 – but it meant I was selling Rolls-Royce, Bentley, Ferrari and Jaguar. Along with it came my old friend Peter Reynolds, as managing director, the man who sold me my father's Rolls.

We used H.R. Owen as the foundation of our motor interests and added other businesses to it, such as Savile Motors in Solihull, Stratford-upon-Avon and Banbury. The following year, we took over Scottish Automobile and then Hollingdrake Automobile. Eventually we merged all of them into the Heron Motor Group. A little later still, we expanded by acquiring a stake in Henley's, the largest vehicle distributor in the UK. At the peak, I think we had nearly every franchise you could think of, owned 175 depots from Aberdeen down to Exeter and made a lot of money.

What I discovered about this business is that the cars you can sell, you can't get enough of from the manufacturers. And the cars you can't sell, the manufacturers have too many of. The deals you have to do are always based on taking back a second-hand car, or on whatever extras you can put on the finance agreement. In the end, the business gets to a point where you're just shifting tin. Unless, of course, you're right at the exclusive top end of the business, which is where H.R. Owen was. But then, that's a business that goes up and down with the economy. The big advantage H.R. Owen had over all the other top-end dealers in the world was that it was based in London, and that market is very special. When the Western economy is on a downturn, there is always somewhere else on an upturn. When the British and Americans aren't buying expensive motor cars, there are always people in London who are, like the Russians, Indians or Arabs.

I sold H.R. Owen to Nick Lancaster for £17 million and keep in touch with him. After all, cars are still a hobby of mine and I'm friendly with a number of people in the business, including the three-time Formula One world champion Sir Jackie Stewart. He's a quality guy, and one of the most down-to-earth and honest people you could ever meet. He made a lot of money building up his Formula One team then selling it to Jaguar. He often invites Gail and me to races, especially the British Grand Prix and Monte Carlo. I've also come to know Bernie Ecclestone – I don't know him as well as I know Jackie – and he has made himself a huge fortune as 'Mr Formula One'.

I don't go to Grand Prix events very often, not just because I don't have the time, but also because I don't have the inclination to go. Formula One isn't my thing. But cars are. I like them so much that Peter Reynolds and I once actually tried to build one. It was called the Owen Sedanca. Most people have never heard of it, because we didn't build a lot of them. The design of the car was influenced by the idea of the Lamborghini Espada placed on top of a Jaguar XJ6 chassis. The all-aluminium bodywork was hand done by coachbuilders Williams & Pritchard. The car had a Jaguar 4.2-litre engine.

We unveiled it at the 1973 Earls Court Motor Show, priced at £8,500, which was very steep. I think at the time the Lamborghini Espada was selling for about that. Still, we took 80 orders. But then war broke out in Israel, the oil crisis hit and all of those orders were cancelled. We scrapped the project and only the prototype survived. Then, in 1978, an Arab gentleman in Oxfordshire ordered one for his son. We farmed out the manufacturing to another coachbuilder and they delivered the car. He liked it enough that, a few years later, he ordered another one for himself. Those two Sedancas are still around, along with the prototype. The 1982 version was sold a few years ago in the Netherlands for 15,000 euros, which was then just over £12,000.

Building the car was a nightmare. If it wasn't the electrics, it was the steering, or it was the suspension, or it was thousands of other little problems that came up while we were trying to get the wrinkles out. The car worked, but you can't really make any money in that business unless you can build in very big numbers.

Like so many things in life, when you start trying to do things that are different, you may get a lot of benefits from the leap forward, but there can be too many other things that go wrong because no one's ever been there before.

* * *

Motorbikes and motor cars were an enjoyable sideline. So was yacht building.

As a young man, when I used to go to St Tropez, I'd walk along the quay licking the steam off the windows. Once, on holiday in the south of France – which sounds very glamorous, but in those days you could stay in a small hotel for £5 a night – Gail and I rented a little car. We parked on the quay and stopped at a café and sat there looking at the yachts. I saw Peter Sellers on his yacht, the film producer Cubby Broccoli on his, the famous American writer Harold Robbins on his and the financier Bernie Cornfeld on his boat with beautiful women hanging around him. And I turned around to Gail and said, 'One day I' – and I did use the word 'I' not 'we' – 'One day I will be on the inside looking out and not on the outside like this, looking in.'

While Gail and I were on our honeymoon, also in the south of France, I bought a single-engine Riva Ariston speedboat, which cost about £4,500. That was quite a bit of money in those days. I learned to drive it and we used to zip up to St Tropez or down to San Remo. As long as the weather was good, that was about as far as you could go, 30 to 50 miles left or right. A year later, I bought a Riva Aquarama, which was the next model up. This was twin engines, but, again, it was a day boat.

A year or so after that, through my friend Harvey Soning, I met Jon Bannenberg, who eventually became a great yacht designer. In those days, he was just doing the interiors of buildings, anything to scrape a living. The first yacht he did was for the German entrepreneur Helmut Horten. That boat, *Carinthia V*, was said to be one of the most beautiful yachts in the world at that time. When *Carinthia V* sank, Jon built *Carinthia VI*, and after Horten died, leaving his young widow a fortune, Jon built one of the world's largest yachts, *Carinthia VII*, for her.

Anyway, I was talking to some friends about boats and I heard that there was a yacht for sale sitting in an Italian shipyard that I could pick up for £200,000. By then, I could afford that, so I asked Jon to have a look at it and said that if he'd design the interiors, I'd buy it. He agreed and I bought the boat.

I called it *Heron III*, kept it in Monaco and manned it with an alcoholic English captain and four crew. We never went very far in it, just up and down the coast and occasionally to Corsica, Sardinia and St Tropez. It wasn't a good sea boat and you could feel that in the water. I'd only had it a few months, and maybe used it four times, when one afternoon in Monaco some grubby Middle Eastern bloke came up to the step of the boat and asked, 'Would you sell this to me?'

My answer was, 'It's not for sale.'

He said, 'I love this boat and I'd like to buy it.'

I replied, 'You don't look to me like a man who has any money to buy anything.'

He insisted, 'Oh, yes, I have the money.'

'OK.' I pointed across the quay. 'See the yacht agents just over there? If you want to buy the boat, go talk to the man who runs the business.'

He promised he would.

The next day we went off to St Tropez and just as I was pulling into a slip there, the man who owned the yacht brokers in Monaco came running up. He was all excited and said, 'You know that guy who wants to buy your boat? Well, he's offering £250,000 for it.'

I couldn't believe it and said, 'But he doesn't have two bob to buy himself a pair of shoes.'

The yacht broker said, 'You're wrong. He's an Arab prince and he definitely does have the money.'

I still didn't believe it, but the boat was no good anyway. 'OK. Get a banker's draft from him for £250,000 and he can have it.'

Two days later, when we returned to Monaco, the yacht broker was holding the draft from Barclays Bank with my name on it. Our holiday was finished in any case, so I took the money, took all our personal items off the boat and handed him the keys. I'd made a £50,000 profit and thought to myself, that ain't bad.

Except that now I didn't have a boat. So I became friendly with an Italian shipyard and built two very fast 33-metre boats. One was for me, the other was for my friend Jack Dellal, another legendary property guy. Jon designed them and I think they cost me £600,000 to £650,000 each. They were wooden hull boats, but not very good, because when they went into the water they lost three or four knots. Boat building in those days was hit and miss, and this time we missed. We had to add three tonnes of extra ballast just to keep the nose up.

We ran the boats for a couple of years – I called mine *My Gail I* – but I was never happy with it. After we had a fire on board, which was a scare, I thought, I've had enough of this, I'm going to build myself a proper boat. The hull was designed by Fritz De Voogt, who was one of the most famous designers. Jon Bannenberg did the superstructure and the interior. It was 44 metres. I signed the contract on my 40th birthday, named it *My Gail II*, and took possession 18 months later.

In the meantime, I started building four 21-metre boats at the yard in Italy, which sort of put me in boat-building business. These were really fast boats for their day, with speeds up to 25 knots. I named them *Blue Bird*, *Red Bird*, *Yellow Bird* and *Fire Bird*. I sold one to a Frenchman, one to a Greek guy, one to an Englishman and one to Colonel Gaddafi, the dictator of Libya. I never met him. It was all done through his representative.

We sailed *My Gail II* for a couple of years, but it wasn't a very good sea boat and the day we got caught in a storm I started thinking about my next boat. You learn by experience.

That was when I received a phone call from David Morris, the jeweller, who was very friendly with the Sultan of Brunei. I was in a board meeting in London and David insisted I take the call, so I did. He wanted to know, 'Would you sell your boat? I'm sitting here with the Sultan of Brunei and he has a brochure of your boat in front of him. I told him, "I know the owner and it's a fantastic boat. I've been on it," and he said he'd like to buy it.'

I'd paid $4 million for *My Gail II*, doubled the price and he bought it. So I went to the Amels shipyard in Holland and built *My Gail III*, which came in at 59 metres and was really special. It had a crew of 13 and my skipper was Jeremy Dawson-Hall, a former Trident submarine captain. But when my troubles hit in 1991–2, I sold it and was boatless for many years. I was punishing myself for having been so stupid, for having lost 95 per cent of my money in the reconstruction of Heron.

In all, I've had and/or built 14 boats. In 2005, I went to the Heesen yard in Holland and built *G-Force*, a 37-metre boat with a max speed of 30 knots. It sleeps eight in four cabins, and has a crew of six. It's owned by a charter company and when I use it I pay for the charter. This is quite a boat and at the 2006 International Yachting Awards in Venice, *G-Force* won the Best Semi-Displacement Yacht Under 40 Metres award. That's really flattering because an awful lot of boats are built under 40 metres.

One other note about Jon Bannenberg. He not only built boats for me, he is also the man who almost introduced me to Fidel Castro. Jon had gone out to Cuba to see Castro, who, believe it or not, wanted to build himself a yacht. He travelled back and forth a couple of times to show Fidel his plans, and the two got friendly. Jon was with Fidel one day when he offered Jon a box of his very best Cohiba cigars. Jon said to him, 'I don't smoke, but my friend Gerald Ronson is a big cigar aficionado.' Fidel said, 'If he is a good friend of yours, then give him this box of cigars.'

So Jon came back to London, rang me up and said, 'I've got a present for you.' I thought, it's cufflinks or something, and was really delighted when he handed me the Cohibas from Fidel. The next thing I knew, I was on Fidel's personal guest list for Cuba's annual cigar festival. He invited me for several years, but I never went. It was a four-day event, which would have taken me out of the office for a week. Maybe I should have gone at least once, because I know a few people who did and they found it interesting. But then, I was doing business in the States in those years and I wasn't sure what the Americans would think about my hanging out with Fidel. Anyway, I told myself, I don't need to go all the way to Cuba to smoke myself to death. I can do that in London. Eventually, the invitations stopped.

* * *

Expanding my frontiers into areas other than property – like motorcycles, cars and boats – did not mean I was neglecting property. During those same years, I grew my property interests by taking on projects in Northern Ireland, Glasgow, Liverpool, Warrington, Oldham, Crosby, Bristol and Cardiff. I had a small house-building company, decided to make it much bigger and took over one of our biggest competitors, Stanshaw Estates. That brought us an additional 3,000 houses and excess land of 400 acres with planning consent. Over the next two years, our commercial property programme grew in capital value from £8 million to £20 million. We also had nine overseas schemes that were valued at £30 million. By March 1973, Heron's pre-tax profits were just over £43 million.

As our business expanded, so did my staff. In 1974, I hired Alan Goldman. I'd known him since the early 1960s. He was a chartered accountant, had become a partner in his firm and had acted for us. I hired him away to be my finance director. He later became my deputy chief executive. Alan helped guide me into businesses that became our new frontiers. We diversified into clocks and watches when we bought Ingersoll. The company was fine, but we introduced quartz to Ingersoll watches and the business really took off. The same year, we sold our stake in Henley's to the Bank of Scotland, doubling our money. Our interest in motor sales then took us into motor insurance, and we bought the 80-year-old National Insurance and Guarantee Corporation.

About this same time, I became aware of a big new consumer market opening up fast – electronics. So I opened a chain of shops called First Computer. We were trying to sell hardware, software and training, but we were too early. The market wasn't ready for it yet and we managed to lose £10 million. Being the only person in Heron House who doesn't have a computer, I sometimes think First Computer is the reason why.

We also acquired the UK's sole distribution rights to Atari. This was at a time when Atari was a state-of-the-art electronic toy and sales were going through the roof. I went to Silicon Valley in California to visit the facility and meet the managing director, an unpleasant character named Ray Kassar. We had a lot of hope for the business, but it got off to a bad start because I didn't get on with him and he didn't like me. It was a difficult afternoon that didn't get any better when I arrived back at our hotel in San Francisco. Gail had been shopping with a friend, and the two of them had gone mad buying a lot of frivolous stuff. Gail and I had a row about it, and I got hold of her credit cards and ripped them up with my bare hands.

A year later, I went to the Las Vegas electronics show and met Steve Ross, who was chairman of Time Warner, the company that then owned Atari. I was escorted up to Steve's suite, where he was sitting in a chair like the king of the castle. Kassar was with him. I knew right away this wasn't going to be fun.

Steve said to me that Kassar had told him, 'We should be doing a lot more business in the UK.' He said, 'You've only sold 400,000 units and a million cartridges last year.' He then started bandying about some big numbers, which Kassar had obviously fed him.

Well, I know the details of all my businesses, and I also knew that Steve Ross and Ray Kassar didn't know what the hell they were talking about. Could we have done 10 per cent more? Maybe. But not the kinds of figures he was throwing around. So I said to Ross, 'Neither one of you knows the UK market, you're talking rubbish, and what your managing director here is telling you is bollocks.' Ross was a man used to having everyone in front of him down on one knee. I said, 'If you and he think you can do it better, why don't you buy me out and do it yourselves?'

Ross was stunned. He wasn't used to being spoken to like that. So now he asked me if I was serious about selling it. I said that if he made me an offer based on what Kassar thought this business should be doing, I'd consider it. That put Kassar in a tough situation because if Ross wanted to make an offer, Kassar would have to stand by his inflated figures. And, sure enough, two weeks later they showed up in England, paid me $20 million for my sole-distributor contract, bought back all the stock in my warehouse at cost and the following year managed to lose $10 million. Not long after that, Kassar was shown the door.

* * *

Around the same time that Alan Goldman came to work with me, a British entrepreneur contacted me about buying a piece of property. I hadn't met him but invited him to stop by the office to discuss it. That was the beginning of my friendship with Robert Maxwell, known in certain circles as 'The Bouncing Czech'. He was quite a character and, personally, I liked him.

Maxwell was born Jan Ludvik Hoch in a small Czechoslovakian town in 1923, which put him just past his 50th birthday when we met. By the time the Nazis had overrun his country, he'd escaped and joined the British forces fighting Hitler. He always claimed that Field Marshal Montgomery had personally awarded him the Military Cross, a story I'd heard before meeting him but always doubted. He changed his name to Ian Robert Maxwell, although he only ever used his middle name and everyone called him Bob.

After the war, Bob found himself in Berlin, where he somehow acquired, probably stole, Russian and German scientific papers, which he brought back to the UK. He translated them and published them and used the money he made to acquire Pergamon Press, a small textbook publisher. He skilfully turned that into a major publishing house.

In 1964, he got himself elected to the House of Commons as a Labour MP. He was eventually unseated and returned to publishing, with the dream of one day owning a national newspaper. Ten years after I met him, he purchased the *Daily Mirror*. Then, in 1991, Maxwell was found drowned after he went overboard from his yacht while cruising off the Canary Islands. He was buried on the Mount of Olives in Jerusalem, the highest honour that the State of Israel can bestow on someone. And, in his case, that was pretty interesting, because until 1948, Maxwell always denied he was a Jew. I was the one who helped him rediscover his roots.

In an odd way, Maxwell reminded me a bit of my father. Maybe that's one reason why we got on well together. Was he a bully? Yes. Was he clever? Yes. He showed up for that first meeting in a scruffy old shirt and suit, driving a banged-out old Rolls-Royce. I told him, 'You can't go around like that.'

He said, 'You dress smartly. Who's your tailor?'

So I introduced him to my tailor and my shirt maker and then sent him over to H.R. Owen so he could get a new Rolls. When he decided that he wanted to have some art on his walls, I tried to convince him that he could afford some really good pictures. Dealers started offering him very expensive art, but Bob wasn't interested. He told me, 'I'm not spending a million quid on pictures when I can get some that look real for a few hundred,' which is what he did.

After he bought the *Mirror*, in 1984, I took him to Israel for the first time. He usually told people he wasn't Jewish, but he told me he was and had given it up. So I said to him, 'What's all this crap? How come all of a sudden you're not Jewish any more? I'm going to Israel to see the Prime Minister, Yitzhak Shamir. Why don't you and Betty come with me?'

I had a plane in those days, so Bob and his wife came along with Gail and me and Marcus and Lily Sieff. Marcus was by then Baron Sieff of Brimpton and had not long stepped down as chairman of Marks & Spencer. As we were flying into Tel Aviv from over the Mediterranean, Bob could see Israel in front of us, and he started crying. There were tears coming down his face. He kept saying, 'I should have come here years ago.'

We checked into the hotel and a few hours later I saw him furious and ranting at the staff because his fax machine wasn't working. The following morning, we went to see Shamir.

Bob and the Prime Minister got on very well. It was funny to see them standing together, because Bob was so big and Yitzhak was so small. And while we were in the PM's office, Maxwell announced, 'I want to invest in the country.'

Shamir asked, 'How much do you want to invest?'

Bob said, 'At least a quarter of a billion dollars.'

That was a huge amount of money and, needless to say, Shamir was impressed. I didn't have any idea whether or not Bob had that kind of money – he certainly wasn't shy when it came to telling people stories that weren't true – but, sure enough, he started investing and really got into Israel in a big way. He even bought a football team there.

Now that he was a Jew again, I guided him into the Community, where he became chair of Israel Bonds. I also helped him become involved with the National Society for the Prevention of Cruelty to Children (NSPCC). His charitable work culminated in a Royal Command Performance of *The Nutcracker* at the Royal Opera House, with the Queen in the royal box. Bob and Betty Maxwell were in the box next to her. Gail and I were in the box on the other side of her. We had more royals there that night than ever before, including the Queen Mother, Princess Margaret, Princess Diana, Prince Charles, Prince Andrew and Prince Philip. The whole family.

Maybe he was using me for a certain amount of respectability, because a lot of people were highly suspicious of him, and some of his business practices had attracted bad press and Department of Trade and Industry enquires. And maybe I was using him for the money he could contribute to worthy causes. But still, we became good friends, even to the point that when he wanted a yacht and an aeroplane, I helped him buy a second-hand plane and then built his yacht for him.

It was at the time I was building *My Gail III*. I'd heard that the brother of Saudi financier Adnan Khashoggi was building a boat but had abandoned the project, so I helped Bob buy that boat. I think he paid $11 million to $12 million. He wasn't at all bothered how it was finished inside and said to me, 'You deal with it all,' so I did. I didn't make money out of it. I did it for him as a friend. I even found him a captain and crew. That was the *Lady Ghislaine*, the boat he was sailing when he died.

For a few years after he bought it, if I was sailing somewhere over the summer holidays, he would follow us on his boat. But he was never on his boat for more than three days at a time, and when he was, he was always working two phones. He could never relax. And he didn't have a lot of personal friends. There were plenty of people he could use and abuse, but there weren't a lot of people he could sit down and have a genuine talk with.

It turned out that he didn't like most people, even though he often invited the good and the great to his home for parties. Then he resented the fact that they all came. He lived in a big old house in Oxford – it was awful and I wouldn't have lived there if you paid me – which he rented from the local council. Gail and I would get invited to his parties, and one night he said to me, 'Let's go in the library because I don't want to talk to these people.'

He referred to them as 'a bunch of arseholes' who would go anywhere if someone invited them. He knew I felt the same way about some of that crowd, but I wasn't throwing the party – he was – and if I had been throwing the party, I wouldn't have invited those people. Anyway, he said, 'Come in my study, I want to show you something.'

He took me in there, said, 'You always thought I was joking when I told you I had the Military Cross,' and brought down a big book. Inside was a photo of him with Montgomery pinning the Military Cross on him.

I said, 'I take it all back Bob. I'm sorry if I didn't believe you. But you tell so many stories . . .'

He laughed, then told me how he got it. He ran away from his native Czechoslovakia at the age of 17 to join up with the British to fight the Germans. He must have received several field promotions because he was already a captain when they came across a machine-gun post at the top of a hill. The Germans were firing down at them and had already killed a number of British soldiers. Maxwell said he was leading a charge up the hill when, halfway, he looked around and saw that no one else was there with him. He couldn't retreat without getting killed, so he went on alone, threw some hand grenades into the machine-gun nest, killed the Germans and knocked out the machine gun. I'm not sure how much of it was true, but that's what he told me.

After the war, while he was publishing those Russian and German scientific books, he become some sort of spy for the British against the Russians. He had access through his contacts in Russia to certain information that he fed back to British Intelligence. But the British felt he was a double agent. He probably was. After all, he was a businessman trading to get scientific books from the Russians and I'm sure that, in return, they wanted information from him about the West.

However, Bob did do some very good things. In 1986, just after the Chernobyl disaster, when the Russian nuclear plant went into meltdown, Bob used his contacts with the Russians to fly Jewish children affected by the radiation to Israel. The Russians weren't letting Jews out, but Bob got a few planeloads of those children to Israel. Which was why the Israelis had respect for him. Forget all the other bullshit. He saved a lot of lives. That said, I can't think of many other good things he ever did for Israel. He put a few million dollars into Israel Bonds, but that's not the same as giving money, because a bond is a bond and Israel has never defaulted on its bonds. Anyway, it wasn't his personal money, as he did it through a pension fund and after he died the pension fund got it back.

I think I was one of the few people he trusted enough to spend personal time with. He knew that I'd give him a straight opinion on things and would also tell him if he was talking bollocks. Unfortunately for him, he didn't always listen to my advice. He wanted to own a New York publishing house and a New York newspaper, so he borrowed something crazy like $2.6 billion to buy Macmillan Publishers and then another big chunk of money to buy the New York *Daily News*. He also acquired Berlitz, the foreign-language business, and the Official Airline Guide. But his publishing venture in New York was the beginning of the end. He paid $95 a share for Macmillan when they were only worth $60–65. It was obvious that Bob was being run up, but he had two obsessions. He had to be in America. And he had to be bigger than Rupert Murdoch. This was during the period when Murdoch was having some financial problems and had to restructure. Bob saw an opportunity to beat Murdoch at being Murdoch and took it. He was a total megalomaniac.

I knew the inside of the Macmillan deal because I had dinner one night with the director of an investment bank acting for the publishing company. He asked me, 'Do you know this Bob Maxwell?'

I didn't want to let on that he was a friend because I knew this fellow was going to talk, so I said, 'I've heard of him.'

He said, 'I'm going to bid him up on this price for this company.'

The following weekend, I was sailing around Corfu, Bob was on his boat and we had a drink together. I told him, because I thought I owed it to him, 'Those Americans are going to bid you up.' But he still had to have an empire in New York. He was like a child at Hamleys. He had to have his toy right away, even though you could go down the road to Toys R Us and get it cheaper. So Maxwell borrowed all that money to buy into New York, most probably pledging all his shares. Then the shares in New York went down and he got caught in a bad squeeze. He still bought other companies after that, but New York was his downfall.

It was all very sad to see. He did a lot of stupid things and got carried away with himself. Not that I'm a genius, but I warned him about New York and even though I never set myself up to be his adviser, if he'd asked me about the deals he was also doing in the property business, I would have told him that they, too, were dumb. Same goes for his investment in an engineering business. It was dumb. And the people he had running his business were even dumber.

I used to see him every couple of months, but towards the end if I wanted to see him, I had to go to his office because he was too important to come to mine. He had a grand penthouse suite at Holborn, stocked with all these pretty blonde secretaries with whom he would be very flirtatious. It was surreal. I'd sit there, and of course he'd want to show off, so he'd pick up the phone and bark at one of his secretaries 'Get me Gorbachev' or 'Get me [Neil] Kinnock' and all the time he'd be winking at me while talking to them.

Game playing, ego, a crazy power trip – call it what you will. Was he getting anything personally out of it? No. It wasn't about money, because when he went he didn't have any money. It was a myth. This was just some bizarre kick.

It was a bit like Conrad Black, the Canadian who used to own the Telegraph. He took money out of the business to pay for whatever he wanted. Black couldn't see anything wrong in it, any more than Maxwell could.

On 5 November 1991, he was on the Lady Ghislaine off the Canary Islands and suddenly went overboard. There was a whole to-do about whether he fell or was pushed – you know, murdered – or if he just committed suicide because he was afraid he'd wind up in jail.

I don't believe he was murdered. I don't think people crept onto the boat in the middle of the night and threw him off. That's nonsense. I knew the boat well and I saw him on it many times. He would get up in the morning and he didn't care who saw him naked when he went to have a pee over the side of the boat. He was so fat, with his stomach hanging over, that he looked like a hippopotamus on two legs.

My guess is that he got up that night – maybe he couldn't sleep for thinking about all his troubles – and went for a pee. If he was planning to top himself – and I've had this conversation with his son Kevin and with his widow Betty – he would have written a note saying, 'It's all my fault, don't blame Kevin. Right or wrong, I take full responsibility. Goodbye.' But he didn't. So he got up to pee at four or five in the morning while the boat was cruising along through a lovely breeze, leaned over the side and the boat hit a little bump. He weighed 24 stone and wasn't that steady on his feet to begin with, and he simply fell over the side. He most probably held on for all he was worth, but he was in the water and nobody knew he was gone until two hours later. That's what I honestly believe. And nobody's ever proved anything different.

Bob was a friend to me, especially when the Guinness affair blew up. He made suggestions about how I could get out of it, which were not really suggestions I'd contemplate, because his idea was that I should lie my way out. However, he did introduce me to Victor Mishcon, whom he knew well and insisted was the best lawyer to defend me.

There were several rumours at the time of Bob's death that he was a spy for Israel. I don't think he was ever officially working for Mossad, but if the Israelis had ever wanted him to find something out about the Russians, sure, he might have met with some people and passed the information along. But he and I never discussed it, so I don't know. I can say that the Israelis never approached me to do anything like that.

Bob was a lot of things, but, believe it or not, he wasn't boastful. If he did something on the quiet, if he did something that needed to stay secret, he wouldn't tell everybody about it the next morning. He understood military intelligence and understood how the game is played. That said, whenever he did anything, he always kept a note of it in his own little mental accounting ledger. If he did you a favour, he expected you to do one for him in return. He knew who owed him what.

He was buried in Israel, on the Mount of Olives, which is prime property. I'm sure that was payback from the Israelis, not necessarily because of his investments, but because of what he did for those children after Chernobyl. Of course, owning newspapers made him powerful enough that he could have been useful for the state of Israel at various times, so maybe that helped, too. But saving those children – that alone was probably enough to seal the deal.

* * *

In 1979, Laurence decided to leave Heron. I know that he would have succeeded very well, but, deep down, his heart wasn't in it. I was sorry that my father's other son did not want to carry on in the family business. It was clear that he didn't really like being in business with me and maybe part of the problem was that I was a hard act to follow. Still, he gave it a try, worked hard, learned a lot and showed his abilities. He stuck with it for 12 years. I'm afraid that, because of the age gap between us, at least in the beginning, I regarded him somewhat as a pupil, a protégé and a junior partner. He sometimes thought of me as his second father. I also thought of him as, one day, my successor. So I was sad to see him go.

Maybe if Laurence hadn't come into the business and had gone out to do his own thing at the very beginning, his relationship with our father would have been a lot better.

Laurence had always been fascinated by the world of music and entertainment, and when he left Heron, he took over the management of the pop group Bucks Fizz. Together, they won the Eurovision Song Contest. His company was called Missing in Action, a name I had unwittingly inspired. While he was working with Dad and me, every now and again, he would go through a phase of not speaking to either of us. I would try to end whatever feud we were having by telephoning him and asking, 'Where the hell have you been? Missing in action?'

His publishing company, Paper Music, teamed up the established lyricist Pete Sinfield with the young jingle writer Andy Hill, and together they wrote the Bucks Fizz hits 'The Land of Make Believe' and 'Making Your Mind Up', which won Eurovision. Laurence handled Carl Palmer and his group PM. He also handled Bill Wyman when he left the Rolling Stones and produced his hit 'Je Suis un Rock Star'.

Laurence loved the music business, possibly because nobody came into the office until half twelve, then from half twelve to half two everyone disappeared for lunch, and after lunch, back at the office, there was mayhem for the rest of the afternoon. After music, he went into the video business, then into the DVD business. But the DVD business changed radically when newspapers started giving them away for free. The customer base disappeared and Laurence got out in 2006. I suggested he use an office at Heron House, and, as long as he was coming in anyway, when certain opportunities arose, I saw that he got involved. Today he's back at Heron full time, and our relationship is the best it's ever been.

He has six children. One of his twin daughters, Charlotte, lives in New York and is a designer with her own label. The other twin, Samantha, is the free spirit of the family. She's a disc jockey in Los Angeles. Then there's Henrietta, who recently graduated from Leeds University, where she read history. Her brother David is a year younger and is very ambitious. The little one, Joshua, who is seven years younger than David, is a natural born diplomat.

The famous one in the family is Laurence's oldest son, Mark. He got into the music business early on, saw it as a business, worked very hard at it and moved up from disc jockeying to producing to taking bands on the road. Mark has produced for Amy Winehouse, Adele, Robbie Williams, Christina Aguilera, Lily Allen, the Kaiser Chiefs, Daniel Merriweather and Duran Duran. He's also had a successful solo career, with his own album Version, which won him three Grammys and a Brit Award for Best Male Artist in 2008. I'm pleased to see his success. I'm sure if my father was still alive he would be proud of Mark, because my father loved winners.

Sadly, the same year that Laurence left Heron, Dad had a stroke and decided to retire. I don't think for a moment he would have given up the reins had he not taken ill, but his doctors warned him that he couldn't afford to ignore his health. He was then 65. The saddest part of the next 5 years was that he finally tried to do some of the things that my mother had always wanted him to do for the previous 30 years, like take holidays and spend more time with their friends.

Most people liked him, but some did not. His blunt, straightforward manner put them off. He was a bull of a man, but you always knew where you stood with him. And I never met anybody who did not respect him. He was an old-fashioned man of his word, straightforward, larger-than-life, loyal and absolutely fearless. He never sulked or bore malice. He was physically very powerful and could have knocked me down with ease on the times when I provoked him, but he never did. We had some awful rows over the years. When things went wrong, he would raise Cain. But the storm would soon blow over and after that he'd forget it.

Dad was a remarkable man by any standards, and when he died in 1983, he left a great empty space behind him. God rest his soul. My father had the satisfaction of knowing he had built a highly successful company in which everybody knew what it owed to Henry Ronson. More than anybody else, Dad shaped my character and taught me my business. He gave me the opportunity to succeed. I loved him and I am forever grateful.

CHAPTER 5

······················

GAIL AND THE GIRLS

We met on a blind date in 1966.

I was in my mid-20s, and I was out and about all the time when I wasn't working, chasing models and actresses who weren't always of the highest calibre. A friend of mine was dating a friend of Gail's, and I was always saying to my friends' girlfriends, 'Do you know any good-looking girls that I haven't met?'

Most of the time they'd say, 'You know them all already.' But this time, this one said, 'I'm working with a girl at the moment who's one of yours.' That was her way of saying she was Jewish. 'Her name is Gail Cohen, she's very pretty, very nice and she lives at home.'

I said, 'Give me her number and I'll give her a call.'

She said no. 'I have to talk to her first.'

I figured, that's what happens when you deal with nice girls, and pretty much forgot about it. Ten days later, I was out with my friend and we bumped into this girlfriend and now she said, 'I spoke to Gail. If you ring her, she'll talk to you. Maybe you can go out together.'

Never too shy to pick up the phone, I called, she sounded very pleasant, so I invited her out for dinner. What Gail didn't know at the time was that there were other things going on. One of my friends was going out with a girl who shared a flat with a young actress I was quite keen on, but she was playing hard to get because her career was more important to her than having a relationship with me. With hindsight, that was her mistake. Anyway, my friend and the actress's flatmate and Gail and I made a date. I came to collect Gail, and in those days I had a white Bentley Continental with a personalised number plate. The car also had gold fittings. I admit it was a bit flash.

Gail was just 19 and I must have been 26 at the time. She was living in Wembley with her parents, Joe and Marie. Her father was the manager of a furniture store in Harlesden. I came inside, but when she introduced me to her parents, she couldn't remember my name. The moment her father saw me, he took an instant dislike. In his mind, I must have been a threat, someone who might take his daughter away from him. Which I did, of course, but that had nothing to do with him at the time.

Over dinner, Gail was good company but very nervous. Today she says it was love at first sight. Which is nice and I like that, but it wasn't exactly the case for me. Gail was a lovely, attractive and respectable Jewish girl. But at that stage of my life, I wasn't into respectable Jewish girls.

A week or so later, I was invited to a respectable dinner function and when I looked around at the girls I knew, I realised that I couldn't invite any of them along, so I rang up Gail and asked her. It was one of the best decisions I made in my life.

I was going out seven nights a week – the madness of the 1960s – seeing four or five of those less respectable girls, but I started moving some of them aside. The more I went out with Gail, the more her father disliked me. He'd stand outside waiting for me to bring her home.

After about a month, I was seeing more and more of Gail and she was promoted to number one. So we'd go out on Saturday nights and maybe once or twice during the week. Then, somewhere around the six-month mark, I invited Gail to come with me to a wedding. We had a good time, but when I took her home, while we were sitting in my car, she said to me, 'Are we going to date much longer?'

This was a girl who wouldn't say boo to a goose, so that startled me. I asked, 'What do you mean?'

She said, 'If you only want to keep taking me out, I mean, if you're not serious about me, then I think we should stop.'

I asked what she wanted.

She said, 'Are we getting engaged?'

I agreed, 'OK, let's get engaged,' because I didn't think that necessarily meant getting married.

She said, 'No. If you want to get engaged, you have to ask me properly.'

So I said, 'OK, do you want to get engaged?'

She said, 'No. You have to ask me to marry you.'

I said, 'All right, do you want to get married?'

She said, 'Yes.'

The moral of the story is, 'Never take a girl to a wedding if you're not already engaged.'

* * *

If ringing Gail that first time was one of the best decisions I have ever made in my life, then marrying her was the best. We had the religious ceremony at Norrice Lea Synagogue, which is where I had my bar mitzvah and, as it happened, it was even the same rabbi. Our reception was a dinner-dance at the Dorchester.

Unfortunately, Gail's parents didn't attend. Her mother and father were totally different from Gail. It's funny how you can see family characteristics in some people. I look at photos of my late father and I see myself. I look at photos of my mother and I see her in me, too. But I never saw that with Gail and her parents. Sometimes, I'd look at her and then at her parents and think, maybe she's adopted. She wasn't anything like either of them. Besides the fact that she's tall and beautiful – her parents were short, although her mother was not unattractive – they had very different dispositions. Gail gets along with everybody. Her father was unbelievably difficult. He was the dominant member of her family and saw me as the man who took away from him his greatest jewel, his only daughter. I understand how, when you have only one daughter, your whole life can revolve around her, so when somebody comes along and takes her away from you, you won't like that. Of course, I was able to give Gail more than her father ever could, in terms of material things, but he still resented me.

To be frank, I didn't do a lot to like him, either. I look back and, in many ways, I understand it. But I couldn't understand it at the time. If I brought Gail home half an hour late – it wasn't as if we were out all night or coming in at 4 a.m. – he'd sulk and wouldn't talk to her for a week. Over the period of six months that we were dating, that became very debilitating. I tried everything to make peace. I even had the rabbi come to speak to him. But my rabbi wasn't important enough. He was the sort of man who wanted the Chief Rabbi.

For her father to get into that situation with his only child was sad. Maybe because her parents are both long gone, I feel a bit sorry for him. He saw very little of his grandchildren. Gail's mother missed out too, because she went along with her husband. My auntie Rosalind and my uncle Tubby, who were both special people, treated Gail like their own daughter. It was Uncle Tubby and Auntie Rosalind who walked her down the aisle.

We honeymooned at the Carlton in Cannes and moved into a three-bedroom flat in Heron Place, which was then a brand-new development at the end of Marylebone High Street. As it happened, I'd built it. We leased the flat from the company, Gail furnished it with her characteristic good taste and we lived there for a year or so, until 1968, when our first daughter, Lisa, came along.

Gail and I both wanted a house, but we didn't want a huge mansion. We wanted a home that would be manageable for Gail, who was only 22 and now a young mother. We wanted something we could grow into. Ironically, I found it across the street from my parents' house in Hampstead. I saw it, described it to Gail, told her I thought it was ideal for us and thought she'd like it. She went to see it, loved it and we bought it. So Gail went from her family home to making a home for me, and I went from my family home to making a home with Gail.

We still live in that same house today. It is not what I would call a rich man's house. It's not over-opulent. It's a nice upper-middle-class family home. And for me there's a big difference between a house and a home. You walk through my front door and you feel comfortable. It's not like walking into some impersonal grand palace. It doesn't say, look how rich I am. It says, I live here and I like living here. It's comfortable, I have a pretty little garden and, in fact, everything I need. Anyway, my personal needs are really quite modest.

I think that Gail and I are a great team and I am very lucky to be married to her, especially because I'm not the easiest person to live with. Gail is warm and friendly and doesn't have a bad bone in her body. She doesn't have agendas. She's totally genuine. She is more gentle, more open, more outgoing and friendlier than I am. She is very good-hearted and a truly special person. That isn't to say that I'm not any of those things, just that she's better at them than me.

I'm much more outspoken, probably because I am my own man and have always been. There are some people who are intimidated by me. After all, I'm not four foot nothing. I can be brusque and tough – at least, that's the reputation I have developed over the years – and I don't stand for bullshit. Some people dance around the mulberry bush rather than say what they think. Not me. I'm upfront and I don't mince my words. If I upset some people, so be it. When someone asks me for my opinion, I give it to them. Not everyone likes that. But it's simple. If you don't want to hear the truth, don't ask me for it.

Gail is more subtle and goes out of her way to avoid confrontation. I don't ingratiate myself with people, don't go out of my way to be liked. Mingling with the social set doesn't interest me. I stay busy with my business, my family, my Community and my charities. I get respect, but there is no doubt in my mind that a good part of the respect I get is through Gail. My daughters sometimes refer to me as Gail's 'schlepp-along'. She is well known in her own right and works hard for several charities. She was already volunteering with children's charities before I met her.

Community work is something that we have been able to share, though over the years each of us has taken on our own individual commitments. Apart from her interest in children's charities, Gail is deputy chairman of Jewish Care.

As a lover of the arts, she really came into her own when she became involved with the Royal Opera House and has raised many millions of pounds for them. Gail started going to the opera when we were first married and loved it, and she worked on her first opera gala in 1978. She was invited onto the development committee, where she worked very hard for many years raising money, and is now on the board of directors, which is a government appointment.

For all of her work, in 2004 Gail became a Dame of the British Empire (DBE). I hope it shows that I am very, very proud of her.

* * *

Although I have only had one house and one wife, I have been blessed with four daughters and six grandchildren.

Lisa was just a year and a half when Amanda arrived in 1970. Not quite two years later, in 1972, Nicole was born. Eighteen months after that, Hayley joined us. If they have been raised well, and I know they have, it's because of Gail. That doesn't mean I haven't played my part, but she has to get most of the credit. And while some people may see me as tough and intimidating, having daughters softens you up in many ways. The four of them can twist me round their fingers, to different degrees, so obviously I must still be human.

Do they sometimes think I'm a bit of a control freak? I suppose they would say yes. Have I set certain parameters? Absolutely. But I think every parent should. Parents who let their children roam free to do whatever they like don't give their children a proper structure. Children need to learn manners and need to learn respect. Come on, I see kids today who need to learn how to eat with a knife and fork.

Today, everything is over-psychoanalysed. You can't do this because the children will resent you when they grow up. You have to let them do that or they will rebel. You can't impose your values or they will never develop values of their own. Gail and I imposed our values on our girls because we felt it was our responsibility to do that, and the four of them grew up with those values. I expected them to work hard at school and to do their best. I didn't care if they didn't get straight As, but if their report card ever said 'could do better' then I wasn't happy. 'Satisfactory' wasn't good either, because that said to me they weren't doing enough work. At the same time,

Gail encouraged them to have lives of their own, to use their brains, to accomplish the things they set out to do. Obviously, they were raised with many privileges, so it was important to Gail and me that they understood that with privilege comes obligation. That when you are fortunate, you must help those who are not as fortunate. We involved the girls in our charity work and they take an active role in the family's commitment to Community activities.

I don't think my daughters are spoiled, because they all earned their own living. Each of them has a good university degree, in areas such as business management, science, economics, education and fine arts. My youngest daughter, Hayley, is a fully qualified teacher for children with special needs. And I was every bit as proud of her when she took a job for peanuts as I was when Lisa was working in the City. Nicole made us proud producing television shows, and Amanda made us proud being successful in retail. She went to Israel and did product development first for Macy's, the New York department store, then for their parent company Federated Department Stores, which also owned Bloomingdale's. She also opened Topshop and Miss Selfridge in Israel.

If they are unspoiled, it's because we haven't overindulged them. They live in nice homes, but unlike other wealthy parents whom I happen to know, I never said to my daughters, here you go, buy yourself a house for three million. I gave them money as a down payment, but then they each had to pay their mortgages. They needed to work because they had bills to pay every month, and I wasn't going to pay them. When the girls were young, they had a weekly allowance, but it was less than most of their friends'. When they turned 17, I bought them each a Suzuki jeep. It was when I owned the Suzuki franchise for the UK. So they had a car, but it wasn't an expensive car. Out front, our house looked like a Suzuki parking lot. None of them had another car until they were in their early 20s and could afford to buy their own. Even when they were much younger, from the age of about 14, we insisted that they have part-time jobs. They weren't allowed to stay home during the summer or on school holidays with nothing to do. All four of the girls had Saturday jobs.

Lisa likes cars almost as much as I do and when I had my last Porsche Turbo, which was in absolutely immaculate condition, I told her she could have it, but on the condition that she couldn't put her dog in it. I didn't want some big hairy animal crawling all over that beautiful leather. She loved the car, but she loved her dog more, so she bought herself a Mini. That's her only car.

I suppose Lisa is her father's daughter. Not that they're not all their father's daughters, but she's the one who came into the business. She is very able, likeable and gets on well with people. She's smart, has a good business head and good intuition. She's not her father, and she may take exception to this, but she's not entrepreneurial. Then again, I wouldn't want her to be her father. She's very capable in her own right and has earned the respect she has in business.

Of course, when you have four daughters, it's the oldest one who goes through most of the pain. Number two gets some of it, but less. By the time you've gone through it with the first two, you've had enough, so numbers three and four get away with murder. Well, sort of. If they wanted to go out with some young man, they needed to ask permission. And when it came to that, they quickly discovered it was better to ask their mother than me. Then, any young man taking my daughter out had to come to collect her. If they were going to a party, I wanted to see an invitation, even though the girls were forever insisting that their friends didn't send out printed invitations. And curfews were real. Most of the time, the girls were smart enough to get home early.

As each one reached 16, I took her with me to the States for a week to learn how the business worked. We'd fly to New York on the Sunday, do a meeting, go on to Dallas, Houston or Phoenix and from there to Tucson, Los Angeles and San Francisco, before flying home to London late on the Friday. I also took each one around the UK with me, especially on my Saturday petrol-station tours, and into Europe. I wanted them to see where they might fit into the business. I also wanted them to enjoy those trips and never understood why they didn't necessarily like the petrol-station tours. But in 2006, when Gail and I celebrated our 40th wedding anniversary, the girls wrote an essay about their parents, which included a section called 'Payback Time'.

They insisted that Saturdays are defined in the Bible as a day of rest, not a day to get up at 6 a.m. and cover 500 miles inspecting 12 petrol stations. 'For your working daughters, Saturdays are sacred for shopping, hairdressing and nail appointments, as well as a proper lie-in and a good long lunch. This is why we don't always choose to join you each week in the back seat of your car, with you and your cigar, walking around wet and cold forecourts.'

But just maybe there was method to my madness. Amanda and her husband recently built a new house. Her husband is in construction and probably thought he knew what he was doing. Like the other girls, Amanda had a grounding in our house-building business and also rode with me to inspect building sites. So while her husband was constructing their new house, she was there with her opinions about finishes. It wasn't long before he turned to her to scream, 'You sound just like your father.'

Even if all four girls do know about finishes, I'm happy to say that they have grown into responsible women who are doing well in life. Sometimes, of course, there are bumps along the road. Amanda fell in love with an Israeli and they weren't right for each other. Before they even became engaged, I told them that it would end in tears. Amanda was in denial for seven years and went through a lot of pain, which is a shame. But they had two lovely children, which is a consolation. Today, she is happily remarried to a nice man. Nicole and Hayley also married decent young men and as long as they're good husbands to my daughters, earn a living and are good fathers to their children, Gail and I are pleased.

Of the four, I suspect I am most protective of Hayley. Not just because she's the youngest, but because as a child she developed a stammer. Gail and I were aware of how that could affect her, so we did everything we could to help her, to encourage her and to give her the strength to deal with it. If Lisa is the most like me, I have to say that Hayley is the most like Gail, because of her inner strength. She found school hard, worked her way through it and took a job teaching underprivileged children. I'm talking about children from broken homes who had been abused or had been on drugs. She even spent three months in Israel working in a school with problem children.

As for my six grandchildren, they are the responsibility of their parents. I am happy to provide them with the best education, to put a roof over their heads if their father and mother can't afford to do that and to give them an income so they can get started in life. But it is not my desire in life to leave a great fortune to my grandchildren or, for that matter, to my daughters. They will have enough to keep them and enough to pay their mortgages. But it won't be enough to buy Savile Row suits and Porsches. I hope my grandchildren and great-grandchildren are happy with their share, but it's down to their parents to see that they're brought up properly, with respect and a sense of responsibility. If a few generations down the road they choose to screw it up, there's not a lot I can do about that. I know that my children won't, but if my grandchildren do, well, their parents will have to deal with it.

What I am really leaving them is a great asset that I hope they will take very good care of, and that's our family foundation. For me, that's the most important.

* * *

As a family, Gail and I made a point of us always having holidays together. We had boats, so in summer we'd be on the boat. In winter, I would take the girls skiing. Now, I'm not a lover of skiing. In the beginning, they'd go off with their mother – and they're all first-class skiers – I'd take a walk, read a paper, smoke a cigar and meet them at lunchtime. Did I personally enjoy it? No, I didn't. Then I decided to learn how to ski, but by that time I was in my mid-50s. Having fallen down 100 times in the course of that week, once I could ski down the mountain unaided, from the top of the slope back to the hotel, I took my skis off and never did it again. The girls love skiing, so I took them, but it's not my idea of fun. Anyway, I don't like the cold.

It was important that we did things as a family. If they had a sports day at school, I made a point of being there, because you never want to say, later on, I should have been there. I always had time for my daughters. As the girls got older, we took them on longer trips, like to a game park in South Africa and around the islands in Hawaii, and to the usual places like Disney World and Disneyland. I liked that. I took the girls on every major ride. I enjoyed Magic Mountain. Especially because we had VIP passes at Disney, so we didn't have to queue.

I really don't like queuing. I am also not fond of birthdays and New Year's Eve. I don't necessarily have a problem with weddings, but I'm not sure about big, noisy, crowded parties. New Year's Eve I find particularly irritating – all that stupid behaviour and the belief that everything is going to get better next year. As for birthdays, the older I get, the less comfortable I am about birthdays. I think people make an unnecessary fuss, but that's because I am of an age now when it would be nice to be younger.

When someone asked me recently if I would like to be 10 years younger, my answer was, 'No, I would like to be 20 years younger.' I say that because if I knew then what I know now, I wouldn't have believed in certain people whom I shouldn't have believed in, and I would not have been sucked into things I shouldn't have been involved with because it wasn't my business. But I can't be younger, so I remind myself that my greatest assets and my greatest blessings are my wife, my daughters and my grandchildren. I remind myself that so many wonderful things have happened to me that they outweigh the bad things.

Also on my list of things that irritate me are airports. I hate them. Gail calls me a travel snob. But airports are inefficient and you're always queuing up for everything. It doesn't matter whether you're going first class or tourist, you're treated like cattle from the moment you check in until you step onto the plane. Then, nine times out of ten, the plane will take off late. When you work to a tight schedule, like I do, it's inconvenient and creates stress, so that by the time you get to your first meeting, you want to strangle somebody. Also, I hate waiting for bags to come out. Many times when Gail, the girls and I would go somewhere as a family, Gail and the girls would go out a day before me with all the luggage and I would follow with my carry-on. Gail is much more patient than I am.

I guess I'm just not a good traveller, and because I have travelled so much for business, when I do take time off, the last thing I want to do is go someplace. But Gail enjoys travelling, so we go away on holiday. Thankfully, holidays for me almost always mean the boat. As soon as I step on board, I switch off. Give me a couple of days and I look a different person. I don't have a care in the world. Yes, I ring the office every day to see if anybody needs me, but being on a boat is the only time in my life that I can say, after two days, I'm relaxed. The problem is, I can only manage it for about a week. If we go away for anything more than that, believe me, I've had enough after ten days and I have to get back to work.

So between travelling for business and spending time on a boat with Gail, the family and some friends, I'm pretty much travelled out. You can imagine, then, what I thought in 2005 when our friends and neighbours, Nimel and Sitra Sethia, invited Gail and me to go to India. They wanted us to see their country. Gail really wanted to go, so we went.

We began our trip in Delhi and met a number of the senior business people there, then visited Udaipur, Agra and Jaipur. Of course, we visited the Taj Mahal, but after seeing it up close, I don't see why it's supposed to be one of the wonders of the world. It's very impressive. But so is St Paul's Cathedral, and any number of other buildings in Europe. And to see them, you don't have to go all the way to India, where, by the way, you take your life in your hands on the roads. The drivers are manic. And then there are all the animals walking on the roads. It is indeed another world.

We stayed in magnificent hotels, in magnificent suites. Now, I don't normally stay in suites when I go to hotels. I'm quite happy with a good double room, especially when I'm on business. I try to watch expenses because I know that if I start staying in big suites, my co-directors will have similar ideas. It's just not necessary. But Gail booked this trip and I think she went a little mad with the travel agent. In Jaipur, for instance, we had the presidential suite and, just to explain how big that was, it had its own swimming pool.

I'm not a lover of Indian food – or Chinese food for that matter – because I get uncomfortable when I don't know what I'm eating. So we tried to eat most of our meals within the hotel. We'd order room service and stick to things like roast chicken and lamb. Then, just in case, whenever we travel, Gail brings a medical kit with her so that if, God forbid, we're stung by a bee or poisoned by the food, we have the antidote with us.

The Sethias are friendly with the Maharaja and Maharani of Jaipur, and one night we were invited to the palace for dinner. There were four other maharaji from other states there with their wives. Some of them are extremely wealthy people. Others have a title and not a lot of money. But they all have a great respect for each other, and they were very charming and very hospitable. The evening didn't start until about 10.30. We arrived at the palace – where, by the way, they have 600 staff – and for the next hour or so, a lot of whisky was consumed. Neither Gail nor I are big drinkers, and we were both suffering from jetlag, so we only sipped at a single drink and hoped it would last us for the entire evening.

Dinner was an amazing experience, because it was held in the main dining hall, where we sat on solid silver chairs – it took two men to lift them so you could sit down – at a Lalique glass table. Around the room were portraits of presidents and prime ministers – every major leader for the last 75 years – who had also once dined there.

I looked at all the maharaji, and at all the food laid out on this spectacular table, and thought about all the world leaders who'd sat where we were sitting, then turned to Gail and whispered to her, 'Here we are, two north London Jews in the midst of all this. We've come a long way.'

CHAPTER 6

....

ASSUMING OTHER RESPONSIBILITIES

Sometimes in life you meet people who see qualities in you that you don't recognise in yourself. If you're lucky, those people are in a position to give you the benefit of their experience and to develop you into a leadership role. I was lucky enough to have known Marcus Sieff. He was a mentor to me. He pushed me forward, encouraged me and recognised in me a potential leader in the Jewish community. Whether he was right or wrong, only time can tell.

Starting way back in the 1960s, and over the course of many years, I went with Marcus on a number of missions to Israel. It was, I suppose, because of the power of my money and not my great intellect. In those early days, I was a very big supporter, probably one of the biggest UK donors, giving £1 million to £2 million a year for various projects in Israel. On one of those early missions with Marcus, I guess it was in 1973, Golda Meir invited us to her home for breakfast. I remember that my dad was on that trip with us. She was Prime Minister and served us breakfast in her kitchen. I mean, she actually served it herself. We had a bit of smoked salmon, a bit of herring – to be quite frank, I don't like to eat either for breakfast – a bit of bread and some coffee. We sat around her table and, of course, she gave us her views on things.

Over the years, I've spent time with most of Israel's prime ministers and leading politicians, from Yitzhak Rabin and Menachem Begin to Yitzhak Shamir, Shimon Peres, Bibi Netanyahu and Ehud Olmert. I got along with all of them, probably because I'm a good listener. I also knew Moshe Dayan. The general with the patch over his eye who led Israel through the Six Day War in June 1967 and was Defense Minister during the Yom Kippur War in 1973 was a bit abrupt, a bit sharp and not exactly a man of a lot of words. But the most memorable time of all was having breakfast with Golda, a wonderful old grandma, with whiskers growing out of her chin, who was super-intelligent, tough as old boots and looked like a man.

Marcus was internationally known for his role as an important leader of the worldwide Jewish community. To support organisations like the Joint Palestine Appeal (JPA) – later the Joint Israel Appeal (JIA) and today the United Joint Israel Appeal (UJIA) – he would host social functions in his home with various political leaders from Israel and the UK. He always made sure that Gail and I were invited. He knew what he was doing, bringing me on so that some day I could follow in his footsteps.

Thanks to Marcus, I also went on a mission to Washington, where we had lunch with President Jimmy Carter at the White House. This was in the late '70s. Henry Kissinger was on my table and spoke brilliantly. He's very smart, a real operator and, as it turns out, he and I share a birthday. Not the same year, mind you. I've seen him once or twice since and we joke about our mutual birthday. But I found Carter weak and wet, and I wasn't impressed. Being in the White House was memorable. I wasn't in awe, but I was impressed because it's always an experience to have an audience with the President of the United States. I was still in my 30s, and that's a big deal when you're young. At my age, today, it's not such a big deal, but it was then. As for the food, it wasn't great, but then you don't go there for the food.

Then there was the day when the Chief Rabbi, Immanuel Jakobovits, almost got us killed. About a dozen of us were visiting the Golan Heights – escorted there by the actor Topol, who was doing his Israeli military service and was the officer in charge – when the Syrians opened fire. We were all looking down into the valley on the Syrian side at 800 tanks that had been blown up during the war. I remember thinking that they looked like little smashed-up toys when, all of a sudden, a 120-mm shell flew over our heads. Topol yelled, 'Get down!' so we dived into a bunker, covered our heads and stayed there like that while the Syrians fired seven or eight more shells at us. We were wearing flak jackets, but I kept thinking to myself, this isn't going to do me much good if I get hit by one of those things.

As soon as they stopped, we didn't hang around. Not what I would call a pleasant experience. Looking back, maybe it was the Good Lord's way of toughening me up for the real aggravations that would come later.

* * *

Marcus Sieff started working at Marks & Spencer, the company founded by his grandfather, in 1935 when he was 22. He became chairman when he was 59. Having worked his way up, he really knew the business. Even though his family no longer had financial control, he always ran M&S as a family business. He spent 12 years as chairman and the profits under his leadership spoke for themselves. Unfortunately, when the family members left, M&S went backwards.

I would often meet with Marcus and other members of the family on a Monday morning to talk about Community charity matters. Marcus's uncle Edward 'Teddy' Sieff would be there, and he was a real tough dynamo. Teddy was chairman from 1967 to 1972, when Marcus took over, and a man who would not compromise easily. He was also tough enough to have survived a terrorist attack on his life. In 1973, a South American murderer named Ilich Ramirez Sanchez, known as 'Carlos the Jackal', burst into Teddy's home and shot him point blank in the face. Teddy survived because the bullet ricocheted off his teeth. Marcus's cousin Michael Sacher would also be at those meetings, although he was a much quieter man than Marcus. Michael was managing director and played a big part in M&S's success.

I'd arrive at head office at 7 a.m. to find that the rest of them had been there since 6.30, going through the figures from the week before. They discussed what they'd seen at the weekend, because every one of them, and especially Marcus, would go out at the weekend to visit stores. He knew everything about his business, to the point where you couldn't really talk to him about other businesses. Unlike a lot of people who pretend that they understand everyone else's business, Marcus was the first to say he only understood retailing. I think it was Marcus who taught me that retail is detail.

His was the old-fashioned, hands-on approach. I liked that, because it's the way I do business. He knew that in the retail trade you have to understand the merchandise. You have to be able to feel it, to touch it, to know what the customer wants. Sure, he had a lot of professional management to depend on. But professional managers aren't entrepreneurs. He used to tell me that his late father, Israel – who was chairman from 1964 to 1967 – knew where absolutely every item in his stores was supposed to be. He had the plans in his head. As the story goes, Israel went into a store one day up in Yorkshire and saw that the knickers were not where they should be. So he summoned the manager and said, 'This isn't where they go.'

The manager tried to explain, 'I moved them because I think we do better business this way.'

Israel was a prickly old man who never swore but still told his manager, in no uncertain terms, 'Young man, you are not paid to think, you are paid to do. You've got the plan of the store and that's how it should be. If I come here again and those ladies' knickers are not where they should be, then you will not be here as the manager of the store. Do I make myself quite clear?'

Like his father, Marcus also had the plans of the stores in his head and knew where everything was supposed to be. Whenever he told me that story about his father, I'd say to him, 'Your father and I read from the same script, because when I go round my petrol stations, if they don't have the Pringles where they should be, or the biscuits where they should be, or the sandwiches and the milk where they should be, then I blow up. The difference between your father and me is I do swear.'

Israel and Teddy and Marcus were a different generation, and those were different times. You don't find families like the Sieffs any more. Today, everybody is so over-educated that managers don't have the killer instinct. In retailing, you have to understand the merchandise, you have to understand the marketplace, you have to understand what people want. You need staff who smile and know their job and are willing to take the time to look after the customer. You need to put together a lot of little pieces and can only really do that if it's in your blood. You can't just take a university exam. Retailing requires an entrepreneur's mentality and without it you're just a cookie-cutter business. If it's not in your blood, you won't put the focus and energy into what is required to be numero uno on the high street. Business schools can't teach detail, commitment and focus. You have to bring that to the business yourself.

What I learned from Marcus about business is the same as what I learned from Marcus about charity work. Today, even though I work 80 to 90 hours a week, I spend at least 20 per cent of that time as a charity worker, dealing with the good causes that I chair or otherwise support. The Gerald Ronson Foundation gives to a large number of different good causes in society. I try to set an example, not only within my own Community but also in the wider community. My wife does the same. My daughters are also involved. As Marcus eased me into a leadership role in the Community and I became more involved with various good causes, I discovered that many charities were being run like hobbies by people who did not understand business. They want to help, they want to do some good, but running an organisation properly isn't in their blood.

I have always been prepared to do things that I believe in even if it means a lot of time, a lot of irritation and a lot of aggravation, because it also, often, means a lot of personal satisfaction. But then, I'm a doer. The problem is I often find myself sitting round tables with people who have left their brains outside. That's particularly true with certain captains of commerce and industry who join boards of charitable groups to further their CV in the hope of obtaining an honour. I have also found with a lot of English charities that everybody around the table is too polite. They won't be confrontational, take risks or ask people for money. But if you don't want to ask people for money, what's the purpose of being on a charity's committee?

Some charities are overburdened with people who think that since they are putting up money they are entitled to exercise patronage. Some charities are just badly organised, wasteful or poorly run. Some have too many jobs for the boys. Some are staffed by people who may try to do their best but are not really qualified to be there. Charities need to be run like a business and the staffing of them should be as lean as the tightest-run business. If they're not, then the charity's reputation suffers, and so does the reputation of the people who support it.

If I am enlisted into a charitable cause, then I'm entitled to have views about how it is to be run and to express those views. Saying things that people don't like may not make you popular, but if you believe you're there to do good, then the people working with you are entitled to have your honest opinion, even if it's not an opinion they like to hear. If it becomes clear that the organisation cannot be run in a way that I can accept, then I prefer not to get involved. I take my efforts and resources elsewhere. This upsets some people, while many others welcome it. I make no apology for my approach or method.

More often than not, I end up being the member of the committee who breaks the logjam that invariably comes about as a result of everyone else's reluctance to deal with delicate issues. I do my homework in advance, and I do it thoroughly. I'm not afraid to haggle with anyone, or everyone, until I'm satisfied that we're all on the same page. Many people who serve on charitable committees with me come away thinking I'm too tough, but it's important to be tough, especially when you're talking money for a fund-seeking organisation. When charities are joined by somebody like me, who insists on as much competence and efficiency as in a properly run business, the trustees may become ruffled. It's easy to understand, because they're all giving freely of their time and effort, and they don't necessarily understand, or accept, that they need to be disciplined. They don't always like it when I remind them that both the donor and the trustee have a duty to get every ounce out of every pound given and received.

There is nothing magical or holy about money given to or spent by a charity. It's like any other kind of money, and it behaves like any other kind of money. It will only buy so much and not a penny more. If the trustees say to me that they want a million, I ask them why three-quarters of a million won't do. Or, I ask why a million when it's clear to anybody who can add and subtract that what they really need is a million and a half. It's fundamentally important to hold everyone involved accountable. That way, those who are already contributing can see that they are getting their money's worth, and potential contributors can see that they won't be taken for a ride.

It is also important to me, personally, that when my name is on a list of supporters, other people can be sure that the charity is being managed properly. They can rest assured that their money is being well looked after. If it weren't, my name wouldn't be on the list.

In September 1967, I put my name on the top of one list that was extremely important to me – the Ronson Foundation, which I set up and funded with my own money. In those days, Heron had two lots of shares, dividend shares and non-dividend shares. I bequeathed all of my dividend shares to the foundation to provide an income. The foundation became Heron's single largest shareholder. I was comfortable doing that because I wasn't taking any income from my shares, and I never did. Believe it or not, I've never taken any money out of the business. The only money I've ever received is my salary and the capital growth from my shares.

For administrative reasons, I reorganised that first foundation into what became the second Ronson Foundation in 1979. But nothing much changed, because I continued to make contributions to good causes through the foundation, and also personally.

I have always felt very strongly that if you have had the good luck to possess or to acquire wealth, then you should give something back to those who are not so fortunate. Whilst I hope I would have had the same attitude towards charity no matter how I'd been brought up, I was told when I was still very young that you cannot be a good Jew if you are not ready to give to the poor and the needy. And from the time I formed that first foundation until 1990, I gave away more than £35 million from the foundation, the company and personally.

If there is a downside to being charitable, it's that a lot of people drive you mad. Almost right from the start, I received two or three requests a day for money, most of them from people I'd never heard of. All these years later, nothing much has changed, except that I now get four to six requests a day. These are people I've never met who write to me, 'Dear Gerald'. Not even 'Dear Mr Ronson'. The reason they write to me is because they think I'm an easy touch. And in many cases, I am. At least compared to other people. If I recognise someone's name, or if I knew their father or if I once met their uncle, or if it's somebody I only remotely know, they get a small cheque from me. It encourages them, so that's good. Just as importantly, I'm not going to let anyone in that category say, I wrote to Gerald Ronson and he told me to take a hike.

Of course, I get sob stories, but I'm not in the sob-story business. I know there are many people who have major problems, but we don't have the resources to deal with everyone. So if I don't know someone or can't find a connection to that person or his charity, then they get a polite letter saying, if you don't hear from us, we haven't approved your application. But everybody who writes gets a response, even if it's a no.

I also receive letters from people who figure that as long as I've asked them for money for my good cause, they can do the same thing for their good cause. That's fine, except that many of them aren't smart enough to make a proper face-to-face request. For every 20 letters they send out, they probably only get a couple of responses back, because it's usually some schmuck charity.

The reason I do what I do is not for any acclaim, not for any reward, but because it's what I need to do. In the end, it's the Good Lord who will judge me. When my days are over and I knock on the door, hopefully he will say, looking at the checklist, you've done a lot of good things in your lifetime, so I'm giving you a luxury pad. On the other hand, I may wind up in a basement bedsit. Who knows?

Many people who give money don't give their time and energy in order to encourage other people to give. I do both because I believe that a person is not discharging his charitable duty if he only gives money. For busy people, time is a much more valuable commodity, strictly limited and therefore precious. Then, too, it's no good asking other people for money and telling them that all you're doing is donating your time. You have to be a good giver if you want to be a good asker.

I give and urge others to give. There are people who openly say that I am one of the best fund-raisers in Britain. If so, it's probably more to do with my shortcomings than any good points. I have no hesitation in approaching people to contribute or suggesting to them the amount they should consider contributing. Some people find this brash, if not downright rude. Apparently, in polite British circles, there is a difference of opinion about which subjects are suitable for polite conversation and which are not. I've heard it said that it is easier to talk about sex than about money. But I find that people prefer my uninhibited, straightforward approach rather than pussyfooting around the subject. If nothing else, my more direct approach saves time.

I know a man, for instance, who is worth three to four billion pounds and one night when he started talking about how he loves to spend money on yachts and planes, I asked, 'Why don't you do something useful instead, like create a foundation, put £500 million in and give it away?'

He started huffing and puffing, 'Why should I? I pay my taxes.'

It baffles me that a man who has made so much doesn't understand what it is to help the underprivileged. Sure, he worked hard for his money, but how can he be so stupid? He and others like him hide behind the misconception that there aren't any underprivileged or poor people in the Community. That's crap. People are entitled to have different ideas about their own responsibilities, but here's a man who could give away tens of millions and never miss any of it. If you have a heart, how can you say, why should I give it away?

I'm sure there's a reckoning somewhere. Someone's keeping score. But until that man gets to that point, he's got to deal with me, and I'm not shy about telling him what I think. I don't have a problem with someone giving money to anything, from the Battersea Dogs Home to a cure for the common cold. Fair enough. But when a man like him does nothing – considering the amount of money I give away and the amount of time I spend raising money – I believe I have every right to speak up.

* * *

The experience I received working alongside Marcus Sieff soon paid off for several charities outside of the Jewish community. Word got around that I could organise fund-raising and, in 1984, I was approached by the Duke of Westminster on behalf of the NSPCC to join the Centenary Appeal Committee to help raise £12 million from commerce and industry.

I agreed to become joint vice chairman of their financial development board, along with the late Sir Maurice Laing. He was an executive at his family's construction company, John Laing PLC, and also the first president of the Confederation of British Industry. My job was to set out the blueprint for a fund-raising campaign. I suggested we bring together key figures from each industrial and commercial sector of British business, put them on the financial development board, let them set targets for their own sectors and make them responsible for meeting those targets. We also appointed a special director and staff, because this fund drive was over and above the ongoing appeal of the NSPCC.

Everyone thought this was a revolutionary approach to major fund-raising in the UK, and it worked, because we surpassed our £12 million target. But all I did was take the model I'd used with Marcus at the JIA and adapt it for the NSPCC. Since then, that model has been used successfully by many other major charities.

That same year, the late Sir Angus Ogilvy – husband to Princess Alexandra of Kent, the Queen's first cousin – rang to ask if I would be interested in joining the steering group that was going to lead an appeal to form the Prince's Youth Business Trust (PYBT). The idea was that the PYBT, founded by the Prince of Wales, would champion the cause of underprivileged young people by funding them to set up their own enterprises. The trust had traditional beginnings among the good and the great, but these were men who didn't necessarily concern themselves with issues pertaining to women or minority groups. In that respect, they weren't unique. There are many people in our society who work on long-established problems with all the best intentions in the world, but never come to see that there are new problems that need to be tackled.

Being invited to lead that appeal meant two things – getting people together and writing out a big cheque. I accepted right away, but for my own reasons. I'd become concerned with the problems that non-Jewish ethnic communities in the UK were having establishing themselves. I saw similarities between West Indian and Asian communities and the Jews who came to Britain at the turn of the century. That was one of the reasons I also got involved with the Windsor Fellowship, which takes sixth-formers from various ethnic communities who are going on to university and links them up with companies and organisations who give them work experience while helping to support them throughout their degree course. It's a wonderful programme because it puts these young people onto the first rung of the ladder of opportunity.

Now, I saw the PYBT as another opportunity to help young people from ethnic communities. But the appeal got off to a shaky start because there was no real fund-raising structure in place. So the first thing I did was put together a good team, then focus our campaign in two directions. There would be a national appeal on a regional basis. Then we would look to captains of commerce and industry. I think the original target had been a conservative million, which was nothing.

Together with Lord Boardman – he'd been a Conservative Minister for Industry, president of the Association of British Chambers of Commerce and chairman of NatWest Bank – we set up a number of small but high-level lunches and dinners, giving business leaders a chance to get involved. I set the pace with the first million-pound gift. All in all, we raised £7 million for the appeal. But we knew we could do a lot better, and, after careful consideration, we set a target for £40 million by 1988, in honour of Prince Charles's 40th birthday.

There was a high level of unemployment amongst young people

in those days, and the wide feeling was that this money would be well used. So when we went to see Lord (David) Young, who was head of the Department of Trade and Industry, and told him what we were planning, he was rash enough to agree that the Government would match, pound for pound, whatever we managed to raise. I'm sure he never expected to have to stump up as much cash as he did, because we raised £20 million. With his match, we hit our target.

A few years later, we asked the Government, if we go out and raise some more money for the PYBT, will you match it again? I don't think we told them what our target was, because we didn't want to frighten them, but they said OK. So I went out and hit a lot of people for some big chips. Angus and I were a terrific double act. I'd bring prospective donors into St James's Palace, we'd chat them up over a drink, and by the time they left, we had their cheque. This time, the two of us raised a lot of money and happily took another £50 million from the Government.

It was great fun, and Angus and I must have done it for ten years. But then, the Government could hardly complain, since our efforts and the PYBT were helping to solve problems that would otherwise have ended up on the Government's doorstep anyway.

Everything was fine until the PYBT was merged into The Prince's Trust. Prince Charles welded all these different charities together under the one umbrella, and at that particular point, I felt everything suffered. I don't think he was getting the best advice. He had people around him telling him what they thought he wanted to hear. When I first became involved, I insisted that my money was only to be used towards programmes supporting ethnic minorities. Angus Ogilvy was on side, and so was Tom Boardman, but it didn't make me too popular with some of the other people there.

As I was only on the periphery, I decided that was where I would stay. The Prince's Trust still keeps me informed and often invites Gail and me to whatever big events they hold at Windsor. And I get on with Prince Charles very well. I have known him for a long time, respect him and know that he respects me. He is very good at what he does for young people and is genuinely committed to helping them have a better life. But I honestly think he could achieve a lot more if he had better people advising him. Unfortunately, royalty attracts a certain type of person and they're not always the most dynamic, down-to-earth, middle-of-the-road kind.

I also have a lot of respect for his mother. Gail and I have had tea with the Queen and met her on many occasions. She is a very good woman, a very committed lady. Her husband and I get along, but that's about it. We have met several times in the context of various charities and I've found that at times he can be quite charming. But at other times, he can be prickly.

I should add that when I went through the Guinness problem, the royal family was supportive and considerate. Prince Charles wrote a letter to the judge speaking up for my character, and one night Princess Anne spotted Gail at a function and made a point of going up to her to ask how I was. None of them ran away or turned their backs. In fact, within a few weeks of my leaving HMP Ford, Gail and I were at a black-tie reception at Buckingham Palace. Bizarre, when you come to think of it.

Princess Diana and Gail were friends, and she showed real concern about how Gail and the girls were coping. We were guests at her 30th birthday party at the Savoy. In fact, Diana and Gail used to have lunch together, and she came to our home on a number of occasions. But I remember saying to Gail that Diana was a woman who couldn't hide her emotions. I didn't mean that she was unbalanced. I just warned Gail that if they became too close and didn't agree on something, Diana would be unhappy and drop her like a stone. So Gail maintained a certain distance. Diana used to send Gail little notes all the time, but Gail keeping her distance was how they stayed friendly to the end.

* * *

Around the same time that I began my involvement with the PYBT, Mrs Thatcher decided that the Government could no longer fund the nation's museums at the same rate as they had in the past. She needed a way to encourage museums and galleries to become more businesslike in the management of their activities and to seek their own opportunities to increase resources.

The Natural History Museum in South Kensington is a world-class scientific organisation, but until she came along it was run by scientists. It was also unionised and employed most probably over 1,000 people. Mrs Thatcher wanted entrepreneurial know-how on the board to help them cut down on overheads and put the museum on a profitable footing, so she asked if I would serve a five-year term. This was a non-paid post that took time to do properly, brought with it no status and a lot of aggravation. I accepted. Shortly after I arrived, she appointed Sir Denys Henderson, chairman of ICI, to serve as well.

The museum already had a corporate development plan in place, but they weren't used to the ways of business or particularly familiar with the techniques of fund-raising. So together with Sir Owen Green – he was chairman of the industrial conglomerate BTR – we created the Museum

Development Trust. It then struck me that an establishment of such international prestige should have royal patronage. But proposing that would be controversial, because no other museum in the country had a royal patron, and our trustees, being somewhat cautious by nature, might not wish to be the first to put forward this new concept.

There are many ways to skin a cat, so I proposed that the Museum Development Trust take the lead and seek patronage in its own right. That way, the museum's trustees would be shielded from any fallout. Princess Diana had recently visited the museum privately with her two sons. I suggested she'd be the appropriate patron, and when it was agreed, Gail presented the idea to her. And she said she would be happy to be associated with us. Knowing that, I felt maybe we could up the ante by inviting her to become patron of the museum itself. I went back to the trustees to tell them what I was thinking, they extended the invitation to her, she accepted and that's how she became patron of the Natural History Museum. She visited the museum on a number of occasions and her involvement was invaluable.

Owen and I then set out to launch a new era of more aggressive marketing. We brought in a director for commercial services and raised millions from the private sector to fund new exhibitions. In the name of my family, I gifted the museum £500,000 to establish a new dinosaur gallery, which opened in the spring of 1992.

I was also able to assist the museum with my experience in property. I hadn't realised how breathtaking the museum's space requirements are. Quite apart from providing for the studying and cataloguing of its collections, which is carried out by more than three hundred scientific staff working in the museum, it needs to house five million plant specimens, eight million fossils, fifty million animals (including insects), a quarter of a million samples of minerals and rocks, and more than two million books, manuscripts and pictures. Each year, the museum libraries receive more than 10,000 different periodicals published on natural history. In those days, the museum's storage space was in Park Royal, but the lease was due to run out and the funds set aside for new storage premises by the Treasury were very limited. What was more, the economy was booming during the latter part of the 1980s, which meant property prices were buoyant. It seemed unlikely we would be able to afford suitable premises close to London. Then came the economic depression of 1990–91, and suddenly, just when we really needed it, more property became available. I negotiated a deal for a major storage facility in south London and saved the Treasury a million or two.

I enjoyed the people I met at the museum – they were very different from property people – but I'm not sure that all of them quite understood me. And I did not always understand the scientific work they were doing. Needless to say, I learned a lot from them, but in return I gave them a lot of my heart and soul.

My time on the board included the six months I was in prison. The directors were under a lot of pressure to get me off the board, because the unions hated me. They had far too many people doing nothing and I watered down their influence. It wasn't the scientists I got rid of, it was all the schleppers, all those people who were just taking up space. Institutions that have been going for God knows how long always resent somebody coming in from the outside and deciding, you don't need 50 people doing this. But the directors were true gentlemen, never suggested that I resign from the board and welcomed me when I came back. And, as with all such things, when it came time to move on, after my five years, I moved on.

In March 1989, I received another request from Angus Ogilvy, this time in his capacity as patron and chairman of trustees of the Chindits Old Comrades Association. The Chindits was a special-forces unit made up of British infantry soldiers and Gurkha rifles, together with some Burmese and West African troops. It was the brainchild of Brigadier Orde Charles Wingate and fought brilliantly in the Burma campaign during the Second World War. Angus told me that permission had just been granted for a memorial on the Embankment, next to the Department of Defence, in honour of the Chindits and Wingate. He wanted my help to raise enough money to pay for it. I jumped at the chance, not just because the Chindits were such heroes, but also because General Wingate, a devout practising Christian, had been a great friend and benefactor to Israel.

During his service in the British army in Palestine from 1936 to 1939, Wingate established relationships with the Zionist leadership and was outspoken in his support of their aspirations to create a Jewish state. His close links with them did not necessarily endear him to the British high command. But when he saw the damage being done by Arab guerrilla forces to the oil pipelines that went from Haifa to the Jewish settlements, Wingate trained the Special Night Squads, which were small, swift-moving, lightly armed Jewish military formations designed to answer Arab attacks. Amongst the fighters he trained were Moshe Dayan and Yigal Allon, later to become a leading figure in the Israeli government.

The British authorities became so embarrassed by Wingate's commitment to the Jewish cause that they transferred him. During the Second World War, he helped rout the Italian forces in Ethiopia and helped to put the Emperor

Haile Selassie back on the throne. He then persuaded Winston Churchill that great damage could be inflicted on the Japanese in Burma through the use of unconventional forces parachuted behind Japanese lines. These 18,000 guerrillas were officially known as Long Range Penetration Groups, but Wingate himself nicknamed them after the mythical Burmese creature the Chinthe – half lion, half eagle – and they will forever be remembered as the Chindits.

One face of the memorial would be dedicated to Wingate, who was killed in a plane crash in 1944 during the Burma campaign. The inscription, from Winston Churchill, describes him as 'a man of genius who might well have become a man of destiny'. Next to it, Wingate is praised as 'an important influence in the creation of the Israel Defense Forces and the foundation of the State of Israel'.

It was an honour to help with the Wingate Memorial, so I went to Marcus Sieff and asked him to join me as co-chairman of the fund-raising committee. He'd not only served as an officer during the Second World War and spent time in Palestine but had met Wingate. Of course, he accepted. We launched the appeal at a reception given by the Prince of Wales at Kensington Palace, and 18 months later the memorial was unveiled by the Duke of Edinburgh.

CHAPTER 7

....

MAKING MY WAY THROUGH MRS T'S '80S

The 1980s saw business in Britain climb out of the Dark Ages thanks
to Margaret Thatcher, a dynamic and strong leader who liked self-
made entrepreneurs. I got to know her reasonably well – she was MP for
Finchley, which is the area where I live – and when she became Prime
Minister she sometimes invited Gail and me to dinner parties at No. 10.
Other businessmen I used to see there were James Hanson and Gordon
White of Hanson Trust, Terence Conran, who was running Habitat, Philip
Harris, who was CEO of the carpet company Harris Queensway, David
Alliance, who made uniforms for the army and the navy and turned the
textile company Coats Viyella into a £2 billion empire, and the legendary
American tycoon Armand Hammer.

Mrs Thatcher liked entrepreneurs, encouraged them and put the
country into a position where entrepreneurial businesses could succeed.
That doesn't mean to say there were a million great entrepreneurs under
her time, because I don't believe there were any more then than there are
today. But she understood what old Labour didn't, that entrepreneurs are
good for the country because they create jobs, create wealth and make
other British businesses more competitive.

She also understood that for business to flourish, someone needed to
take on the unions, who were holding the country to ransom. Doing what
she had to do made her deeply unpopular in certain quarters, but the
unions were tyrannical. They had a stranglehold over business and there
was no way Britain could survive in the competitive world of enterprise if
they were allowed to continue to dictate terms. I'm not anti-union, but you
couldn't have unions demanding 15–20 per cent pay increases at a time
when we were living with inflation in double digits. The miners' union was
especially difficult, and the strike in 1984 nearly destroyed our economy.

Mrs T was not prepared to bend. She was a very dynamic lady and a leader who did not tolerate nonsense, even within her own party.

I'm neither a Conservative nor a Labour supporter. In fact, I'm a declared independent. I support good people whether they are left or right. I supported her because I shared her convictions. I'd known her husband Denis for about ten years before I met her. He was a director of Castrol, the lubrication oil business, which was sold into Burmah Oil, and we'd done some business together. He was a nice man, although I couldn't say he was a great businessman. I think he was capable in the job that he did. He was an Englishman of a certain era. Remember, we're going back more than 40 years, when businesses were run differently and the people running them were a different breed. We've moved on, in some ways for the better, in some for the worse. Anyway, I'm sure that before we got to know his wife, Denis said to her, I know Gerald and he's a good chap.

Publicly, she could be intimidating. Privately, she was genteel. If you were one of her ministers sitting around the table at No. 10 and you said something she didn't agree with, she would make it quite clear that you were wrong. She wasn't the most tolerant lady in the world, and you knew it when she was angry, but socially she was charming.

One Christmas, many years ago, Gail, the girls and I were in South Africa. The phone rang in the hotel suite, and when I answered it, a familiar voice said, 'Hello Gerald, it's Margaret here.'

She was visiting her son Mark, who lived there at the time, and, completely out of the blue, wanted us to come over for a drink. Frankly, I thought twice about it, because I've never wanted to get too close to any politician. Maybe that's because I don't want to be associated with anyone else's politics. So I said I didn't know what arrangements Gail and the girls had made and that I'd get back to her. When I asked Gail if she wanted to go, she said, 'It won't do any harm.' So we went. And it turned out to be very pleasant. She made a lot of nice little hors d'oeuvres for us and was very motherly towards the girls.

That surprised me because we were always so used to seeing her political face. But then, I understand how people show different faces depending on the situation they're in. If I'm in a board meeting battling with 18 people because all I'm getting from the people around me are problems – and as Prime Minister, she had problems every day of the week with hundreds of people – then, of course, I'm a different person from the one who sits down with the family at home for dinner on Friday night. I'm much more approachable in a family setting than I am when I'm in the ring fighting to get things done. It was the same with her.

She was a woman with great strength of character, which is a terrific personal asset in politics and business. But in her case, it was also a liability. Her strength of character drove her to stay on too long. In politics, like in the rest of life, there's a time to go, and I think she should have gone after seven years. Instead, she stayed until she was so isolated that she lost sight of the true picture. It happens to lots of politicians, because they surround themselves with yes-men who don't tell them the truth when they're wrong or when they overcomplicate what needs to be done. Politicians want to please as many people as much of the time as possible so that they can get re-elected. When they come up with a scheme, they think the civil servants are actually going to make it happen. But every time they put something forward in the House – Commons or Lords – there are the 'fors' and the 'againsts', and the scheme gets watered down. Even after it's passed and makes its way through the bureaucracy, the fors and againsts carry out some parts and conveniently ignore others. A year later, the grand scheme has become like one of those big hosepipes that winds up at the bottom of the garden with only a little drip coming out of the tap.

That's what happened with Margaret Thatcher. I think that's what also happened with Tony Blair. He's a first-class man. I like him and always found him to be a man of principle. But there were a lot of things he wanted to do, and some he did, that came to very little. It's a shame. But that's the nature of British politics. It's not a lot different in America, France or anywhere else. Which leads me to wonder, why would anyone actually want to be a politician? I'm not someone who believes that politicians are people who can't get jobs in the real world, because a lot of them did have jobs in the real world, but I haven't seen too many politicians who were very successful in business before going into politics. At least with British politicians, it's rare that one follows the other. Possibly politics attracts people who are not very good at anything else besides speaking on their feet and making people believe they can deliver what they say they will. It's what actors do. That's the art of acting. They make people believe.

There is a Yiddish word, 'tachlis', that could be translated as 'the quality possessed by doers', and, to me, that's the difference between politicians and businessmen. Politicians aren't doers, except when it comes to getting elected. They're actors. At heart, I'm a doer. To be frank, doers may not be the most charming people or the best people to make a wonderful speech, but doers make things happen. Mrs Thatcher had that doer quality. That's one of the reasons why I always had a lot of respect for her.

Of course, when you're young and you meet people who are older, you're naturally more impressed than when you're, say, 70 and meet politicians who are maybe 35 or 40. With the benefit of age, you look at those younger men and women, and you can tell straight away that they do not necessarily have the same conviction to see things through that Margaret Thatcher did. What's more, in today's world, tachlis isn't necessarily always politically correct. And I'm the first to admit that I don't live in a politically correct world. In my world, if you don't do, then all you've done is talk. In my world, no one really wants to listen to talk. If I believe in something that I have a passion for, I get on with it. Doers follow their passions, and passion is one of the qualities for success. Passion creates commitment and focus.

That's another reason why I respected Margaret Thatcher. She had passion for the things she believed in. Before she came along, England was perceived differently. And maybe there have been times since her when we've gone backwards. But she had passion for restoring the 'great' in Great Britain. She dragged the country out of the nineteenth century and brought it into the twentieth century. She saw the need for free enterprise, the need to encourage people and the need to get the machine going. That's why she encouraged her ministers to cut out as much red tape as they could, which is rare. She understood how to make decisions, how to drive things forward, how to make you proud to be British.

* * *

With the Thatcher years came a booming market, and a lot of people made a lot of money. Yes, there was greed, but there was also jealousy. Whenever you have a lot of people making a lot of money, somewhere in the shadows there are people who resent the rich and successful. These are people who think wealth creation is some sort of evil ambition, who don't understand how business is done, who hate entrepreneurs, who have convinced themselves that rich businessmen must be crooks. These are people who have decided that, when the time comes, they're going to make an example of the rich bastards.

Though the stock market and the City were never a major interest of mine, I found it an interesting world. In some ways, it is very complex. In others, it is very simple. In industry, you have to deal with many people and a great deal of plant. People have to be managed, and plant has to be constructed, maintained, manned, supervised and operated. Running a business is arduous, and emotionally it drains you. Playing the stock market is essentially the opposite. You sit in the office or at home, study the form, pick up the phone, tell your broker what you want and put the phone down. Today, you can do it all by yourself online with your laptop from the beach. Over time, you may make a lot of money, or you may lose a lot of money. There is a dramatic aspect to it, but it is an untaxing process. In business, it may take you ten years to build up a good investment, or get rid of a bad investment, with all the aggro that goes along with it. Playing the market, you can build your stake or get rid of it immediately, even if it costs you a large amount of money. A quantum leap in profits and a quantum leap in size are two different things. The market makes its own demands and has its own challenges. But compared with life in industry and commerce, playing the market is very smooth, simple and impersonal, even if you are ruined as a result of it.

My own interests have never revolved around money. I'm interested in running a big, complex and successful business. Making money is a result of being good at that. But I could see how a well-chosen investment followed by a takeover could give me a big business to run without having to wait all the time it normally takes to build one up from scratch. Temperamentally, I have always liked speed and have never been long on patience. So in the '80s I spent quite a bit of time shadowing likely targets for takeovers on the Stock Exchange and enjoying the excitement and the challenge of it.

Heron was generating lots of cash. As I remember, we were sitting on more than £500 million, which was a huge sum in those days and is still a great deal of money today. There was no sense leaving it all in the bank, so we took positions in companies and got involved in takeovers. I am no great financial expert, but it was a good time to do that and I could see companies that were undervalued.

Being cash rich meant we could buy anything we wanted to. I have always believed that cash is king – I still do because it's all the more true today – but just because you can afford to, you don't have to jump on every bus coming along the high street. You have to be patient. A proportion of our acquisitions did not come out of some scientific development plan, it came out of picking and choosing opportunistic deals. And any entrepreneur who says he's never done any opportunistic deals is either kidding himself or not telling the truth.

This was a time when entrepreneurs like Jimmy Goldsmith were getting involved in 'greenmail'. That was when you started bidding on a company, threatened the board with a takeover and let it be known that once you had control, you were going to fire the senior managers and fire the board, then break up the assets of the company. The senior managers and the board would panic and use whatever funds they had to buy your shares back from you at a big profit. We deliberately stayed away from games like that. It wasn't the way I did business. It's not who I am. I knew our reputation in the City – the reputation I wanted to maintain – and there was no way I would jeopardise that. We are serious business people running a serious business. I maintained then, and I maintain now, that we always play by the rules.

It was also a time when the entrepreneur Jim Slater wrote, 'When the world is selling, then you should be buying, and when the world is buying, you should be selling.' He's not wrong. I don't think you can generalise, because it depends on the assets, but it's usually best to sell into a market when everybody else wants to buy. That's one of the reasons why, in 1982, when Lew Grade's empire came up for sale, we took a serious look.

Lew owned Associated Communications Corp (ACC), which included the television production company ATV, which made programmes like *The Saint, The Prisoner, Thunderbirds* and *Sunday Night at the Palladium*. He owned Central Television and was therefore one of the men behind the creation of the ITV network. He owned several London theatres and had a considerable property portfolio. He also owned ATV Music, which owned a company called Northern Songs, which meant that Lew Grade owned almost all the Beatles' hit songs. But a few years before, when Lew had run into some financial trouble, an Australian entrepreneur named Robert Holmes à Court had put money into ACC. Taking the devil's shilling was a mistake, because once Holmes à Court was inside, he plotted to take the company away from Lew.

I knew Lew quite well and wasn't surprised when he rang me to ask that I come see him. As soon as I arrived, he told me that Holmes à Court was going to seize control of ACC, and he was adamant that he did not want Holmes à Court to have it. He disliked the man, and rightly so, because Holmes à Court was devious. Lew asked me if I would be prepared to make a counterbid there and then. Lew said that if I did, he was sure the board of ACC would approve it.

Though I often do things by instinct, and sometimes get them very wrong, I am by nature cautious and don't like to rush. I said I'd think it over that night. One of the people I spoke to was Jarvis Astaire, who was a well-known entrepreneur in his day. He thought we could buy the company for around £55 million. Considering that we would then own Central Television, a big film catalogue, that music catalogue and some prime real estate, at that price, the company was cheap.

I also spoke to Rupert Murdoch. He was nowhere near as powerful in those days as he is today, but he rang me up to ask how I was getting on with the takeover, how I was getting on with Holmes à Court and if he could help in any way. I like Rupert and have always found him to be a straight-talking guy. He didn't much care for Holmes à Court either and told me, 'He is a man who can't sleep straight in his bed at night.'

Unfortunately, the shares of ACC were in a two-tier structure, meaning that there was voting stock and a much larger block of non-voting stock. I'm going back a lot of years now, but I think ACC was then probably worth £100 million. The board had control of the company through their ownership of the voting stock. Knowing that the company was in dire straits, Holmes à Court said that he would make a rescue bid for the company provided that the board gave irrevocable undertakings to accept his bid. I think his offer was £35 million. Astaire and I raised him 30 per cent with a £46.6 million bid. As I remember, Holmes à Court matched us, we went to £49 million, he came back with £60 million. He then gave the board only a few hours to accept. They panicked, turned us down and Holmes à Court walked away with the company. We sued the board for breach of fiduciary duty and won our case, but since Holmes à Court had control of the voting stock, he still won the company.

I tried to block the sale with the broadcasting authority because there was a rule on the books that foreigners couldn't own Central Television, but somehow Holmes à Court got around that. Thanks to us, he had to pay an extra 15p per share, but none of the shareholders ever seemed grateful.

I'd said publicly that I thought it would be improper to buy shares before announcing to the general public that I was going into battle for control, and whilst no one said I did anything wrong, I was criticised in the press for being too self-righteous. They wrote that because I didn't buy my shares first and then lost the bid, I was too naive to play this game.

The usual predatory way is to buy a chunk of stock before launching a takeover, which not only gives you a head start in the race for control, but in the event you lose to a rival bidder, at least you have the inevitable jump in the price of the shares to cover the costs of your foray. We'd spent thousands on legal fees, and I have to agree that my ignorance, or naivety, cost us money. We should have bought shares to make money as Holmes à Court and the speculators bid them up. Not doing so was stupid. But, at the time, my reasons for not buying seemed sound to me. It was a game that others were playing and getting criticised for – running up a company's share price, then bailing out with a big profit instead of actually winning the company fair and square – and I wanted to be Mr Cleaner-than-Clean.

Of course, as soon as Holmes à Court won control, he did what corporate raiders always do. He ripped the company into pieces, sold off Central Television and everything else that had any value – like all the Beatles songs, which he sold to Michael Jackson – and probably made

£100 million out of the deal. Interestingly enough, the only asset he kept was one song from the Beatles catalogue. He insisted, as part of the sale to Michael Jackson, that his daughter Catherine – whose nickname was Penny – be given all the rights to 'Penny Lane'.

I never really understood why Lew sold out to Holmes à Court. In Lew's autobiography, *Still Dancing*, he doesn't have many kind words to say about him. Maybe Holmes à Court had something on Lew. Who knows? But at some point in his dealings with Holmes à Court, Lew and the rest of the board had given their word, and Lew was an old-fashioned guy who believed, like me, that your word is your bond. Lew told me he just couldn't break himself out of the deal.

Robert Holmes à Court died of a heart attack at the age of 53 in 1990, leaving his widow so much money that she became the richest woman in Australia, thanks in large part to his ACC connections. Lew Grade died 8 years later at the age of 92.

Some people thought that the real motive behind my bid was to get into show business. This was an era when entrepreneurs were being written about like movie stars, and a few even thought they were. But show business never interested me. I just saw money to be made in those assets, and I am in the business of making money. It turned out that ACC was burdened with lawsuits, carrying a £38 million overdraft and £67 million worth of debt, so maybe we didn't lose as badly as some people thought we did. Anyway, I don't ponder over deals we didn't do.

Ironically for someone who didn't want to be in show business, I did get into the entertainment industry, at least for a while, when in 1984 we bought a company in Los Angeles called Media Home Entertainment. It wasn't because I aspired to be a movie star, it was because the company was one of the largest independent operators in the video business, and there was money to be made in videos. The way it worked in those days, you had to finance a movie in order to get the video rights. So we financed over 100 movies. Today, they're considered cult movies, but I always considered them rubbish. They were things like *The Delta Force*, *A Nightmare on Elm Street* and a remake of *The Texas Chain Saw Massacre*. I built up Media Home Entertainment but can't say it was a lot of fun. Show business was a lot of aggravation with a load of shitty people.

Not that I ran Media Home Entertainment personally. It was run by management, and in the early days it made a lot of money. But the video business is yesterday's business. It wound itself down, lost its way, fell into the hands of the big boys and died on its feet. The only people making money in that business today are the major studios, producing big hits and selling millions of videos, which have subsequently become DVDs. I was never tempted again. Once was enough. Too many people in the entertainment business are not our style.

* * *

Back in London, we made a bid for the United Drapery Stores (UDS) group, which included manufacturers and retail outlets like Richard Shops, John Collier, Allders department stores and the duty-free shops at Heathrow and Gatwick airports. It was 1983 and only the second major bid we attempted. We came up short when James Hanson joined the action. We were at 32p a share and declared our bid final. He was very good at doing these deals, cleverly sidestepped us with a reverse rights issue at 33p and walked away with the company. Although we failed this time too, at least we did not make any major mistakes.

So I continued share building and share dealing. In some cases, we bought shares to create a platform from which we might acquire the company through a takeover. In other cases, we bought shares because we thought they were undervalued and stood a good chance of appreciating. But I have to admit that I was not then, and am not now, totally at home in the City. And I wish I had realised that more clearly before we got into all of this. My experience is that of a trader in the marketplace, and the marketplace that I understand is property. If you are buying and selling property in my marketplace, there are rules. But they're nothing like the legal apparatus you have to cope with when dealing in the City. When we were trying to acquire ACC, I found myself sitting around with lawyers, accountants and bankers every day, and the first item on the agenda would be some section of the Companies Act. Most of it was gibberish to me and drove me round the bend. I wanted things simple. I wanted dealing in the City to be like dealing in property. If I hear there's something for sale in Luton, I drive there, look at it and decide whether to buy it. If I buy it, I decide whether to redevelop it or sell it at some future date. But you can't deal that way in the City.

After UDS, we bid for Debenhams department stores. In 1985, Ralph Halpern was running a company called the Burton Group, which had several chains of clothing stores, and decided he wanted to own the Debenhams group, which also owned Harvey Nichols in Knightsbridge. Ralph's bid got particularly complicated because after he built up a stake of 38 per cent of the company's shares, it did not seem likely that he would be able to acquire any more. Debenhams had no intention of being taken over and had found an ally for the time being in the Fayed brothers – Mohamed and Ali – owners of the House of Fraser, which included Harrods.

Though they had openly ranged themselves in support of Debenhams, and against Burton, there was speculation that once they had succeeded in helping Debenhams to fight off the Burton bid, they would move to take over Debenhams themselves. I only got involved to help Philip Harris – now Lord Harris – because we were close friends at the time. He was selling his carpets in Debenhams and had heard that if the Fayeds bought the company, they would throw him out. So he came to me to say, 'If we buy shares, we can block anyone from taking over.'

I asked, 'Why do I want to do that?'

He said, 'So that maybe somebody else will come in who I can have a relationship with.'

Cutting a long story short, we wound up with £30 million to £40 million worth of shares. I did it to help Philip. At the same time, I couldn't really see any downside to the deal, but then, there wasn't any great upside to it either. Halpern won his bid and I think we might have made a couple of million pounds' profit. Philip was able to sort out his arrangements to sell his carpets at Debenhams, and that was it. Except, for whatever reason, it received a lot of huff and puff in the papers.

Newspaper people sometimes make up stories or add a twist to fill space. With all those deals going on, I became an unwilling favourite of the crystal-ball gazers. If a company looked ripe for a bid, some newspaper would whisper to its readers, with a knowing nod, Gerald Ronson. My name was linked to a bid for Burmah Oil so often that I might have been the only businessman in England who doubted that Gerald Ronson was going to buy Burmah Oil. As it happened, we did own shares in that company, but I often read about companies I was supposed to have stakes in and didn't. I'd open the Sunday papers and actually laugh, because one week I was bidding for some company alongside a Saudi consortium, the week after that I was bidding for another company on my own. It still never surprises me how irresponsible certain newspapers can be. They don't do their homework. If you're a 'colourful character' you can wind up with a lot of space in the papers. And for whatever reason, they see me as a colourful character. But I am what I am, and I can't change that. Then, too, neither do I wish to.

The upside is that when people know you're in a position to sign a big cheque, they pick up the phone. In the UK in those days, there were maybe only half a dozen people in a position to make the decisions we could. In 1984, when I was awarded Businessman of the Year by the Chancellor of the Exchequer, Nigel Lawson – in the presence of 400 leaders from every section of the community – a lot of people with something to sell found our phone number.

All the brokers in the City knew our phone number and we were working with several of them. One in particular, whom I considered to be a good friend at the time, was Tony Parnes. He had a reputation for being pretty flamboyant, having started as an office boy and worked his way up to become a big deal at the brokerage house Alexanders, Laing & Cruickshank. His nickname in the City was 'The Animal', not because of any way he acted but because he had a lot of hair on his head.

I'd known Tony for some years. He was a personable fellow, our families were friendly and he had a good reputation. Because he knew we could write big cheques, he would ring me every day, usually at the end of the day, or stop by to talk about what deals were around or propose that we buy 2 per cent of this company or 3 per cent of that company. Obviously, his own desire was to make commission out of the shares that he was selling, but at the time I regarded him as honest and capable. A lot of people were quick to slag him off after the event, but they'd been happy to do business with him. Over the years, we did tens of millions of business with Tony. Some deals made money, some didn't. But that's the nature of the stock market.

Looking back, I overestimated his ability to know what he was talking about. He may have had a good nose for a deal, and maybe I'll give him credit for spotting an opportunity when one came along, but he didn't understand the rules and regulations as well as he pretended to. I took it for granted that, as a top trader, he knew what he was doing, knew the rules and would always tell the truth.

That became the biggest and most costly mistake of my life.

* * *

Towards the end of 1985, the liquor and drinks company Distillers, who made and distributed Dewar's White Label Scotch, Johnnie Walker Scotch and Gordon's Gin, was ripe for takeover and two companies went after it. One was the Argyll Group, a food and grocery conglomerate run by a Scottish entrepreneur named James Gulliver. The other was Guinness, a brewing company started in the mid-eighteenth century in Ireland and still largely owned by descendants of the Guinness family. Distillers was twice the size of Guinness.

The man running Guinness, Ernest Saunders, was a tall, impressive, capable businessman who could put on all the charm. He also had a very high opinion of himself. I'd met him socially at a cocktail party given by our mutual friend, Sir Jack Lyons, in support of an art exhibition to raise money for charity. Saunders had been an executive at J. Walter Thompson advertising agency, then at the Swiss food company Nestlé, before being recruited by the Guinness family to fix a company that was in serious trouble.

I felt that family had a lot to answer for and found many of them to be wet, useless people who'd done nothing more than inherit a fantastic business. I knew some of them, not particularly well but enough to know that they were not my sort of people. One of the exceptions was James Guinness, who was a nice man. I liked him. And I think he was embarrassed by the rest of the family.

Saunders took a company that had long ago lost its way – there were about 50 different companies inside Guinness, manufacturing toothbrushes to toilet rolls – cleaned the place up and turned the family's fortunes around. In return, it seemed to me that the family treated him poorly. Even after he made tens of millions for them, they considered him nothing more than a hired hand and were not very generous. But Saunders also had an ego to feed and his plan was to turn Guinness into another Nestlé. He saw his future not selling beer but running a company with all the wonderful brands that Distillers owned. He was clever. The fact that he was an egomaniac, a liar and everything else is another matter.

So he went after Distillers and took on the fight with Argyll by offering to pay for Distillers with a combination of cash and Guinness shares. Obviously, the higher the Guinness share price, the better their offer seemed to be for Distillers. There was nothing unique or even remotely sneaky about this. When the bid for Distillers was first launched, the Guinness share price was quite high, so Argyll's friends started selling Guinness shares short, forcing the price down. At the same time, Argyll's friends were buying Argyll's shares to keep their own share price high. That's how this game was played.

I was reading about it in the papers but didn't have any particular interest in it until Tony Parnes came around one evening during the week of 20 January 1986. He wondered if I'd be prepared to purchase some Guinness shares because Saunders and Guinness were looking for people to join their fan club. I asked Tony what the terms were. He said we would be covered for our costs and indemnified against losses. I said, 'I take it you've cleared what you are saying to me with Ernest Saunders?' He said he had.

As long as Guinness would reimburse us for our costs and any losses, we had nothing to lose. The interest on the money we were spending and the brokers' fees would be covered. If the shares went down, we would be reimbursed at the price we paid. If the shares went up, we might even make some money. It was like loaning them money. That was fine. But what really interested me was that Distillers owned a very good portfolio of properties. I especially liked their brewery site at Alperton, which is off the North Circular Road, and also their hotel portfolio, which included the Meridian in Piccadilly and the best hotels in Edinburgh. My thinking was that if Guinness won, they would sell off those properties to help pay for the takeover. Helping Guinness should create enough good will to put me at the front of the queue for some of those properties.

I told Parnes we'd go in for £10 million. It wasn't a lot of money, considering that the Distillers takeover wound up costing £2.5 billion. Parnes said he'd take care of it, and I left the timing and the buying of the shares to him. I didn't think there was any reason to get in touch with Ernest Saunders, because Parnes said he'd already cleared it with Saunders, and, at that stage, his word was good enough for me.

Some time afterwards, Saunders rang me to say he understood we were being helpful and that it was appreciated. I wanted him to understand what my interests were, so we fixed a date to have breakfast. We met at the Meridian around eight in the morning on 7 February. My conversation with him was about the properties Distillers owned in central London. He asked me if I had an idea what they might be worth. I said I would do some research. Halfway through breakfast, we were joined by Olivier Roux, who had been a consultant at Bain & Company in Boston and was now serving as Guinness's finance director. Saunders and Roux had an 8.30 meeting, so they had to leave.

Over the next few months, Saunders rang me every ten days or so to ask if I was hearing any good or bad news about the bid. Any time he felt a newspaper editor had been unfair to him, he'd ask me if I could put in a good word. I had to remind him, 'I'm not in the PR business.'

Parnes was also ringing me sometimes three or four times a day, in addition to popping in every other afternoon or so. We'd talk about business, not just about Guinness. But one afternoon, some time after the £10 million had been spent, he wanted to know if I would consider adding some more. So we went from £10 million to £15 million and then to £18 million. When that was expended, Parnes asked if we'd go further. I was prepared to go to £25 million, but that was the maximum. It was about 5 per cent of our entire portfolio, which was the most we would invest in any one share. From my point of view, that was now a lot of money. But for Saunders, Roux, Guinness and their £2.5 billion deal, my £25 million was only 1 per cent. Before this was over, Saunders and Roux had raised more than £200 million this way. Clearly, I wasn't the only one. There were a lot of other people who put in a lot of money. And that's important to remember.

Before I agreed to the additional stake, I said to Tony, 'We can't have an open-ended situation.' I reminded him that I wasn't in the share-buying business and that I was only getting involved to have first pick of those properties. I was concerned that after I helped Saunders and Roux, they'd turn around to me, demand stupid money for the properties and I'd wind up with two fingers. So I said to Parnes, 'This is all well and good, but what is our success fee if we go to £25 million?'

He decided that a 20 per cent fee, based on my £25 million stake, would be reasonable. That was £5 million. I wanted to know, 'Do you have the approval of the company?' He came back to me the next day to say yes.

On 3 April, I went to the Guinness head office on Portman Square in central London to have lunch with Saunders. Roux came in and so did Thomas Ward, who was an American lawyer and a director of Guinness. It was a bit like musical chairs. At that lunch, I asked them to clarify what they understood our deal was. I didn't want any misunderstanding in relation to what Parnes told me and what the arrangement was. Saunders said, in front of Roux and Ward, that we would be covered on the downside in terms of any capital losses, any interest and the costs of the transactions. Then, Saunders said, if they were successful, they'd pay us a fee of £5 million, which was 20 per cent of the exposure. Saunders also said that, by helping them, I was in pole position to buy those properties.

Guinness was underwriting its fan-club members' losses because that's the way it worked in the City in those days. There was never any suggestion that there was anything illegal or underhanded about this. Here I was, dealing with chief executive Saunders, finance director Roux and legal director Ward, never thinking for one minute that they were dishonest or that they would ask me to do something dishonest. It was only afterwards that I found out they were crooks. It was only afterwards that I found out that Parnes was getting £3 million for bringing me in and that I wasn't the only person he was bringing in. It was only afterwards that I found out how Ward had brought in the American arbitrageur Ivan Boesky and the American investor Meshulam Riklis, and how Saunders had recruited the Bank Leu in Zurich to buy shares. There were dozens of people circling around this deal, in it because there was money to be made. But I was only in it to have first pick of those properties. If Saunders and Roux were willing to underwrite my losses, so much the better. I knew I'd have to pay a fair price for whatever properties I could buy – they weren't giving anything away – and everything I did with Saunders and Roux and Parnes was in the open. There was never any wink-wink. If there had been, I would have run away. If someone had whispered, don't tell anyone about this, I would never have been within 100 miles of this.

I mentioned Sir Jack Lyons. I'd known him for many years. He was a financier, a nice man, not the cleverest in the world, but not a crook. He was a rich man who'd already retired and probably missed the game of big business, missed playing with the big boys, so he got himself a seat on the Bain & Co. advisory board. Jack and Tony Parnes were also joint directors of J. Lyons Chamberlayne. Saunders brought Jack in as a political adviser because Jack knew everybody and this takeover was very political. Here was an Irish company based in the UK buying a Scottish company, which raised all sorts of questions in the halls of government about employment, brands, management, etc. Jack was good friends with Ted Heath and marginally friendly with Mrs Thatcher. But Jack may have oversold his relationship with government. He was getting a fee from Guinness, but that had nothing to do with me. I didn't know about any of this until much later.

After that lunch with Saunders, I came back to the office and told my own directors what Saunders and the others and I had agreed. It never occurred to me to ask lawyers and accountants. I have every right to expect that when I'm dealing with the CEO and chief financial officer of a major public company, whatever they do is within the law. If they break the law and deliberately hide that fact from me, how am I guilty of breaking the law too? If Saunders and Roux conspired to do something illegal, which they did, and as long as I acted in good faith, which I did, why should their crimes be my crimes?

On 18 April 1986, the Guinness offer for Distillers became unconditional and the war was won. Some time in May or June, Parnes told me that Guinness was planning a big placement of shares and our shares would be included. He said it was being organised with Cazenove, a blue-blood brokerage in the City. I told Parnes to let my finance director know so that he could deal with the necessary paperwork. I didn't deal with any of this. I never knew when the shares were sold or who sold them. We were paid what Guinness promised to pay us, including the success fee, and, as far as I was concerned, that was the end of that. I didn't spend a lot of time on this while it was happening, and once it was over I didn't spend any time at all on it.

In fact, I didn't give the Guinness takeover of Distillers a second thought for the rest of the year. That is, until the Department of Trade and Industry decided I had to.

CHAPTER 8

....

GUINNESS

van Boesky was a Wall Street trader who amassed a fortune by betting
on corporate takeovers. His timing was so uncanny – buying and selling
shares just before news reached Wall Street that prices were going up or
down – that he was investigated by the Securities and Exchange Commission
(SEC). They found irregularities and charged him with insider trading. In
the plea bargain he worked out to avoid a long term in prison, he confessed
to having been involved with Ernest Saunders and the Guinness takeover
of Distillers. The SEC passed that information along to the Department of
Trade and Industry (DTI).

I didn't know what was going on until 1 December 1986. I was in Brussels
inspecting some property and heard on the late-evening news that the DTI
was looking into the Guinness takeover. The next morning, on my way back
to Britain, I read more about it in the papers. Frankly, I didn't really have
a reaction to the news, because I knew I had not done anything wrong. I
thought perhaps, at worst, it might create a bit of aggravation. But I never
thought for a minute that it was going to be a major concern. I'd been dealing
with a public company and the men running it had assured me that they had
the authority to do what they were doing, that it was perfectly legal. Why,
all of a sudden, would I think differently? Boesky had got sucked into it in
America. I didn't know what he'd done or anything about what Saunders
and Roux had promised him. They certainly never discussed that with me.

I admit, though, that I was the one who gave them Boesky's phone
number. Saunders and Roux told me that Thomas Ward wanted to meet
Boesky and asked me if I knew him. As it happened, I had his number, but
I didn't make the introduction. My secretary passed the number along to
Ward. That's all. And Ivan – not that I was his big buddy – never asked me
if I knew any of them.

No, I didn't give the DTI enquiry a lot of thought, at least not until a month or so after it was announced, when Tony Parnes came to my office to tell me, 'This is going to get serious.'

I blew up at him. 'You introduced me to these people. You got me into this. You said it was perfectly legal. Now you're telling me this could be serious?'

That's when he confessed to me, 'I was paid a commission.'

It was the first I'd heard of this and I was furious. 'A commission from them on top of the commission you made on the shares you bought for me?' It was dishonest of him, and if I'd known about it when he first came to see me about Guinness, I would never have become involved. 'Yes, you are in big fucking trouble. But there's no reason why I should be in trouble with you. You were my adviser. Just tell the truth, because the truth is very simple.'

He answered, 'That may be difficult. My legal advisers have said that if I tell the truth, I could go to prison for five years.'

I yelled at him, 'I don't give a fuck if you go to prison for 55 years. I don't have any secrets about what I did and it's no secret that you said to me it was perfectly legal. Just tell the truth.'

He sat in my office crying, telling me, 'I love you like a brother.'

But he dropped me in it with his lies and if this had been a movie about the Mafia, they'd have put a contract out on him.

* * *

I needed legal advice, and Bob Maxwell insisted that I speak to Victor Mishcon, one of the most eminent lawyers of his time.

Victor was born in Brixton, the son of a rabbi, and rose from humble roots to become Baron Mishcon of Lambeth, and Shadow Lord Chancellor in the House of Lords. His law firm, Mishcon de Reya, was renowned for handling many high-profile cases, especially Princess Diana's divorce. Victor died in 2006 at the age of 91. When I met him, he was already in his mid-70s, but still had his wits about him. He was a small man who spoke slowly and deliberately, was very clever, very honest and very articulate. So many other lawyers I've met pontificate and drag things out. Not him. He would sit behind his desk, listen carefully to your question, then, right away, give you a precise answer.

Stepping into his office was like stepping back to the 1930s. Books and papers were everywhere. He didn't use a computer. His secretary, an older woman with a bun tied up on the top of her head, always carried a notepad and pencil. He addressed her as 'Mrs Joseph' and she addressed him as 'Lord Mishcon'.

Our relationship was strictly professional. We never became close friends. There's a certain style with old-school professionals, not just lawyers but doctors too, who draw an invisible line between themselves and their clients and don't usually cross it. I understand that. If you're advising somebody, you don't want to allow yourself to become emotionally involved. That doesn't mean he didn't care, because Victor was a very caring man, just that he was a very formal man, even a bit chilly and distant.

When Bob Maxwell saw that I was playing with a very straight hand, he decided that maybe I needed a tricky, devious lawyer and suggested that I fire Mishcon and hire someone he knew who would help me lie my way out of this. I refused because I'm not a liar. I stayed with Victor because I don't walk in crooked lines. Bob, on the other hand, was a great liar, and look where lying got him. I wasn't going to allow myself to be associated with any shady deals. And even if I didn't do anything wrong, I also wasn't going to keep any money that might somehow appear to be tainted. So on 18 January 1987, I returned it all to Guinness.

The next thing I knew, the Department of Trade and Industry required me to appear before their inspectors. The inquiry was headed by a lawyer named David Donaldson and an accountant named Ian Watt. I was allowed to have a lawyer present, but it did little good, because the rules of British justice didn't apply. This was a Star Chamber where I was obliged, under duress, to testify. I did not have any right of silence. I had to answer every question truthfully and fully. If I did not, the inspectors warned me, I could be held in contempt and sent to jail for up to two years. I told the truth and, naively, expected that would work. But the transcripts of my DTI under-duress interviews were passed to the Crown Prosecution Service and the CPS handed them over to the police. Those transcripts were then used against me. It was straight out of some Third World dictatorship.

From the time my name first appeared in the press in connection with the Guinness affair until the day I was arrested and then for every day of the trial, my family and I went through non-stop harassment by the media. Journalists, photographers and cameramen were parked outside my house and parked outside my office, and they followed Gail and me wherever we went. The only time I was free of them was when I was travelling out of the country, which I was during the second week of October 1987.

I had security at the house because I wanted to be certain that Gail and our four daughters were safe. And on Tuesday morning, 13 October – the day I was due to arrive home in London – the security man said to Gail,

'There's something funny going on.' A car had pulled up in front of the house. A man and a woman got out, one walked one way and the other went the other way. The security man said, 'There's a book in the back of the car and I believe it's really a camera.'

Gail was worried and rang Lord Mishcon. By then, the police had arrested and charged Saunders and Parnes, and Victor realised that the police were getting ready to arrest me at home. To avoid a media frenzy, he arranged for me to pre-empt my arrest. So as soon as I landed in the UK, Victor and I went to the police station. There, I was charged with eight offences, including theft, false accounting, conspiring to create a false market in shares and unlawful share indemnity. I was not put in a cell, and I was never handcuffed. In fact, I have to say that the police were very fair and treated me with respect. One of the senior fraud squad officers who interviewed me actually said, 'We have to go through all the motions, but you shouldn't be here. I don't think you've done anything dishonest. I think you're being turned over.'

Commander Malcolm Campbell was in charge at the time and he was a decent man. I have subsequently met him several times, as he is on the committee of the Philip Green Memorial Trust, a charity I am also involved with. Malcolm knew I needed to keep running my business, to travel to Europe every week and to the States once a month, and let me keep my passport. He said to me, 'I know you're an honest man. I know you're not going to run away.'

The fraud squad investigation was headed by a senior officer named Botwright and his partner, whose name was Craig. Both of them told me they felt this was not a case for the police and that I was being used as a scapegoat. They bent over backwards to be nice to me. They didn't treat other people involved in this the same way because they could see who was telling the truth and who was lying.

I know that Mrs Thatcher felt embarrassed about this, and it was awkward for her, at least until it was over. But there was really nothing she could do, not without serious political repercussions, and afterwards we went back to being friends.

The magistrates set my bail at £500,000. I could have paid it, but in England you have to find third parties to put up bail. I suppose that helps guarantee you'll show up for the trial. There was a long list of people willing to help, but I asked my two pals Trevor Chinn and Harvey Soning, and they guaranteed £250,000 each.

I've known Trevor since I was 16 years old. He's been very successful in business and, as chair of several organisations like the UJIA, has been a real leader of our Community. His wife Susan is one of Gail's closest friends.

Harvey and Angela Soning have been our friends for 40 years. Gail and I met them at a wedding – we were all sitting on the same table – and it turned out that he was in the midst of buying a flat for his father in a block we'd built in Avenue Road. They're a very fine family, very nice people, very loyal. Here, too, Gail and Angela are great friends.

So Trevor and Harvey posted bail for me, which is a complicated procedure, because they had to prove to the courts that they had assets and were good for the money. And I was free to get on with my life for the next two and a half years. That's how long it took between being arrested and the trial. And through it all, we continued to be harassed by photographers and the press. Day and night, they never left us alone.

On the morning I was arrested, after Gail spoke to Victor Mishcon, she phoned Angela to tell her what was happening, and it was Angela who decided that the best thing was to get Gail out of the house. They went into town together and were walking along Sloane Street when they just happened to walk into a card shop. To this day, Gail doesn't know why they stopped there, because she wasn't looking to buy any cards, had never been there before and has never been there since. But as soon as they went inside, news came on the radio that I'd been arrested.

Gail and Angela left straight away, because the last thing Gail wanted was for our children to hear the news that way. So they found a phone and rang all the schools where the girls were and told the headmistresses that they were on their way. By the time they all arrived home, the place was surrounded by the press. Cleverly, Gail got in touch with the security guy inside the house and told him what to do. He went outside and announced, 'They're not coming home. You can go now.' And the schmucks left.

* * *

Unbeknownst to me or to Victor Mishcon, the Government was busy stacking the deck against us.

To begin with, the DTI had set its sights on me. The Secretary of State for Trade and Industry who'd ordered the enquiry was a fellow named Paul Channon. Who was he? A member of the Guinness family!

It wasn't until years later that we saw documents the Government tried to hide from us that proved that the Crown Prosecution Service conspired with Channon's DTI to keep the police out of the case until the DTI inspector could get us to incriminate ourselves in the under-duress interviews. Obviously, the prosecution cannot call a defendant to testify against himself in court. But as long as they had the DTI transcripts ready before the police read us our rights – the right to remain silent – they could read the transcripts to the jury.

The Guinness family held Saunders in contempt and many of them knew what I thought about them. Obviously, Channon couldn't be seen to be closely involved in the case, so he passed the buck way down the line to a very junior henchman, one of his parliamentary undersecretaries, Michael Howard.

I don't know Howard well, but I've never been impressed by him and don't think he was a strong leader for the Conservative Party. I've always seen him as a political opportunist. Channon was much too smart to allow his overinflated ego to endanger his own position by ordering Howard to get the bastards. But then, he wouldn't have needed to, especially in that climate. The City of London had just gone through what was called 'The Big Bang', which made the timing of this perfect. The Big Bang's promise was a titanic change in the way business would be conducted. The Tories wanted a vibrant City to compete with Wall Street and needed to appear as if they were cracking down on white-collar crime. The men who ran the City were desperate to be seen to be transparent or at least to make everyone believe they were. To manage this, the Government created the Serious Fraud Office (SFO). But to make sure that the rest of the world understood that these were the good new days, they first had to be seen doing something about the bad old days. They needed a show trial.

No, Channon didn't have to say or do anything more than hand Howard a golden opportunity to advance his own career. It's understandable that I never had time for either one of them.

The way things usually work is that the police gather evidence and, based on what they find, the CPS decides whether or not to prosecute. But correspondence between two DTI solicitors in late 1986 reveals that they understood how it was better to let Donaldson continue with his Star Chamber rather than bring in the police, because the inspectors could force us to talk and the police couldn't.

In January 1987, Donaldson met with DTI solicitors and a solicitor from the Department of Public Prosecutions (DPP) to discuss when to call in the police. They had already lined up counsel to prosecute us. But instead of passing along any evidence to the CPS, Donaldson was ordered to carry on with his interviews. A few weeks later, the DTI contacted both the Metropolitan Police and the City of London Police to say that the DPP and the DTI inspector felt that 'a police investigation at this stage was not appropriate'. The DTI didn't want the cops screwing up their case.

A month after that, the DTI decided their unfair methods were bearing fruit. Saunders was, in Donaldson's words, 'beginning to come apart at the seams'. That, he believed, confirmed the wisdom of leaving the inspectors to get on with it, rather than calling in the police. So for nearly one year, the DTI continued to plan with the CPS to use unfair powers to obtain statements that the prosecution could use in court.

* * *

The DTI kept saying that the Guinness affair was unique. Except it wasn't, because what Saunders and Roux did was what everyone else in the City was doing. Originally, the Government planned to have at least two trials. The first would be Ronson, Saunders, Parnes and Lyons. The second would deal with a few of the many other people involved in the case – Lord Spens from the investment bank Henry Ansbacher, the American lawyer Thomas Ward, Roger Seelig, a director of the merchant bank Morgan Grenfell and an adviser to Guinness, plus the 'Galloping Major', David Mayhew of Cazenove.

The reason they put the 'non-Establishment' four of us together in the first group was because the Government badly needed to stage a show trial. As scapegoats, each of us brought something to the spectacle. Just about everybody in the City disliked Saunders and, at the same time, thought he was Jewish. Actually, he was Church of England, but nobody cared what he really was. Throw him into the pot. Parnes was a second-line broker, a commission man, working for Alexanders, Laing & Cruickshank, and they're no bluebloods, no ornament of the Establishment, so he'll do. Jack Lyons, poor old man, wandered around on the periphery of the case. He had a good name and a knighthood. To show the country that we mean business, we'll have that off him, thank you very much. And Ronson? Just right. Self-made Jew. Not Establishment and actually has the cheek to say he doesn't want to be. Not a City man, he's in property and petrol, but we can make him out to be some sinister financier. Who cares if he's only a bit player in this? He's a colourful character and we can play him up. So in goes Gerald Ronson.

But consider this. The £5 million fee that Guinness paid was to Heron, which, in those days, was 45 per cent owned by my charitable foundation. If I thought it was wrong or dishonest, or if anybody in my organisation thought it was wrong or dishonest, would I have involved Heron? I might be naive, but I'm not stupid. I could have organised an account in an offshore bank and covered everything up. But I was open and forthright about it. Everything was transparent for everyone to see, because I'm not dishonest, and if I think something is dodgy, I don't get involved.

Notable by his absence in all this was Olivier Roux. If the Guinness share-support scheme was illegal, and if this was really about putting bad guys in the dock, then the first trial should have been Saunders, Roux and Ward. They pulled the trigger. I put in £25 million out of the £200 million plus on the Guinness side. Ivan Boesky put in £60 million. That leaves £115 million and I know who made up 75 per cent of that. What about them? I was the only member of the Guinness fan club to get arrested. And who knows how many hundreds of millions were dropped on the Argyll side. Yet not one single person involved with Argyll was even questioned.

As a result of this £2.5 billion takeover, £178 million was paid in fees to various people and firms. I returned Heron's £5 million. What happened to the others? I never saw any of the people who divided up those fees in the dock. I never saw them return a penny.

In all, there were probably as many as 40 people directly involved in this. But I can say, without any hesitation, that putting them in the dock would have been too embarrassing to certain people that the Government simply couldn't afford to embarrass.

Early on, there was some talk with my lawyers about separating me out from the others. But the CPS refused to allow that because they knew if I was tried separately, I'd get off. And that would jeopardise the entire case. They needed to tar me with the same brush as Saunders, Parnes and Lyons.

Our trial began in mid-February 1990. There was so much interest in it that the Government decided there wasn't a courtroom large enough at the Old Bailey, so they renovated Courtroom No. 2 at Southwark Crown Court just for the occasion and moved the trial there. No expense was going to be spared to convict us and throw us in jail.

A high court judge named Denis Henry was assigned to preside. The jury was composed of five women and seven men, taken at random from the jury pool, none of whom had anything better to do for the next six months than sit in court and listen to the complexities of business in the City. There was no way they were going to understand the case. Which is why, I believe, Henry was there. The people who assigned him to the case probably felt that he was a safe pair of hands.

* * *

The first battle we fought was to get the DTI transcripts ruled inadmissible. Again, if the police had interviewed us under the same conditions as the DTI, those interviews would have been ruled unsound. In order to put evidence in court, the police must obey the very strict codes of practice as contained in the 1984 Police and Criminal Evidence Act (PACE). That includes the right to silence. Safeguards are there specifically to avoid abuses like the use of DTI interrogations under duress for police investigations.

But Judge Henry wouldn't have it. My lawyers explained to me that nobody had to instruct him, that he understood what his role was, that senior judges believe they must protect the status quo by upholding the law as they see it in their antiquated way. In their minds, society has an infrastructure and they are stakeholders, along with lawyers and politicians. Many of them are political, not in the Conservative or Labour sense, but inside the judiciary. They don't ruffle feathers because when you ruffle feathers, you don't get promoted. Instead, they sit on high, looking down their noses at the rest of the world, deciding for themselves if a defendant is guilty, and, once they come to that conclusion, they make sure that the jury delivers that verdict. Their job is to produce a victory for the infrastructure.

It was obvious to everybody that if he threw out the DTI interviews, the case against us would evaporate. So, in his infinite wisdom, Judge Henry decided that compulsory interrogations are not statements obtained through force, coercion or oppression, but instead 'confessions', which are permissible under PACE. That decision always seemed totally wrong to me.

We were cooked. I never got the impression that he cared whether or not my rights as a British subject were being violated. I believe to this day that, from the start, he wanted a conviction. To make sure he got it, he handed Olivier Roux immunity from prosecution, allowing him to turn state's evidence. Roux, who was at the heart of this, could admit to the crimes he'd committed in order to testify that we'd committed them too. But Roux was so closely involved with Saunders and his lies that he would have said anything anyone wanted him to say to avoid going to jail.

Saunders was charged with sixteen various counts, Parnes with eight and Lyons with seven. The original eight charges against me were reduced to five and then to four. They included conspiracy to contravene the fraud-prevention act through an unlawful plan to buy Guinness stock and increase the value of the shares, theft and false accounting.

To set the record straight, I did not conspire with anyone to do anything. I entered into a business deal that I was assured was perfectly legal. I would never knowingly contravene any act or do anything illegal. I did not steal anything. My company was paid a fee for services rendered and when those services were questioned, I returned the fee in its entirety. I did not do any false accounting. When Roux said it was time to submit an invoice, my financial director, Alan Goldman, met with Roux who told him, 'Invoice us for services to Guinness.' That's what we did, because that was the truth. It wasn't for services to British Transport or British Gas. I never even saw the invoice until I was informed that it was to be used as evidence. What's more, I know for a fact that other invoices were submitted to Guinness from other people and other companies – all of whom were more deeply involved in this than me – and those invoices were total fiction. They were for things that never happened. They were invented to disguise anything having to do with 'services to Guinness'. And yet not one of those people was done for false accounting. Not one of them ever showed up in any dock anywhere.

Some people later said I did insider share dealing. Not true. There was no insider dealing. Even after all these years, the word 'fraud' gets used in the press because people who write stories about me and the Guinness affair don't understand what the case was all about. I never committed fraud. I was never charged with fraud. It is wrong and malicious to say that I have ever had anything to do with fraud.

And if I committed a crime, where were the other people who did exactly what I did? I know who some of them are, but I didn't name them then and I won't name them now. Not because I'm afraid to. I'm not afraid of anything. But because I don't drop people in the shit the way Saunders and Roux and Parnes did me with their lies. That's not my style. In early conversations we had with the prosecutors, they asked if I would consider being a witness for the prosecution. They said if I testified against the others, I'd be exonerated. Victor Mishcon didn't trust the CPS, but still advised me to think about their offer.

But how could I do that? It didn't fit comfortably with who I am. I'd be seen in the City as a leper. Who would ever want to do business with me after that? I said to Victor, 'I can write the script. Everyone in the City knows that this is trumped up, but I would forever be "the little Jew boy who grassed to save his neck".'

My co-defendants weren't my friends, so it wasn't as if I owed them anything. By the same token, I was not unfriendly towards Jack Lyons. I probably knew, or at least thought I knew, Tony Parnes best of all. And whilst I was never close to Ernest Saunders, up to the time of the Guinness trial I wasn't his enemy either.

That changed when he went into the box to testify in his own defence and started throwing darts with real venom at the rest of us. That's when his true colours came out. Saunders swore under oath that he knew nothing about indemnities or success fees. He kept saying he did not recall any conversations with me concerning my purchase of Guinness shares or his promise to indemnify me against any losses. But Roux's testimony made Saunders out to be a liar. My DTI transcripts showed that he was lying, too. The prosecution entered into evidence a letter from me that had been published in the press outlining the meetings I had had with him, including our conversations. My lawyers cross-examined Saunders and repeatedly asked him why if the conversations I'd written about in that letter had never taken place, he had told the inspectors he couldn't recall the conversations, instead of insisting that they were a pack of lies. Saunders couldn't say that the letter was wrong, just that he couldn't recall those meetings or that agreement.

Without Saunders' testimony, there would have been no case to answer. But he lied through his teeth to save his own skin, failed at every turn and wound up doing damage to us all. Juries act on impressions, and their opinion of him rubbed off on the rest of us. They saw Saunders as a rich, lying bastard, when all he had to do was tell the truth. And he wasn't the only one who lied. I watched as several people in court lied.

Furthermore, someone with a close working knowledge of the Panel on Takeovers and Mergers was asked, 'Have you been aware of any price support or have you been aware of any similar transaction or scheme?' He ought to have known there had been other inquiries. In June 1986, Turner & Newall PLC had gone after a company called AE PLC. Their brokers, Cazenove and Hill Samuel, had created, with the aid of Barclays and Midland banks, a share-buying mechanism that indemnified the two banks against any loss. But this man sat there, his head up in the air, and answered, 'No, sir.'

Certain men on the Guinness corporate board testified that they knew nothing about any transactions with me. They made out that Saunders and Roux never had any authority to negotiate with me. They lied to protect their own arses, saying that they didn't know what was going on.

I sat in court listening to all this bollocks for months, constantly aggravated, feeling that the judge was dragging everything out for as long as possible, like some melodramatic pantomime. I said to Gail, 'No one on the jury understands what this case is about.' I looked into their eyes and saw some of them staring back at four rich defendants, three of whom were Jewish and one of whom they thought was Jewish, and knew they were thinking to themselves, let's get even with these greedy rich bastards.

At one point, Henry allowed the prosecution to show the jury photos of my home, my yacht and my cars. It was totally irrelevant to the case. Yet he allowed the prosecutors to tell the jury what privileged lives we led, that my yacht was one of the biggest in the world. He must have known that some of the members of the jury were struggling to pay their electricity bills and that a couple of the jurors were on the dole. Yet he told them I was drawing a salary of £5 million a year. What does that have to do with the case?

Henry actually made a point of emphasising my £5 million a year by explaining to the jury that it was equivalent to so many years of his own salary. Where does his salary come into this?

The way Henry primed the jury with what I took to be prejudicial comments suggesting avarice and greed convinced me that his mind was coloured by the amount of money involved. There can be no impartiality where there is envy and, unfortunately, because it is part of this country's problem, there is a lot of envy in the British.

* * *

In the middle of the trial, one of the twelve jurors stole a video camera and was dismissed. Tells you a lot about the quality of people judging us. So we were down to eleven.

Towards the end of the trial, I was contacted by someone who said he could sort out the jury for me. I don't know if he could have managed it, but he said the jury was there to be nobbled. I went straight to Scotland Yard and let them deal with it. If I was dishonest, I would have said, 'How much do you want?' and the result could have been different.

At that point, my lawyers felt the judge should have dismissed the jury and announced a mistrial. He didn't. A dozen years later, we learned almost by accident – because it had been deliberately withheld from us during the trial – that there had been a second attempt to nobble the jury. The police investigated and the prosecution was aware of it, but they didn't tell us and chose not to bring it to the attention of the judge, claiming that it wasn't relevant. Not much!

In all, the trial involved seventy-five days of evidence, ten days of speeches by counsel and five days of Henry preparing the jury to come back with a suitable verdict. As Henry recited his five-day monologue, I sat there telling myself, he wants to be absolutely certain that the jury knows what he expects them to do.

Bizarrely, in his summing up, Henry noted that so many people had been lying but that 'the only person in this courtroom who has told the truth from the beginning of this affair is Mr Ronson'. He spoke in glowing terms of my frankness, my honesty and my helpfulness to the DTI officials. You would have thought that he was recommending me for an honour. Then he came to what he called my 'one aberration'.

Bullshit. There was no aberration. I built up my business in a straight line. That's how I have worked all my life. That is how I always work. If I wanted to have an aberration I could have put millions of pounds in my pocket over the years. But I don't think that way. Did Henry take any of that into account? Not at all. He dropped one charge, which left only three for me to answer, and told the jury it was up to them to decide if I behaved honestly or dishonestly. So now five of the eight charges originally lodged against me had been tossed out. But all eight were interrelated, so if five of them were no good, how could the other three still stand? It defied logic.

The jury was out for five days. They came back on August Bank Holiday Monday, by which time this was the most expensive court case in British legal history. It cost the taxpayer around £7.5 million to find me guilty of conspiracy, theft and false accounting. Saunders and Lyons were convicted of the same charges. Parnes was found guilty of theft and false accounting.

Then they also found me guilty of fraud. That was such a shock to everyone in the courtroom – talk about logic. Henry had to remind the jury that I had never been charged with fraud and that my trial had nothing to do with fraud. It tells you what a bunch that jury was. It tells you how anxious they were to find me guilty. It tells you how 11 people who had been hearing for months about how billions of pounds were changing hands, people whose eyes were filled with envy and jealousy, simply decided, in the courtroom of this dreadful judge, that I'd been dishonest.

CHAPTER 9

....

GUILTY AS CHARGED

On the morning we were to be sentenced, a prison van brought us from Brixton to court. Judge Henry had sent us there overnight, much to everyone's surprise. Normally, when a court in England finds you guilty of a non-violent, white-collar crime, the judge orders you to come back for sentencing at a later date and allows you to go home. Not Henry. He ordered us to be taken down to the cells, then put in a stifling hot, airless prison van to Brixton. I remember sitting there thinking to myself, this ain't the nicest way to spend an August bank holiday.

We'd arrived for processing like everyone else convicted of a crime, but unlike many other people who go through this, no one had been aggressive or nasty to me. There'd been no hostility, no aggro. In fact, the staff there had been quite sympathetic.

Sitting in Brixton that night, I prepared myself for the worst. Throughout the trial, I'd refused to fool myself into thinking that I was going to get off scot-free. I'd made arrangements for Gail to see Lord Mishcon, because I needed to prepare her for the worst, too. He kept saying to her, 'Don't worry, it's not going to happen, but if it does . . .' It was up to Gail to prepare our four daughters.

I knew for sure that I would be going to prison, but I didn't know for how long. Maybe I'd been naive to believe that we would get a fair trial, but it's no good whingeing about it. Take it on the chin, put it behind you and get on with your life. If you don't, you'll eat yourself up and there's no point in that.

On the morning of our sentencing, hundreds of people were waiting for us as we pulled up outside the court. There were family and friends, the media, lunatics carrying banners warning of God's wrath and nutcases done up in peculiar uniforms. We were rushed past them and taken downstairs to the cells to wait for Henry.

134

The cells stank of sick and disinfectant. I sat in that horrible place with Saunders and Parnes thinking to myself, what the fuck am I doing here with these arseholes? It wasn't a happy time. But after a few minutes, a young policeman opened the door, motioned to me and said, 'There's a religious man here for you.'

I didn't know who he was or why he was there, I just knew, 'I don't want to see anyone.'

'He's very insistent,' the policeman said, and explained to me that no one from the outside was allowed down into the cells, except a prisoner's lawyer. But this man had managed to get down there and kept saying he wasn't leaving until he saw me. 'He's not going away.'

I decided, it's better to see what he wants than to sit in here, so I nodded OK and the policeman took me to a little interview room. The man was a rabbi, around 45 years old, tall, dressed in black and with a beard. He had placed a *tallis*, which is a prayer shawl, on the table, along with a prayer book and *tefillin*, which are two tiny leather boxes containing scrolls of parchment inscribed with biblical verses. Orthodox Jews wrap tefillin around their arms and their forehead when they pray.

I'd never met him before but he seemed to know me. 'You're a good man who has done a lot of good work for the Community and you shouldn't be here. I want you to say the morning prayers, lay tefillin and pray to God, because the Good Lord will look after you and protect you.'

I told him, 'I'm not into this Orthodox religious business. I'm a middle-of-the-road Jew. I may talk to the Good Lord when other people have problems, but I don't talk to him for my problems. If he wants to look after me, he will, if he doesn't, he won't. I'm not someone who grasps at straws.'

He didn't care what my excuse was. 'We're going to do it.'

The last time I'd laid tefillin was when my father died, and I wasn't sure I could even *doven*. That's a particular swaying back and forth during prayer. I confessed, 'I'm not very good at this.'

He said, 'Don't worry. I will show you and I will do it with you.'

The man had taken all this trouble for a complete stranger and had somehow managed to get into the cells when nobody was allowed. Gail was upstairs with our daughters, my uncle Tubby and his son, my cousin Nigel. They weren't allowed down here. Anyway, I didn't want to see anyone or have anyone see me in this condition. But I thought to myself, the condemned man still has half an hour, so I said OK. I took my jacket off and rolled up my shirtsleeves. He helped me to put the tefillin on, and we started praying. I could do most of it without his help, but when I fumbled through some of the words, he guided me and prayed with me.

When we were done, as I was unwinding the tefillin, I suddenly felt a jolt through my body.

It was like when somebody pumps a drug into you to take away the pain. Or like when you have pins and needles go through your leg. But this wasn't pins and needles. This was something else. I suddenly felt strong.

And as long as I live, I will never forget that feeling.

You can say it was psychological or psychosomatic. You can say whatever it was that I felt was because I wanted to feel it. You can come up with all the clever answers in the world, but I know what I felt. And that strength stayed with me. It was the strength to know that God was protecting me, that God was there.

I didn't tell the rabbi what I felt. I just thanked him for making the effort to come to see me. But I knew from that point that I could hold my head up high, take whatever anyone threw at me and get on with my life.

* * *

Saunders was sentenced to five years, and he was shaken when he heard that. Tony Parnes was told he would serve three years and passed out. They had to call a doctor for him. Jack Lyons was simply fined. But at that point, his matter was separate from the rest of us. They wanted to review his situation because of his medical condition.

Then it was my turn. I stood up to face Henry, looked him straight in the eye and wanted to say, you're a miserable old arsehole who hasn't got the fucking balls to admit you cooked us. How else should I have felt? Should I have thought, you are such a nice, kindly man who has gone overboard to be fair? He wasn't nice, he wasn't kindly and I will never believe that he was fair.

So even after all those nice things he'd said about me the day before – how I was the only one telling the truth – none of that mattered to him now. Nor did it matter to him that I'd be stitched up on Saunders' lies and on evidence that had been obtained under duress. He could have taken into account the trumped-up case the jury had heard. He could have given me something other than a prison sentence. He had the option to bind me over to keep the peace. Or he had the option to fine me. He could have sentenced me and fined me and then suspended the sentence in lieu of the fine. Instead, he announced that he was going to send me away for one year and, on top of that, he fined me £5 million. It was the single largest fine ever in a UK criminal case.

As if that wasn't enough for him, pouring salt onto the wounds, he said with some satisfaction that for every £1.25 million of the fine that I failed to pay, I would have to spend an additional year in prison. So, in effect, he was sending me down for five years.

Henry's jury found me the least guilty of the four of us and yet, when you add up prison time and the amount of the fine he arbitrarily imposed, he passed the most severe sentence on me.

Five million quid was a horrendous amount of money twenty years ago. It was disgusting. He must have figured, I'll get that rich bastard, and I'll send a message to all those other rich bastards out there. What difference does it make how much I fine him? He can afford it.

How much I could afford should have had nothing to do with it. I'd already given back the £5 million success fee. He knew that. I think this was simply him being spiteful and vengeful. What's more, the money had to come out of my pocket. The company wasn't allowed to pay it, even though all the money from the transaction went into the company. As long as the charges are against the individual and not the company, it's down to the individual to come up with the fine. On top of that, all the costs of the case were down to me personally, too. Forget reputational costs. My reputation, which I'd spent all my life building up, was severely damaged by the Guinness affair. Forget going to prison. Forget wasting six months sitting in a courtroom. Forget the distractions from my business. Forget the emotional costs and the loss of opportunities. Forget all that and I was still looking at a bill for £13 million.

I couldn't say what I wanted to say then and there, so as this man who had once sworn on a Bible to seek fairness and justice read out my sentence, I stood there and stared at him and didn't blink an eyelid.

At least one of us showed some dignity.

Maybe I could forgive the jury their ignorance. They were out of their depth. I cannot forgive them for the expressions on their faces when they heard the sentences being pronounced. They wanted to applaud and shout.

Almost immediately, we were rushed downstairs to the cells. I wasn't allowed to see my family. Gail and our four daughters left the courtroom and walked straight into the glare of the media. It was very nasty. But the picture that appeared the next morning in many newspapers was of Gail and the four girls walking through the press scrum, refusing to be baited or intimidated by the hundreds of photographers. There they were, holding their heads up high.

* * *

As I was driven back to Brixton in one of those horrible cattle vans, there were a lot of things I didn't know then that I know now.

For instance, I didn't know that when the jury came back and convicted me, Barbara Mills, who was the number-two prosecutor alongside Chadwick, turned to one of my lawyers and said, 'Juries never cease to amaze me.' She never thought she was going to get a conviction because she knew there wasn't really a case against me.

Today, I'm on friendly terms with her. Well, I can't really be friendly with any of them because of what they did to me, but I have been to cocktail parties with her and we've been cordial. The first time I saw her after the trial – granted, it was years later – she came up to me and said, 'It was nothing personal, Gerald, you do realise that?'

I said to her, 'It was very personal at the time.'

That's when she repeated to me what she'd said to my lawyer. 'We couldn't believe we got a conviction.' I heard the same thing from some of the policemen involved in the case. They told me that finding me guilty didn't make sense to them. It didn't make sense to me, either.

All these years later, I know why all this happened. It's because Saunders lied to too many people in Scotland. He made promises he couldn't keep, or never had any intention of keeping, that certain people would have their fair share in the newly expanded Guinness. He promised a prominent Scottish banker that he would be chairman, then reneged on all of his promises, because Saunders is a two-faced piece of shit whose ego was out of control. He decided he needed to be chairman and screwed everybody else. He took over a Scottish company, then simply told all the people who'd backed him in Scotland to fuck off.

You just can't do that to the Scottish corporate mafia. They're not only powerful north of the border, they're powerful in England, too. They set out to get even with Saunders, I was in the wrong place at the wrong time and became what they call in war 'collateral damage'.

Yet even then, if Saunders had listened to his lawyers and not testified, if he'd kept his mouth shut, the case against us would have fallen apart. Each of us had the opportunity to testify on our own behalf, and at one point my lawyers and I discussed whether or not I should take the stand. But it wasn't a very long discussion. Victor considered it, but our lead barrister, Michael Sherrard, was dead set against it. He knew I can't lie and he worried that the other lawyers would bait me and I'd get angry. So Saunders was the only one of us to give evidence, which showed him to be a first-class lying schmuck.

In the end, most of Saunders' friends turned their backs on him, although his children didn't. They tried to help him, and good luck to them. Having said that, Saunders brought this on himself. Had he acted responsibly, had he stood up like a man, he wouldn't have received the sentence he did. If he'd played it straight, everything would have been different. Unfortunately, it's not Saunders' nature to play straight.

To a lesser extent the same is true of Parnes. He should have put his hands up, turned round and said, 'I'll tell the truth.' Where he and I were concerned, he should have said, 'If anybody is to blame, it is me. I went to Gerald Ronson and I assured him that everything was above board. I should have known that Saunders, Roux and Ward were crooks.' Instead, he argues to this day that nothing was his fault.

As for Jack Lyons, he avoided a good deal of this because he was a sick man. I am glad that he didn't go to prison, but he lost his knighthood. Henry said that Jack knew that what he was doing was wrong and that he was lying when he denied it. He passed away in 2008 a broken man.

I can only repeat that the £5 million Guinness paid me was meaningless compared to what they paid everyone else. Look at what Cazenove and Morgan Grenfell made. It was ridiculous money. But no one talked about them because they're part of the Establishment. Gerald Ronson wasn't. Gerald Ronson was disposable.

What ever happened to the boys from the Establishment? Exactly what everyone always knew would happen. Nothing! The staging of the second trial ended in disarray. Spens walked, Ward walked and Seelig walked. He was the scapegoat for Morgan Grenfell. Everyone there must have known what was going on, because they made £48 million in fees. So if what I did was illegal, how come nobody from Morgan Grenfell was put in the dock? And what did their invoices say? 'For services rendered'? How come they were never asked to pay back their fees?

It's no surprise that the Galloping Major from Cazenove, David Mayhew, also walked. Some people from Cazenove testified that they knew nothing about the share operation. The same people from the same Cazenove that was involved with the indemnity scheme during the Turner & Newall takeover of AE. Did Mayhew know? Many of those people at Cazenove who said they didn't certainly did. But they were true-blue Establishment, so no one from Cazenove was going to be thrown into the pot with the rest of us riff-raff. I have never understood how on earth anyone could say that justice was done when Cazenove walked free. And, again, what about Argyll and their fan club?

If I sat down and wrote out a list of all the people I know were directly involved with this takeover, people who made money out of it in exactly the same way I did, there could be maybe 40 names. I'm talking about people who, if I committed a crime, also committed a crime. So how come the only people ever held to account were the four of us? And can it just be a coincidence that three of the four were Jews and the fourth was thought to be Jewish?

Oh, well. I guess in life you just have to accept certain things, like who you are, what you are, your position in the pecking order, whether your face fits or your face doesn't fit, whether you went to the right school or not.

Finally, there was the media. It was unforgivable the way they hounded my family. For every day of the trial, they showed us going into court and coming out of court. Every single day of the trial, they reported hearsay as if it was the news.

Three of my girls came to the trial from time to time – Lisa, Amanda and Nicole – but Hayley was only fourteen, and she was too young. Gail wanted to be there every day, but we decided it was a bad idea because the trial was already enough of a circus and I knew what would happen if she showed up. The photographers would go wild, and the captions in the papers the next morning would be, 'Gail Ronson turned up in court today wearing a Chanel blouse . . .' and 'Here's Mrs Ronson looking very unhappy . . .' We didn't want that and certainly didn't need it. But she was there, with all four girls, on the day I was sentenced.

What the media never found out was that I'd rented a flat for the period of the trial along the road from the court and had our cook, Terisita, make us lunch. Gail would meet me there every day.

I have to say that a couple of newspapers were better than the television crews. *The Independent* didn't go off on tangents, and Jeremy Warner at *The Times* followed the trial in a professional, disciplined fashion. But everybody else had a field day. This was the sort of sensational rubbish that sells newspapers, and I was just one of the idiots sitting there forced to take it on the chin.

The media kept talking about 'the trial of the century'. So the jury went home every night and saw the newspapers and saw the TV coverage and heard everyone calling this 'the trial of the century'. The press was in court every day, so the jury heard their opinions of what was going on every night. How could any of that have been fair?

As they drove us back to Brixton prison, there were a lot of things I didn't know that I know now. I didn't know what jail would be like or how long I'd have to be there, or if any judge in Britain would listen to our appeal, or if Gail and the girls would be all right, or how any of this would affect me and my business.

As for the Distillers property, which got me into this in the first place, Guinness eventually sold off many millions of pounds' worth, but not to us. We didn't get any of it. The new management wasn't anxious to do any friendly business with us, and I wasn't in any mood to be very friendly with them.

* * *

Our appeal would take years and we would suffer one setback after another. We were convicted in August 1990, appealed against the conviction in May 1991, and that appeal was dismissed. We appealed again. In October 1995, the Lord Chief Justice, Peter Taylor, presided over the Court of Appeal, joined by two justices, Macpherson and Potter. By this point, there was no doubt whatsoever in my mind that the DTI inspectors and the police had violated my rights. Taylor's immediate response was, 'Absolutely scandalous.' He was appalled at the inspectors' behaviour and wondered out loud in open court, 'How could an inspector abuse his independence by feeding information outside?'

Any statements I made to Donaldson and Watt should have been strictly confidential. My testimony was part of a report that was not to be made public until November 1997. Nothing should have been disclosed to anyone until the report was published. So the arrangement between Donaldson, Watt, the DTI and the police was not only unprecedented but, I claim, illegal. It infringed my rights and, according to my barrister, Michael Sherrard, 'breached every principle of natural justice'.

What's more, the authorities deliberately withheld information from us of a takeover panel decision that had approved the Turner & Newall share-support and indemnity scheme. They also withheld information from us that indicated there was nothing wrong, or illegal, about success fees.

In spite of Justice Taylor's shock and horror, the court ruled that any evidence held back probably wouldn't have changed anything. It was a preposterous conclusion. They dismissed our appeal and, to make certain that we could never embarrass them by having their unreasonable decision overturned, they refused us permission to appeal to the House of Lords. That hardly surprised anyone. Least of all me. Were those three judges going to make a monkey out of their colleague, Mr Henry? Were they going to reverse or change anything that would make the law look like an ass? Were they going to deprive the Government of the political success it scored as a result of this massively expensive show trial?

In the meantime, Saunders applied to the European Court of Human Rights (ECHR) in Strasbourg, France, saying that his rights had been violated when the DTI interview transcripts were allowed into evidence. And in December 1996, just a year after our appeals in Britain were denied, the ECHR found in his favour. Subsequently Parnes, Lyons and I also complained to the ECHR. And the court ruled in our favour, too.

In September 2000, more than ten years after my trial and conviction, the European court decided, unequivocally, that when those DTI transcripts of compulsory interviews had been allowed into evidence, my human rights had been breached and I'd therefore been denied a fair trial. After carefully studying the evidence and the arguments, the court wrote that the DTI evidence had been used 'in a manner intended to incriminate', which therefore tainted the trial and made the convictions unsafe. All seven judges in Strasbourg came to this same conclusion. It was unanimous. They also ruled unanimously that because our human rights had been breached, the UK government had to pay £75,000 towards our costs.

But the Court of Appeal in London quickly overturned the award of costs because that opened up a whole other can of worms, and the judiciary simply couldn't afford to go there. It could have meant that, somewhere down the line, we might have recouped all of our costs. There was no way that they were ever going to admit that the 'trial of the century' had turned sour and that they had to return my £5 million fine and pay me back my millions in costs.

The use of interviews obtained under duress, like those DTI interview transcripts, was another matter. The Attorney General didn't have to wait for the ECHR to make a judgment, he knew from the start they were unsound. He'd already issued guidance that compelled interviews could no longer be put in evidence. Parliament soon followed suit by officially outlawing compelled testimony. So by the time the ECHR ruled in our favour, it was absolutely clear to everyone that we'd been mugged.

Now, if use of those transcripts renders a trial unsound today, how can that verdict from 20 years ago still be considered sound? It isn't logical. But a British court found a way around logic. The Court of Appeal decided, based on a House of Lords decision, that just because a European court had ruled the verdict unsound, that wasn't enough. The European Human Rights Act came into being in October 2000, and there could be no retrospective rights. In other words, because Britain hadn't yet signed up to the European Statute on Human Rights when I was tried, I didn't have any human rights to be trampled on.

Occasionally, I vent some anger about the way Henry treated me – particularly how illogical and prejudicial I believe he was – but I can honestly say, hand on heart, that I am not bitter about the Guinness affair. If nothing else, my pride prevents me from letting the matter get to me. I was convicted and I did my time. I took their best shot, stayed on my feet and just got on with the rest of my life.

CHAPTER 10

....

FORD

I spent three days in Brixton prison, which is a Victorian hellhole. They checked my belongings, boxed up my suit, gave me a medical – really nothing more than a fast look over – handed me prison clothes and read me the rules. Normally, they would have assigned me to a cell, but a senior officer, a Polish man named Sky, was very understanding. He said, 'I've followed your trial. I don't particularly like Mr Saunders and I think Mr Parnes is a little toerag' – those were his own words – 'but you have no business being here.'

I couldn't have agreed with him more.

He said, 'You're only going to be here a few days because you'll be moving on, and we don't want any problems, so I'm going to put you in the medical wing. If there's anything else I can do to make your life more comfortable, let me know.'

I said, 'It would be nice if I had some newspapers to read. And it would be very nice, psychologically, if you didn't lock the door. Also, I'd like to have a bath every day.' That was a real luxury in prison, because normally you only get to have a bath once a week.

He agreed to get me newspapers and promised not to lock the door, except when the governor came round. Then, he said, when all the other prisoners went to work at around 9.30, I could have a shower and he'd put an officer on the door so nobody would interfere. I thanked him and thought to myself, sometimes in life you meet good people, and sometimes, even in the midst of bad things, good things can happen.

The medical ward was clean. I was far away from all the scumbags, but I was still in a cell with bars. I could exercise out in the yard for a couple of hours, where I mixed with lots of other prisoners, but nobody bothered me. If you behave like an arsehole, you get treated like an arsehole, so I went around with a smile on my face and when someone looked me in the eye, I said 'Hello' or 'Good morning'.

When moving day arrived, I asked Sky if he would please ring Gail, because she wouldn't know where I was. I wanted her to know that I was all right, that I was going to HMP Ford and that when I got there I'd give her a call. He rang up Gail and said to her, 'Gerald should never have been here.'

Of course, I was worried sick about her and the girls being alone, but it turned out they weren't on their own for a minute. Gail had great support, not only from the business community but from personal friends. The girls too. So many people rallied to their side.

* * *

They could have driven us from Brixton to Ford – which is in Arundel, West Sussex – in a regular car. After all, I was a Category D prisoner, which means non-violent, not dangerous and unlikely to escape. But just to be nasty, they delivered us in one of those horrible prison vans, with no air and very little light, where eight prisoners sit in a tiny three-foot by three-foot space. They did it for the publicity value, because when the van arrived, the media was there to photograph us. The wardens had tipped them off.

Ford had been converted in 1960 from a Fleet Air Arm station into an 'open' prison – no barbed-wire fences, no guard towers, no cells with bars. Prisoners live in rooms and can move around freely. But just because it's 'open', that doesn't mean you can come and go as you please. Ford is not a country club. Prison is prison. And in some ways, an open prison – where you can see an open gate and traffic going past – is worse than being locked up where you don't see anything, because in an open prison, freedom is an easy 100-yard walk away.

The usual misconception is that Ford is only for white-collar criminals. That's rubbish. You don't meet nice people in any prison, and Ford was no exception. Only about 10 per cent of the prisoners were non-violent and expected to be well behaved. If I remember correctly, there were 550 inmates, including 36 lifers who were there for murders and double murders. If you think you're going to see the right side of life in prison, with all the druggies and loonies there, you're mistaken. I saw violence, people being stabbed and people doing stupid things.

The wardens, called 'screws', are a special breed of weirdo who, because they have a uniform, lord it over the prisoners. They are predominantly right-wing, BNP types, sadists, bullies and racists. Maybe it's too simplistic to say this, but if they were brave and wanted to wear a uniform, why wouldn't they join the army? Maybe it's because they're also lazy. A military uniform comes with respect. A prison warden's uniform is a licence to act out your racial hatred.

I saw at Ford the way black people get a raw time in prison, and I stood up to it whenever I could. I wasn't shy about confronting prison officers when they were out of line with black prisoners. I would say to them politely, 'Is that really necessary? Why would you talk to them like that when you wouldn't talk to me like that?' I tried to use reason. Most of the time, acting like an intelligent man was enough.

When I first went in, they put me in a wooden barracks with fifteen or twenty other men, and I stayed there for a three-week period of induction. Saunders and Parnes were there, too. The place was clean and there were showers. There was a good guy in there, whose name I can't remember, but he was finishing off a long sentence for robbery, and he helped me settle in. It wasn't easy, because this was a depressing place and I was there under circumstances that I considered totally unjust. But he made the induction period easier for me.

For the first two weeks, they didn't give me anything to do. I wasn't in the best state of mind and hadn't yet settled down. I was walking around trying to get the feel of the place, trying to figure out who I could trust and who I couldn't. I put a smile on my face, put my hand out and introduced myself. All of the officers shook my hand, except one arsehole in the gym who refused.

After two weeks, one of the officers said, 'We've got a job for you.' He took me into the dining room and told me, 'You're going to wash up the metal food trays.'

The way it worked was that when a prisoner was finished with his meal, he would take his tray to a rubbish bin, spill everything out and turn over his tray to me. I'd wash it with a brush in hot water, then stack the trays to go into the big dishwashing machine.

I was still unsettled – this wasn't my normal vocation – but I put up a good front. The two guys working with me were helpful enough and showed me the ropes. So there I was at lunchtime, wearing rubber gloves, taking trays from the other prisoners and brushing them clean, when a big black man walked up and handed me his tray filled with his pudding and mashed potatoes.

I said to him, 'Maybe you don't understand. You don't give me the tray filled with food, what you do is empty it in that bin there and then give it to me.'

146

He just stared at me and held the tray out for me to take.

At that point, like a scene from a B-movie, the whole dining room went silent and 500 prisoners watched me. I knew that if I didn't deal with this situation properly, my life was going to be a misery for the next six months. It meant that either he emptied his own tray or I was going to have to whack him in the face, because that's the only language prisoners speak. It didn't matter to me what the consequences were or how big he was, I wasn't going to be intimidated.

I stared back and said to him loud enough for everyone in the room to hear, 'Let's stop playing fucking games. I ain't here 'cause I want to be, you ain't here 'cause you want to be, so if you don't empty your dish, you're going to leave me no alternative as to what I'm going to do about it.'

There was one of those very long pauses – it was memorable – before he smiled, 'You're the guv'nor. You're all right. If anybody fucks you around, you let me know.'

I said, 'Thank you very much, but I don't need anybody looking after me.'

He emptied his tray, put his hand out to shake my hand, and that was it.

When you're in these situations, you have to deal with it. There are always bullies, there are always people testing people. In prison, it's like a load of dogs. Prisoners can smell fear, they can smell which are the weak dogs and which are the strong dogs, and they leave the strong dogs alone. If they make a mistake and get it wrong, they pay the price. It's the same with the officers. They pick on the weaker ones. Standing up to this guy sent a message to everyone that you don't mess around with Gerald. Shaking his hand afterwards was a message that Gerald's not a bad bloke. It stood me in good stead with the other prisoners.

One or two prisoners tried to push Parnes around. They didn't like Saunders, but they thought Tony was a crackpot. I put a stop to it.

After that first confrontation, there was never any violence towards me because everyone saw that I'm not the sort of person you're going to be violent with. Anyway, most of the inmates thought of me as one of the boys. There were a few who didn't like me, but I didn't care whether anybody liked me or not. Behind my back, they called me 'The General' and 'The Godfather'. To my face, most people addressed me as 'Mr Ronson' or 'GR'. I was nice to people and I got things done.

At the very beginning of my stay, one officer spoke to me out of turn. I had a word with him and that didn't happen again. I might have been a prisoner, but that didn't mean I was defenceless. I know that the authorities at Brixton didn't want us and I'm not sure they wanted us at Ford, either. High-profile prisoners create problems for the governors. If anything happened to me, and anything can happen to anybody in a prison, it would have caused problems for them. So I was something of a liability. I had money and access to people in power on the outside, including the press. They knew I could expose things that would be embarrassing to them. They understood that I could fight back.

After three weeks, I was moved out of the barracks to the other side of the prison and into a proper room on the first floor of a building. My roommates were two black men, Irvin and John. Both of them were in their 30s. Irvin, the taller of the two, was in for a burglary, which he said he never did. But then, everybody at Ford said they never did anything. John was there for computer fraud. Irvin would say his prayers every night before he went to bed, and I'd always say mine in the morning, as I have done ever since meeting the rabbi in the cells below the court. Irvin and John and I got on well. I didn't have any issues with them and actually felt better about being in a three-man room than being alone. This way no one was going to come in to mess with me in the middle of the night. Still, I made sure my bed wasn't next to the door.

Our room needed a lick of paint, a proper cleaning and some things to make it more like a home. So I asked around. 'Does anybody know who can do a bit of painting?' The guy who showed up was a Hells Angel motorcycle gang member. I don't know what he was in for, but we talked for a while and when I said, 'I understand you're a painter?' he said, 'Yes, Mr Ronson.' In prison, if you talk to people straightforwardly and show some common respect, they don't have a problem answering you straightforwardly and showing you respect in return.

The currency of prison in those days was tobacco and phone cards. Today, it's drugs, but back then, at least at Ford, if you had tobacco and phone cards, you could get a lot done. Each prisoner was allowed six phone cards a month. Many of them didn't want their cards, some didn't have anyone to call, so they exchanged them for something else, like tobacco. Or they sold them for cash. I went through six to eight phone cards a week. Apart from all the other calls I had to make, I spoke to Gail every day. I was willing to pay for phone cards, but when I asked my mates if they had any, none of them took anything from me for them. Some of them even said, 'Give the money to a charity when you get out.' So I had no difficulty in getting as many phone cards as I wanted.

Actually, I had no trouble getting anything. Nobody was hard up in prison, unless he wanted to be. A lot of people there got quite a few quid together as a result of some racket they were running. In fact, everybody in the prison seemed to have his own racket, peddling this or that. Some of my mates were cleverer than most and had money to spare.

I offered my new Hells Angel friend half an ounce of tobacco to paint the room. He agreed, came back the next day with some paint – obviously he'd helped himself to the prison's supplies – and that's how the room got painted. I then said to Irvin and John, 'This floor needs cleaning properly. It's dirty.' So they showed up with an industrial floor-cleaning machine – I have no idea how they got it – and by the middle of the morning, the floor was spotlessly clean.

We each had a single bed and a little dresser unit. I didn't like what we had, so I passed out some tobacco and got us better furniture. Don't ask me how anyone managed to deliver the stuff to us, but we also got new, double-thick mattresses to make ourselves more comfortable. I then arranged to get us clean sheets regularly out of the hospital ward. I found another guy working in the garden, an Irishman everybody called Paddy, and asked, 'Can you get me plants for the room?' A few days later, he arrived with four plants in pots. I didn't want to know how.

The prison supplied us with clothes, including underwear, which came from the laundry, but that meant someone else had been wearing this stuff before it got cleaned. I hated that, so I went down to the man in charge of clothing, a good London cockney, and made him a deal. Like everyone else, he wanted tobacco and phone cards. I told him, 'I want new pants and new shirts, because I don't want to wear old stuff that's been laundered.' He kitted me out. Every week, he'd bring me all-new gear. Later, I met some guys working in the laundry and arranged with them to do my shirts and underwear by hand. So now every week, I had three or four sets, the new and the hand-washed. In the next room, there was an old army sergeant who took a quarter of an ounce of tobacco every week to spit-polish my shoes. You could see your face in them.

There was a little old Jewish man who must have been about 70 and had been a tailor on the outside. He worked in the tailoring shop inside. When I mentioned that I didn't like the prison clothes, he said, 'I'll make you a pair of trousers.' I wound up with three or four pairs of tailored trousers. And there was a young fellow who lived on the same landing as me who pressed my trousers twice a week.

Before coming to prison, I'd smoked four Montecristo No. 4 cigars a day. But for the first two months in prison, I didn't want to smoke. I didn't want anything. I could get cigars, because you can get anything in prison if you're prepared to pay for it – champagne, smoked salmon, caviar, anything. Various prisoners were always telling me that whatever I wanted from the outside, they could arrange it. A few prisoners even mentioned that they'd received word from the outside that I was to be looked after. That didn't surprise me, because I'd done enough favours for people in my time that now some of the people I'd helped were returning the favour. Eventually, though, I mentioned to a friendly prisoner that I missed my cigars. From that moment on, I was kept supplied. I smoked one cigar in my room after lunch and another after the evening meal. That was like a link to the outside world.

There was a young lad named Lorenzo who worked in the library and he brought me the newspapers every morning. I bought a kettle for the room, coffee, powdered milk and cartons of orange juice. Eventually, I acquired a toaster. Irvin would bring my breakfast back with him after he went down to have his. I ate in the room because I didn't want to go to the dining hall and sit there with a load of rabble and risk having an argument about whether I received one more egg than the other guy. That's the kind of stupidity that goes on with these idiots in prison.

Actually, I ate most meals in my room or in one of the other guys' rooms. Either someone would bring food to me or I'd make a salad for a group of us. I learned a bit about preparing food while I was there, although 'home cooking' took a few days to organise. We had to get tomatoes from the farm, lettuce from the kitchen, eggs and so on. Two or three times a week, a few of us would really put ourselves out and have a very good meal. To arrange this meant quite a campaign, because we needed a lot of ingredients. Good meat and fresh vegetables were precious commodities in prison. Everything had to be acquired by 'various means', which often meant some visitor had smuggled it in.

We always feasted on Sunday night. A Sicilian named Giorgio had been a chef and owned his own restaurant. He'd also been in the French Foreign Legion and a hit man for the Mafia. He was in his late 40s and in the 8th year of a 12-year sentence for either serious drugs or murder. He wasn't big, but he definitely wasn't afraid of anyone twice his size. And he could really cook. He'd spend a few days getting olive oil, Lea & Perrins sauce, fresh eggs and meat, and his steak tartare was as good as you'd get anywhere in London. Another prisoner was an Irishman who'd once been a ship's cook. Somebody would give him a couple of bananas that had been smuggled in that day, and somebody else would give him some sponge cake that had arrived the same way, and he'd get hold of tinned cream, jellies and flavouring. So at nine o'clock on Sunday, three of us would sit down and scoff the lot. Afterwards, I'd light a cigar and one of us would usually say something like, 'Well, here we are in prison, and we've had an excellent steak, a trifle for the connoisseur and cigars. Why go to the Savoy Grill?'

I never went hungry. There were certain dishes I missed in the early days, but in time you lose your taste buds and don't want what you originally missed. What you miss least are the luxuries. The taste for them goes first. Even all these years later, I eat much more simply than I did before I went to prison. Mostly I eat fish, baked or grilled, and plenty of fresh vegetables. A few times a week, I eat some red meat, beef, plain roast or a steak, and a jacket potato. I don't like tea any more. I drink black coffee and, sometimes, hot lemon water. I got to like lemon water in prison. It was difficult to get hold of a lemon, but, like everything else, if you really wanted one, you could have it.

The officers knew this kind of thing went on and took a realistic view of it. They knew food was being smuggled in, but as long as you didn't bring in alcohol or drugs, or openly flaunt the rules, they didn't make an issue of it. The wardens wanted a quiet life, and so did the majority of the prisoners, especially the older ones. The wardens understood that to stretch rules too far would snap the elastic.

There were drugs in prison. But the really dangerous stuff was booze, like the vodka prisoners made out of potatoes. In fact, they made alcoholic drinks out of any vegetables they could find. And it was killer stuff, because it was 100 per cent proof and it rotted your stomach. It also affected your brain. I saw good-natured men take a drink of this poison, turn very nasty, pick up a knife or a bottle or scissors and try to kill someone. One day, four big prisoners had to tie down a drunk so he could sober up before the wardens found out. The only alcohol I touched at Ford was the thimbleful of rum in our Sunday-night banana trifle, and a drop of whisky I took when some of the boys came over at midnight on New Year's Eve and presented me with a quarter-bottle of Scotch. I didn't want it, but not to hurt their feelings I drank a sip to their health and gave the rest to the boys along the landing.

The wardens would come around in the morning to see that you hadn't absconded, then everyone went to work. Anyone who wanted a job could have one. The work day was nine to four, yet not a great deal of work was actually done. Most prisoners just went through the motions, because you got paid £4 a week whether you worked hard or hardly worked at all.

In prison, the passage of time takes on a different and variable dimension. Looking back, time seems to have gone quickly. But looking forward then, time went by very slowly. To make days and weeks move faster, you had to keep busy. Some prisoners preferred to be banged up with three other dickheads and sleep the day away thinking that would make the time go by faster. They wouldn't use their brains to read or go to the gym. The idea of doing something constructive never occurred to them. Even if you were only going to spend a year in jail, a year is still a long time to sit around doing nothing. It's true that for some prisoners Ford wasn't a bad life. They ate better there than they ate at home, and more regularly. They lived in a cleaner room, in cleaner clothes and with cleaner linen than they would have outside.

As for me, I had credit at the canteen and plenty of phone cards and tobacco to barter with. I might not have been living at home in Hampstead, but I was definitely living better than most at Ford. You didn't have to be a rocket scientist or a super businessman to manage yourself there. You just had to keep to yourself and not get into trouble by walking around with your head up your backside.

I was determined that I would not let prison pull me down. I was determined to rise above it. I refused to behave like the rest of the prisoners. I refused to speak like prisoners spoke. Normally, my language is colourful, but in prison I kept it proper. I refused to resort to prison language, like 'snout' or 'burn' for tobacco, like 'screws' for the wardens. Some officers permitted prisoners to call them by their Christian name. With me, it was always 'Mr Smith' or 'Mr Jones', or 'Officer'. If I had acted like the other prisoners, it would have made me one of them. I was not one of them. I could never be one of them.

If you're a lion in the jungle, you should be able to manage life in a little zoo down in Sussex.

* * *

Right after they moved me into the room with Irvin and John, I went to the assistant governor, a nice man named Hall, and said, 'You've had your fun and games for the benefit of the press' – because the press had paid people inside to take secret photographs of me being humiliated washing up food trays – 'why not use my talents? I'm happy to work all day, to go into education, to help people learn something about business. That would be good for both of us.'

He found a job for me in the probation office, where I worked from nine to midday and one-thirty to four. Then in the evenings, from seven to nine, I did business counselling, advising prisoners about whatever ideas they had for when they got out. My involvement with the Prince's Trust meant this was a chance to advise them on how to apply to the trust for funds to get them started in business.

During those six months at Ford, I think I received something like 1,500 letters. Gail must have received 2,000 more at home. It's quite strange really when you're in prison how you actually look forward to letters and communication from people on the outside. I felt a certain helplessness, in a situation that was totally out of my control, at the mercy of other people who had the power to tell me what to do, and I went through the entire range of emotions, from occasional highs to very depressing lows. So letters helped a lot. Post came in not just from the UK but from Hong Kong, India, the United States, Canada, all over Europe, all over the world. Some people wrote to lend support. Some people I hadn't seen or heard from in a million years popped out of the woodwork to wish me well. A lot of my friends wrote very often, sending me résumés of their weeks, telling me where they'd been and what sorts of deals they were doing. It made me feel that I hadn't been forgotten. Only a few letters out of the lot were what you could call hate mail.

Oddly, I got about 50 letters asking for money. I'm not talking about people looking for a fiver because they had a problem and figured it was worth a punt. I'm talking about charities, national charities, seeking a major donation from me. I just can't imagine that the people at those charities who decided to ask me for money quite understood my situation. They should have taken a second look at my address. So here's a little advice to anyone that dumb – don't ask a man for money when he's in prison. Write him a nice letter to wish him well, then ask him for the money once he's out.

I replied to most letters I received, at least the ones that were intelligent and caring, on the principle that if somebody had taken the trouble to write a thoughtful note to me, I owed them a reply. It was especially difficult, at least in the beginning, because I wasn't used to writing longhand, I was used to dictating, and I answered so many that I developed a corn on my finger. In the first few weeks, my handwriting was awful. I was out of practice and not terribly relaxed. Then it got better, to the point where you could actually read what I was writing.

Close friends wrote to reiterate their support and encourage me. A few so-called friends wrote to protect their own backsides. One acted the way he did because he's an arsehole. By the time I came out, they'd developed guilt complexes about their behaviour and tried to be friendly. But I wasn't friendly with them. If you're not my friend up front, I don't need you cheering for me when I'm back on the pitch.

One very old friend was actually willing to go much further than anyone else. Prime Minister Yitzhak Shamir often spent time with us when he came to England. He always said to other people that he thought I was a great man. Of course, that was his opinion. Well, I hadn't been at Ford long when he rang Gail to say that he needed to talk to me. Obviously, he couldn't just ring up the prison and say, this is the Prime Minister of Israel, may I speak to Gerald Ronson? Come to think of it, I suppose he could, but instead he gave Gail a private phone number. I rang and he took the call.

Yitzhak kept asking if there was anything he could do for me. That's the kind of man he was.

* * *

Inside prison, the number-one topic of conversation is getting out of prison. Everybody is always trying to work some sort of scam or make plans for an early exit. They're not necessarily trying to escape, they're just always cooking up a scheme, legal or otherwise, for their freedom.

Parnes was in a three-man room, like mine, and Saunders was in a single, and because we were, on the surface, talking to each other – personally, I would have liked to strangle both of them, which is not a good move in prison – Saunders would come to my room to tell me how he couldn't possibly spend five years there and how he needed to get out.

We hadn't been at Ford very long when he stopped by to see me, sat down on the bed opposite mine and started complaining. He said he didn't like working in the library, which was a cushy job that I'd got for him. And he said he didn't like the other prisoners. He really looked down his nose at them, as if he was so up in the air. I mean, who did he think he was going to find in prison? Then he wondered, 'How am I going to get out of here?'

I joked, 'Make out that you're mentally ill. It wouldn't be difficult for you, because, besides being a psychotic liar, you are mentally deranged.'

He looked at me with a serious expression. 'What do you mean?'

I was teasing him. 'If you made out that you've got Alzheimer's, nobody could ever prove it, because if they looked inside your head, what are they going to find?'

'Oh,' he said, 'I like that idea.'

Irvin was in the room when he said it, and we both laughed at him. When Saunders left, I said to Irvin, 'I bet he'll do that, tricky bastard that he is.'

Soon after our conversation, he asked for clemency on the grounds that he had Alzheimer's. Not long after that, a judge ruled that he was suffering from pre-senile dementia, which is the first stage of this incurable disease.

The judge released him after he'd served only ten months. And as soon as he was free, Saunders miraculously 'recovered', apparently the first person in medical history ever to do so.

* * *

One day, Giorgio, the Sicilian hit man who made such great steak tartare, said to me, 'You're out of shape. My nephew will train you and get you fit.'

His nephew, who wasn't really his nephew – it was a Sicilian term of endearment – was Vincenzo. He was around thirty years old and doing five years for drugs. Hardly the brightest pebble on the beach, he was a good-looking boy who fancied himself as a gigolo. When Giorgio told him to train me, I started finding Vincenzo waiting outside my room. This went on every evening for about two weeks. He was trying so hard that I finally agreed to give it a go. And Vincenzo got me into shape. When I went to Ford, I weighed 15.8 stone (221 lbs). When I came out, I was just under 14 stone (193 lbs). It didn't do any harm. Except that I lost seven inches on my waist and had to send all my trousers back to the little old man in the tailor shop to be taken in.

It struck me as odd that so few prisoners went to the gym. But I wasn't surprised that most of the ones who did were pretty tough. It was interesting because a kind of camaraderie built up amongst us. Maybe it was because we knew we were all giving ourselves a physically tough time when we didn't really need to. We joshed with each other, had our little bit of repartee with each other and vied with each other to make ourselves stronger. Some of these men were pressing 100 kilos plus.

Working out and lifting weights was one way to spend time. But even with that and work, there was still too much time to sit around and think. It's very boring. One of the ways you get through the boredom is by looking forward, which sometimes meant creating something to look forward to. That's why I threw myself into the Christmas pantomime. We wrote a script for *Ali Baba and the 40 Thieves*, made props, hired costumes, staged it and passed the time. We had a few laughs, too.

I often thought about that rabbi who'd come to see me in the cells below Southwark Crown Court, and while I may not be a religious person, I decided I wanted to share some of that experience. So I made contact with the other Jewish boys in Ford. There was a little synagogue in the prison and on Friday nights we held a short service. We had a glass of wine, broke bread and said a few blessings. I also arranged for the local rabbi to come in on Sunday mornings to speak to us about our families. His name was Pesach Efune and he ran the Lubavitch centre in Hove. He's a very decent man who came to see us of his own volition and never asked to be paid for it. Of course, he reminds me of that every year when it comes time to make a donation.

He was a long-black-coated rabbi who was then in his mid-to-late 30s. The first Sunday he came to visit, I was having a friendly meeting with him in the little synagogue when they rang the bell for lunch. The only way he could get out was to walk through the dining hall. I thought, if he's taken the trouble to see me, I can't just say goodbye, I should walk him to the gate. But to do that, we had to walk past 550 inmates. I'd only been there a week or two, so I didn't know what to expect. I wasn't going to deny who I am, so as I walked him through the dining hall to the gate, I held my head up high and nobody said anything.

On a couple of occasions, the prison allowed us to visit his synagogue in Hove. It took a lot of organising and I don't think the governor was happy about it, but the prison chaplain was a good person and he helped arrange it. I remember meeting Gail and the girls there. One or two of the others who came along met their girlfriends and went AWOL for a few hours, allegedly to take a walk around the block. Gail and the girls and I snacked on bagels and smoked salmon.

Because of all that, it didn't take long before the Jews at Ford began to feel a sense of identity, not just as Jews but as individuals. Of course there was anti-Semitism in prison because, however veiled, there is anti-Semitism in most areas of life. Now and again I saw it in the eyes of some of the prison officers. These were men who believed in the National Front and had a swastika on their boots. I could also see it in the eyes of some of the prisoners. But I was never aware of any overt anti-Semitism at Ford, so it didn't worry me. Though we Jews at Ford were far outnumbered, we had nothing to fear. It wasn't a question of numbers, it was a question of inner strength. It's when you hide what you are that people will try to take advantage of you.

During the first few months, the tabloid press made a lot of fuss about the number of times I was able to leave. Some of the inmates were in and out all the time. They'd get permission to go home to feed the canary. To set the record straight, I think that in the six months I was there, I left prison three, maybe four times. Twice to go to synagogue and once to see my doctor. He was a wonderful man named Joe Joseph and wrote to the prison to get special permission for me to come for a check-up. After which, I went to see my mother, who had an apartment in St John's Wood, where the future prime minister of Israel, Bibi Netanyahu, was waiting to have lunch with me.

Bibi was a minister in those days, but I'd known him for several years, since the time when he was Israel's ambassador to the United Nations. I recognised early on that he had the ability to go very far in Israeli politics, so I brought him to the UK because he didn't know anyone here. I introduced him to all the leaders and important people, both in the Community and in the Government.

I always thought that one of the problems Israel has had for many years is that many political leaders can't speak English, or if they do, they speak it very poorly. Bibi went to school in America and had an American attitude when it came to the media. His ability to speak and the way he dealt with the press when it came to explaining Israel's position put him at the top of the list.

* * *

Family visits were limited to one every ten days. The prison authorities didn't like the idea of all four girls showing up at the same time, so Gail would travel down every visiting day while the girls had to take turns. We only had two hours together. On her first visit, it was our wedding anniversary, so I arranged to have two dozen red roses for her. And I wrote Gail a card to tell her how much I loved her. When I walked in carrying the flowers, she burst out crying.

After that, whenever she visited, we'd spend the first hour talking about the family and the second hour talking about the business. There were plenty of other people who wanted to visit me, and I very much appreciated that. I was never out of touch with the business, but it wasn't the same as being in the office or going to see my managers, the way I always had.

I am forever grateful to the Good Lord that I didn't have to go through the Guinness ordeal without Gail and our four daughters. The love of my family was exceptionally important. That isn't to say that I couldn't have survived had things been different. I would have just had to tune into a different programme.

Obviously, I couldn't run Heron from Ford. I would collect my post, which came in about midday, go back to my room and sort through it there. I spoke to my office every day. My secretary, Paulene Clark, handled most things that needed to be dealt with. I'd see my deputy CEO Alan Goldman usually every other week, together with my lawyer. But it was Gail, with her unbelievable inner strength, who really stepped in to fill a big part of the void. When you have a crisis on your hands, you don't sit back and do nothing. Maybe some people do, maybe some people aren't strong enough not to, but Gail proved she isn't like that. She showed up at the office just about every day to look after as much of the business as she could.

She became my roving ambassador to the world. Wherever we had businesses – in the UK and in Paris, Madrid and America – she went there to see my managers and to talk to people and to assure everyone, Gerald's all right. She reassured people that it was business as usual and did a fantastic job. Until then, she didn't know how strong she really was. She'd come from her family home to making a home for us. She'd never been on her own before. But when she had to take charge, she was amazing. She bore herself with great dignity and cheerfulness.

As strong and united as our family was before all this happened, we are even closer today. We have all learned lessons about life and about people. My daughters saw what people can be like and came to understand the value of true friends. They saw at first hand how, in the face of adversity, some people will claim to be your friend and disappoint you, and how others whom you never before considered to be real friends can astound you with their friendship. The girls learned that when an unwelcome and traumatic experience happens, you must make the most of the positive and ignore the negative, and that if you don't behave like that, you let the enemy win. They learned from what we went through that, no matter what, you cannot let the enemy win.

My daughters learned to see the world through their own focus.

There's no doubt about it. I look at them, and I look at their children – my grandchildren – and I look at the stability, the support, the love and the affection they have given me, and at the very centre of it, there's Gail.

* * *

Because I was in a position to help some of the people I met at Ford, I did. One guy from the East End, a fellow named Peter, who must have been in his early 30s, had been a thief, albeit a non-violent one, most of his life. He told me one day that he thought he was a pretty good runner, that he'd already run the London Marathon once and wanted to do it again as soon as he got out. I said to him, 'If you are as good as you think you are and you finish the marathon in under three hours, I'll sponsor you to run for St Mary's Hospital Save the Baby Fund.'

We put in his application and arranged with the governor to let him out for a few days. Peter then worked an angle, saying that he needed a couple of the other guys to help him train, so two of his mates also got out for a few days. Peter ran the marathon in just under three hours and we raised

£10,000. Gail was on the board of St Mary's Save the Baby Fund, so she threw a little luncheon so that Peter could present the cheque to the head man, Sir George Pinker, the Queen's gynaecologist.

Pinker, who only passed away a few years ago, was a kind, upper-crust, polite Englishman. He accepted the cheque and said to Peter, 'What do you do, young man?'

Peter replied, 'I'm a thief.'

Well, Pinker was a little hard of hearing. I was standing next to him so he turned to me to ask, 'What did he say?'

I told him, 'He said he was a thief. But don't worry, because he's not a violent thief, just a well-known thief.'

Pinker smiled, graciously took the cheque, thanked everybody and probably thought he hadn't heard me correctly either.

I helped Irvin, too. He told me that he knew people working in hotels who always had tourists needing a chauffeur and when he came out he wanted to do hire work. Obviously, he didn't have a couple of grand to put down on a second-hand Mercedes, so I guaranteed the deposit and H.R. Owen let him have the car. He paid it off at so much a week.

One of the friendly guys worked in the kitchen. Norman Parker, a convicted double murderer who stayed inside for 22 years, always made sure I had fresh bread. When he came out on parole, he was looking for a quiet life somewhere. I have a 50 per cent share in a nightclub in Valencia and decided I needed somebody I could trust to head up the security, to keep drugs and the wrong people out of there. In that business, it's not the people who own the club who control what goes on, it's 'he who controls the door'. Norman is still working for me there today.

Giorgio was released and came to my home one Friday night with his wife for dinner. I heard later that he was murdered in a Dutch prison. Vincenzo has done quite well for himself. When he came out, he found a rich woman to keep him. I saw him once driving around in a Ferrari.

On the day I was due for release, instead of keeping me there until mid-morning the way they usually do with everyone else, the governor allowed me to leave at one minute past midnight. He did it because he wanted both of us to avoid the media. By dawn, photographers, reporters and cameramen were camping out at the gates to get those first pictures and first interviews of me walking free. But I was long gone.

I climbed into my waiting car, drove to Gatwick Airport and flew with Gail to the Mediterranean, where we had five days together on my boat. Refreshed, I returned to England to get back to work. I made a speech to 550 people at a major dinner in the Dorchester Hotel, and a few days later, I presided over the annual conference with my top managers. After a week in the office, it was as if I had never been away. Within a month, I was visiting my businesses in every part of the world and dealing with most people as if nothing had happened.

Some people didn't know quite what to say to me. They appeared awkward and left it with, 'Good to have you back.' But then the British are not very good in situations like that. Of course, there were some who seemed self-conscious, probably because they'd been glad I'd been 'taken down a peg'. Those same people probably thought the Guinness affair would have changed me. I disregarded them, because you can't expect to be liked or respected by everybody. The important thing to me is to be respected by the people I respect, liked by the people I like, and, especially, loved by the people I love.

If you have that, you are very fortunate.

* * *

Prison crushes men and destroys families. But it doesn't have to. Prison can make a man stronger. The experience of being inside should be a positive one, not one that pulls you down and makes you see the worst in people. If a man's mind can be compared to a camera, six months in prison should cause a man to look at life in manual focus instead of automatic focus. A spell in prison, if you make positive use of it, should teach you not to take things for granted, not to see things as the automatic lens shows them to you, but to focus for yourself on the priorities of life – family, friends, community and your own values.

You have to be strong in prison, not only for yourself but for your family. You have to survive. If you can do that without getting hurt and without becoming embittered, you become more compassionate, more understanding, more tolerant. I find that when I sit around a table negotiating with people, listening to people, watching people assessing other people, I do it differently from how I used to. I see people differently, and I see myself differently. I didn't think of myself as a bad person before I went to Ford, but I am a better person now. I'm more compassionate. I'm more confident. I'm more tolerant, far more so than I would have thought possible. This sense of extra strength, of uplift and inner equilibrium, came to me as soon as I walked out of those gates.

The first few weeks after I came out of prison, a few acquaintances who had often invited me for lunch at their offices now invited me for lunch outside their offices. They found some excuse for not giving me lunch on their home ground. All right, I understand that. They weren't saints and I wasn't a martyr. Some were thinking, there but for the grace of God go I. And some were thinking, he handled it like a man. These people were willing to extend the forgiving and forgetting hand of friendship because they wanted to continue doing business with Heron. Or because they had received money from the Ronson Foundation and hoped to get more. But the lessons of prison would be lost if I lingered too long on such cynical thoughts. I want to believe that at least some of the people who asked me to lunch did this because, in their hearts, they knew that I had been a victim of injustice.

* * *

I have only been back once. It was on Saturday, 29 June 1991, for the Open House Day charity event that I organised while I was still inside. We invited Angela Rumbold, the Home Office Minister for Prisons, and she showed up, which pissed off the governor, who was a schmuck anyway and didn't like having his boss there. He liked it even less when Gail and I arrived in my blue Porsche and were treated like VIPs. Admittedly, it was strange, because everybody there remembered me as a prisoner.

We had 20 companies sponsoring the day, so this didn't cost the taxpayer anything, and we put on a celebrity cricket match. Jeremy Beadle and the agent Anita Land organised it, with a lot of celebrities. David Essex was there and so was the 'Forces' Favourite' Vera Lynn. We had a Salvation Army band and eight Red Devils parachuting down from the skies. It was a day for my pals who were still there to spend with their families, and more than 10,000 visitors showed up. They were welcome to tour all parts of the prison, except the residential areas, and to meet the prisoners. Television crews filmed an interview with the governor, who told viewers what Ford was all about, and Angela Rumbold announced to the media that the Home Office would consider having open days at other prisons. We raised £10,000 for the Gulf War Families Trust Fund.

It was a successful day, and a healthy outing for the prisoners. Doing things like that, which help prisoners' families and the prisoners themselves get back a bit of self-respect and self-esteem, is important. But they never did it again and you have to ask yourself why. The man in charge didn't like it and was uncomfortable with me being there. The officers were also totally pissed off at me because it put a lot of pressure on security. Whether they had anyone abscond, I don't know, as I wasn't going back afterwards to find out.

Most of the people I met at Ford had been in prison before. I think the figure is around 85 per cent of the people in prison keep going back.

Which says to me that there is something wrong with the system. Part of the trouble is that when a man comes out of prison it's hard for him to get a job. He may have the good luck to meet a Gerald Ronson who will help him find his feet, but chances are he won't. Where are his references? He may not have a fixed abode. He may not have a family any more. If he's been in prison for, say, a year, he might have a chance of holding his family together, but if he's been in for five years or fifteen years, it's a different matter. If you aren't very intelligent and don't have much willpower and strength of mind, or a few good friends waiting for you on the outside, chances are you'll wind up back in prison.

I thought about this a lot when I was there, and I asked questions because I wanted to understand. I knew two prisoners who had been inside for long stretches, one for seventeen years and one for twenty. They were spending the last twenty months getting themselves ready for the outside world. Because they were intelligent men who knew what they were doing, I decided they would be all right. But they were the exceptions. Of the lifers in Ford, only three or four still had their act together. There's something very wrong about the way this works. Society should not assume that some people are so bad there's nothing to be done about them.

Many years after I came out, Gail and I were going to a concert at Wembley Stadium. We'd just parked when two big black men started walking towards us. One of them said, 'Mr Ronson, do you remember me?'

I looked at him, nodded, smiled and extended my hand to shake his. 'You were on E Wing at Ford.'

And before he shook my hand, he turned round to his friend and said, 'See, I told you – he's the guv'nor.'

CHAPTER 11

....

CRASHING IN AMERICA

Property in Europe took a beating in the late 1970s, so I looked around for better investments and turned my attention to the United States. For me, America has always been the last bastion of capitalism. I'd never done business there before, but I'd spent a lot of time in the States and I knew there were lots of opportunities waiting for the right entrepreneur to come along. My plan was to build a property business in America the way I'd built my property business in England and the rest of Europe. But America is a big country and I wasn't looking to do business just anywhere. I wanted to be in a high-growth area. What I had to learn for myself is that doing business in America is like swimming in a pool of sharks.

Until the early to mid-1970s, the trend had been for people in the cold northern states to seek retirement sunshine in Florida. But jet travel made it easy to head for the warmth of the desert, and by 1980 Arizona was the third-fastest-growing market in the country. The annual influx of 50,000 people a year showed no signs of doing anything but getting stronger. Tucson and Phoenix were both in the top six of America's fastest-growing cities.

Around the same time, President Jimmy Carter loosened controls on the Savings and Loan (S&L) industry to open up the market. An S&L is the American version of a building society and it does exactly what it says on the tin – it specialises in personal savings accounts and home mortgage loans. For many Americans, their S&L was their bank. For me, an S&L looked like just another form of property business. So in December 1980, when the Pima Savings and Loan Association in Tucson came onto the market and the business looked solid, we bought it for $25 million. We also bought the Western American Mortgage Company in Phoenix for $10 million.

We paid full price for both, but it was a fair price. With hindsight, we shouldn't have bought either, but being an entrepreneur means opening out and going into things, not taking risks but minimising risks. Even then, you know right from the beginning that some things will be more successful than others. The last thing you want is a major failure on your hands, which can happen. That's what business is all about. You can't win big every time. On the other hand, it's a fact of life that if you have to depend on being clever with hindsight, maybe you shouldn't have done the deal in the first place. But you have to keep trying, and the entrepreneur who doesn't do anything, who doesn't expand his activities or his business, isn't an entrepreneur. If you are single-minded and manufacture widgets and all you want to do is make widgets all your life, that's fine. But that's not entrepreneurial.

I went into the US to build a business. I wanted us to be players. And sure enough, right after I bought Pima, two fellows came to see me to ask if I was interested in some prime Tucson land.

Tucson was Hicksville in those days, but it was growing, and this was 12,500 acres, almost 50 square miles, right next to the airport. These guys also offered me 5,000 acres in Las Vegas. The land had belonged to the late billionaire recluse Howard Hughes. He'd been an industrialist, a film producer, an aviator and, for a time, one of the richest men in the world. He died in 1976 and his executors were just getting around to selling off parts of his estate. I was interested in Tucson because, with our bank there, I was flying in every month, so I knew the area. Learjet and IBM both had big plants in Tucson, and the airport was set for a major refurbishment. Modernising the airport meant expanding, and this land came with planning permission for whatever we wanted to do, residential and commercial. I told the two guys yes for Tucson.

But I told them no for Las Vegas. I knew nothing about that town, wouldn't go into a deal if I didn't know everything about the deal and had no interest in spending time in Vegas to find out. I was happy with what we had in Arizona. Schmuck that I was, today that land in Vegas is worth so much . . . well, let's not even go there.

The price for the Tucson land was $75 million. The two men bringing me the deal wanted me to know that, by carefully breaking it up, it could be worth as much as $200 million. I didn't know what it was worth, so I worked out a deal with them where together we pre-sold 50 per cent up front and bought the rest. We built roads and we built homes, and over the next four or five years, we did very well there. I think we wound up making $150 million profit.

We soon expanded our interests to Texas, where we bought 8,500 apartments, and into Colorado. Unfortunately, when we sold the land in Tucson, I made the mistake of putting all the money back into the bank to build up the balance sheet. Pima was making profits of around $30 million a year, and I ploughed that back into the business, too. At the time, that was the right thing to do. That's how we built Pima into a $4 billion institution. And in those days, that was a lot of money.

* * *

In the mid- to late 1980s, the UK property market started to slide. Interest rates were going up and rents were coming down. I could see some commercial property eventually losing as much as 50 per cent of value. Broadgate in the City was a good example. I think rents were originally being projected at £30 to £40 per square foot, but when demand dried up, you were struggling to let space for £20. I could see this beginning to happen, so we started selling assets. My intention was to get rid of everything – especially our investment properties – and keep only the very best assets that we had. But then along came Guinness, and rumours started spreading that I would sell up and go abroad. I never intended to leave the UK, but Victor Mishcon was concerned about us being seen to be selling assets and worried that if we continued, it would look like I was cashing in to leave. In his mind, that could be seen to be an admission of guilt. Under different circumstances, we would have sold things that we didn't sell, but, on his advice, we stopped.

In the States, things weren't looking much better. Interest rates were climbing and bank failures, including S&Ls, were on the rise, too. Also, the housing market had slowed down. Between 1986 and 1991, the number of new houses constructed annually in the States dropped by nearly 50 per cent. As it did, recession set in.

Whilst I was in prison, I began to feel that the property market was only going to get worse. Things were definitely moving in the wrong direction, and I could see a potential collapse in the property business. Heron was all right. We made £69 million profit in 1989 and had something like £700 million net worth of assets, but our debt was £1.4 billion to £1.6 billion, and I needed to reduce that. So I planned the sale of 150 petrol stations to Elf for £150 million, which would have taken me 95 per cent out of petrol retailing, and started looking around for other assets which we could dispose of.

That was when events overtook themselves. Suddenly everything was going wrong. The global property markets crashed, there was a credit

165

squeeze, my car-retailing business ran into trouble, the house-building business crashed and the 'Savings and Loan crisis' in the United States took on a momentum of its own. Carter had triggered what was to come by loosening credit for the S&Ls. By the time he left office in 1981, there were 3,800 S&Ls in the States, 3,300 of which were losing money. Pima was not one of them. Pima was making money. Congress then spent the next 15 years mismanaging control and regulation over the industry with incredible incompetence.

In the midst of this, Guinness almost came back to haunt me. After the trial and after serving my time at Ford, my lawyers were concerned that I might not be allowed back into the United States. If you have a conviction, you have to declare it to the authorities and they can refuse you entry. That would have been embarrassing and costly, so I filed for a waiver, which had to be approved by a lot of people in Washington, including the immigration authorities. We decided that I needed some eminent Americans on my side. So we got in touch with the former US ambassador to Great Britain John J. Louis Jr, who was part of the Johnson & Johnson family. He was happy to help, and so was Dennis DeConcini, one of the two US senators from Arizona. I'd met him a few times in Tucson through our Pima Savings business. We also got in touch with the other senator from Arizona, John McCain. I didn't know him – all we did was shake hands once at a function in Arizona – and yet, without any hesitation, McCain joined with the others and went to bat for me. I have never had a visa problem since.

But I still had S&L problems. When we first got into the business, American banks had fixed rates of interest on deposits. I think at the time the rate was set at 5 per cent. To help S&Ls become more competitive with banks, the government allowed them to take deposits at 5.25 per cent. But the politicians in Washington didn't have a clue what they were doing, and now banks and S&Ls were both offering house mortgages at 7 per cent. Increasing interest on deposits squeezed the S&Ls, which was the exact opposite of what they wanted.

S&Ls started to go bust, so the politicians now threw the market into turmoil by deregulating deposits. They allowed banks and S&Ls to charge whatever they liked. Interest rates went up to attract more deposits, but the money the S&Ls could make on those deposits were house loans and mortgages, which were at a fixed 7 per cent. As deposit rates reached 10, 11, 12 per cent, the geniuses in Congress realised that neither the banks nor the S&Ls could stay in business like that, so they allowed banks and S&Ls to expand their loan books. The thinking was that by doing that, banks and S&Ls could bring in new assets at higher rates. But in order to make that work, Congress needed to allow them to increase the amount of money they could lend out. I think at the time they were limited to 20 times their capital. Congress increased that to 33 times.

It was crazy. And then it became worse. By statute, S&Ls were not permitted to lend money on commercial property. That was the domain of banks, and S&Ls were not banks any more than building societies are banks. They're set up differently and regulated differently. But because S&Ls couldn't bring in enough residential business to stay in business, Congress allowed them to get into commercial-property loans. Suddenly, with fresh money available, a vast quantity of commercial property came onto the market. And the S&Ls jumped in head first. Some of the property they put on their books was OK and some of it was bad, but a lot of it was very bad. After all, S&Ls were new in this game. The really good property deals went to banks because they were the traditional lenders. What the S&Ls wound up with was a lot of property that banks wouldn't lend money on. Everyone in the business was praying for property prices to go up, because banks and S&Ls needed higher property values to cover all this new lending. Which is when Congress, unbelievably, took away the tax advantages on property.

It's obvious that when you take away tax advantages, demand falls and prices come down. In this case, they came down so hard and fast that the market collapsed. Everywhere was overbuilt – Colorado, Texas, Arizona – and it didn't matter whether you were looking at apartments, office buildings or shopping centres. People built whatever they could and part-let the properties. As interest rates shot up, the loans got too expensive to service. And they couldn't dispose of the assets in the marketplace to repay the loans.

The American government screwed up the S&L industry, not Gerald Ronson. And in America, when a market collapses, it really collapses. It doesn't draw back 5 or 10 per cent, it sinks without a trace. From 1986 to 1995, nearly 1,600 S&Ls shut their doors. That was half the industry. It cost American taxpayers somewhere around $125 billion. Making things worse, as more and more S&Ls went under, all sorts of fraud and theft were discovered. It was one unbelievable mess.

* * *

I didn't know if things could get worse but I was hoping to save something of the business and, literally, almost got killed trying.

Travelling to the States every month, I bought a British Aerospace 125, a twin-engined jet, which was a very good way to get back and forth. I had a crew of two and one hostess. It was a mid-sized corporate jet, which means it could go from London to Tucson with one fuel stop along the way. We always stopped at Gander, Newfoundland, and on one trip from Los Angeles back to London, Gander almost became my own last stop, ever.

We fuelled up and took off for Luton Airport, which was five and a half hours away, when the pilot came back to tell me that we had a problem. He said that the nose gear was jammed and hadn't come up, that they had already tried everything they could but it was broken and that we couldn't fly the Atlantic with this problem. He said we had to go back to Gander and make a crash landing.

There were three other passengers with me. I can't remember who they were, not friends of mine, just some people hitching a ride. They weren't with me on the trip to the States, and they were understandably upset about our mechanical problem. But I needed to know some things from the pilot before I became upset, so I asked what the procedure was. He said we'd have to circle for four hours to dump fuel. Then, once we were light enough, the crash teams at Gander would foam the runway and we'd come in. He said we would come in with all power shut down, we'd be on our belly and he would have to get his timing just right so that the plane wouldn't break in two or sparks from the belly landing wouldn't ignite a fire.

Thinking to myself that I had four hours to live, I took a nap.

The hostess woke me in time for the crash that was going to kill us all. She said everything was ready on the ground – fire engines, crash crews and ambulances – and showed us how to assume the crash position. I turned my seat around, took off my glasses, took off my shoes, put my head down on my knees and clasped my hands under my legs. Actually, I was unbelievably cool about it. The brain switches off, which is a good thing, because you can imagine the state you'd be in otherwise. The other passengers were crapping themselves, which isn't surprising, but in circumstances like that, you don't think about anyone else. All I could think of was, what the fuck am I doing here?

My pilots brought the jet in slowly. Then, suddenly, there was a bump and scraping noises as the plane slid along the runway. We skidded until we stopped, and at that point my mind was blank. The next thing I knew, I was through the exit, out over the wing and down on the runway.

As I hurried away from the plane, I still couldn't figure out, what the fuck am I doing here?

Inside the little passenger terminal, I phoned Gail in London and told her that I was all right, that everyone else was all right, that the plane hadn't caught fire but that it was lying there on the runway looking very sorry for itself. I told her it could be a while before I got home, then hung up, looked around and wondered, now what?

Gander wasn't exactly a thriving airport. I didn't know when the next scheduled airline stop might be, or even if there was a scheduled airline that came into Gander. The only other plane I could see was a Falcon on the tarmac getting fuelled. I asked someone who it belonged to and was told that the four people on it were currently in the VIP area waiting to reboard. So I walked into the lounge and found four men in business suits. I introduced myself – a bit of chutzpah – and asked where they were going. One of them looked at me a little suspiciously and explained that they were headed to London.

I said, 'That's great. Would you have room for another passenger?'

He said to me, 'Why?'

I pointed to the runway. 'If you look out there, that's my plane and we just crashed.'

He said they were having an important board meeting and made it fairly clear that I'd be intruding. I asked him who they were. He told me this was the Philip Morris plane and they were all on the board of directors. So I mentioned that I was friends with one of the directors, and this guy finally said to me, 'You can come along if you don't mind sitting at the back of the plane.'

'Don't pay any attention to me,' I said, because this was self-preservation time. Those other people from my plane would have to sort themselves out. So that's how I came home. But before I left Gander, I had a picture taken standing next to my plane with its wing folded back. The next morning, because it was a new plane, I rang Raymond Lygo, who was chairman of British Aerospace, and asked him if he'd heard about my crash. He said he hadn't but was very sorry to hear about it now.

'Well,' I said, 'I'm still alive, or I wouldn't be talking to you. I'm ringing because I don't want this to develop into a whole legal issue, but the bottom line is, it was a mechanical fault and I don't want the plane back. I want a brand-new aeroplane. A law suit won't do you any good and I've got this great photograph of me standing next to the plane with its wing all broken. You wouldn't want to see that in the papers tomorrow, saying, how would you like to buy this plane for your managing director?'

He said, 'I'll have my chief executive ring you.'

I didn't want to leave it running, so I said, 'Would he ring me please by twelve o'clock?'

Lygo promised he would, and right on time, at noon, the chief executive was on the phone. I told him my plane was smashed and I didn't want it back. He said they would give me a brand-new plane but that I'd have to wait three months because planes were committed to customers as they rolled off the assembly line.

'Meantime?' I asked.

'Meantime,' he said, 'we'll pick up the old plane, take it apart, put new pieces on it, and sell it almost like new. And I'll see that you get the use of another jet until your new plane is ready.'

I asked him to send me a note to that effect, but he said he couldn't. He said I'd just have to trust him. So I did. And three months later, they handed me the keys to my new plane.

We continued to refuel in Gander and never had another mechanical problem. But as my business in the States worsened, and I began to understand just how bad things were, I started asking myself a new question – what the fuck am I doing in America?

* * *

Pima almost made it. We didn't go broke. In fact, Pima was the last S&L standing on its feet in the state of Arizona. But I didn't want to keep sinking money into it – we'd already lost the equity we'd put in and we'd lost the money from the sale of the Howard Hughes estate – so we offered to hand it back to the Federal Home Loan Bank in Washington, the agency that oversaw the industry. But they didn't want it either and refused to take it back because we were the idiot English people who had been pumping money into it to keep it afloat. As long as we were keeping it alive, the FHLB was prepared to support us, but we had to continue running it. And that's not what I wanted to do.

It was also costing us a lot to keep American Mortgage open. Adding that in with Pima, and with all the problems we were having collecting on bad loans, I think I was down by about $500 million. I use the word 'I' because this was my money. Heron was me, so this was out of my pocket. The real estate in Texas was under a $480 million wrap with an institution and we had to pay our way out. That added another $100 million to $200 million to my losses in the States. So I decided enough was enough and we cashed out.

I've thought back on Pima often, and from time to time I've analysed our US experiences in my mind. Maybe I should have called this chapter 'How to Make a Billion and Give It All Back, and More!' Sure, that's part of being an entrepreneur. It's part of the game. We were right to go to the States, and many of our problems there were beyond our control. If you wanted to work out a way of destroying an entire industry, Congress demonstrated how to do it. But we made mistakes too. The American management we had in place was very good at running a peripheral institution, but couldn't run what the business became when Congress changed the laws. Our losses came about because, once Congress changed those laws, we wound up loaning money to people who, by my standards, were not honest. Builders and developers signed bits of paper to get money from us, then ripped up those bits of paper when it came to paying us back. They were not only dishonest, they were financially aggressive. When we tried to force them to pay us back, they sued us for 'lender interference'. It's not the way we operate in England.

Even if this part of the country is known as the Southwest, the business environment was the Wild West. I assumed I could let American management look after my interests and I was counting on them to work to our much stricter standards of doing business. They didn't. And we hadn't yet gone through the 'how some Americans do business' learning curve. It's a costly mistake that many English businesses make. And it was a hard-learned lesson. But if you're going to do business in North America, you personally have to be there. When Marcus Sieff took M&S to Canada, he assumed that Canadians would be happy to shop in the same way the British do, but they weren't. He had similar problems when he bought the American fashion chain Brooks Brothers. In fact, wherever M&S went overseas, they lost money because they didn't understand the market and couldn't figure it out sitting in London.

Two people who didn't make that mistake were James Hanson and Gordon White, partners in Hanson Trust. I knew them both very well and, as soon as you mentioned the States to them, they'd tell you, King George III tried to run his American interests from London, and look what happened. That's exactly right. The deal guy was Gordy White. He was a bit off the wall and had a few bad habits, but he was smart enough to understand that if their businesses were going to make money in the States, he had to be there.

What I should have done was send Alan Goldman, who by then was my deputy chief, along with a management team from London, to America. It's not that I had bad people running the business, it's that they were functionaries who couldn't see the bigger picture. When you only show up once a month, you're like a visiting fireman, so the Americans will tell you what you want to hear. If Alan had been there full time, he would have exercised more caution, been more careful who we made loans to and not lost the money that we did there. It was an expensive lesson.

We wrote off the whole of our investment in Pima in our 1990 accounts, though some newspapers in the UK wrote stories to the effect that it was in 1990 that we incurred the losses. They got it wrong. As a result, they made it seem that our overall position at the time was less good than in fact it was. But the UK was never the problem. Europe was never the problem. We only had one problem – the States – but it left an enormous black hole in the middle of Heron.

Heron was unique in the financial markets, as most property companies borrowed secured. In other words, they put up their properties against the loans. We borrowed unsecured, which meant we didn't have to worry about the value of the properties. This was long-term money, mainly ten-year bonds, very keenly priced. So even though our net worth was falling, we were very liquid. If you look back to 1989, Heron's net worth was in the neighbourhood of £700 million. That means a $700 million loss – with the pound at around $1.40 – so we blew out nearly two-thirds of our net worth in America. That was very painful.

I don't dwell on how much money I lost, because I reckon you have to take the rough with the smooth. It's one of the lessons I learned in America. Being able to accept a loss and say, OK, let's move on, is one of the reasons why big business in America is so successful. When Americans make a mistake and register a loss, they don't take fright like the English do and pull in their horns. Needless to say, you can't make too many losses or they'll bury you. And after one setback, if you decide not to take any more risks, you're as good as dead.

* * *

Jumping backwards to spring 1983, a Spanish entrepreneur named José Maria Ruiz-Mateos got into financial difficulties and the government took control of his company, Rumasa. At the time, it was Spain's largest banking and industrial conglomerate. Rumasa owned all sorts of businesses, including Augustus Barnett, which was at the time England's largest chain of cut-rate liquor and wine shops. Rumasa also owned a lot of real estate.

We'd been seeing opportunities in Spain for ten years, having developed our first property there in 1973. It was on the Avenida Castellana, the main street in Madrid. I had faith in the country during the many years most people did not. They saw Spain suffering through a very long and deep industrial crisis. I saw a wonderful country with wonderful people who would one day work themselves out of the mess. So we continued to develop properties there. And in June 1985, our patience and belief in

Spain was rewarded when Spain and Portugal joined the European Union. It was the beginning of a new world for Spain.

That same year, the government decided to sell off the Rumasa real estate. They put together a huge package of properties and put them on the auction block but couldn't find a single suitable buyer. So a year later, they decided to try again. They announced the second auction for September 1986. Some time in August, I was on holiday on my boat off the coast of Turkey when I received a telephone call from my director in Spain, Antonio Eraso. He said, 'The Spanish government are going to sell off the Rumasa properties. Would we be interested in buying them?'

I knew most of the major properties that were for sale – they were landmark buildings – and I knew something of the Rumasa history, but I didn't know all of the properties. How could I? There were 11,500 properties all over Spain, as well as the Canary Islands, including building plots. We needed to study it, go through a huge amount of due diligence, submit our tender on 1 September and be prepared to pay cash for the entire amount on the day that the winning bid would be announced, which was 10 September. Still, I immediately answered, 'Yes.'

Time was of the essence, so I told Antonio that I needed a full analysis of the portfolio. But he could only get about three-quarters of what I required. Here I was in the middle of the sea on a boat with little more to hand than a piece of paper and a pencil. The hours were ticking by and that wasn't enough to proceed on.

Richard Ellis, a real-estate services company, had a senior man in Spain called Francis Pons, who I knew and trusted, so I rang him on the satellite phone, told him what the situation was and emphasised that we had to submit our bid in the next couple of days. In my simple arithmetic, on the back of an envelope, I had already worked out what the major assets were worth, but wanted to know what he thought we would have to pay for the rest. I asked him to look at the properties himself, talk to people he had confidence in and come back to me as soon as possible.

When he phoned with a figure for the lot, I told Antonio that we would buy. Our tender was submitted on the deadline, the Spanish cabinet met on 10 September and announced afterwards that they were awarding the portfolio to Heron for 10.6 billion pesetas, somewhere north of £52 million.

There were ten to twelve other bidders, including a big Spanish group, but they gave it to us because we offered the best professional track record for property development in continental Europe. There was rural land that needed agricultural attention, there was retail space that needed to be torn down and rebuilt, and there were residential properties that needed to be refurbished. The portfolio was a nightmare to manage and it took more than ten years to deliver everything. But in another sense, this was, absolutely, a once in a lifetime deal. It turned out there were actually many more properties in the portfolio than had been listed. And it was probably the best deal that we have ever done.

Three years later, Banesto Bank, which now belongs to Banco Santander, was forced by the Bank of Spain to dispose of its property assets. The government put them on the block in a small auction, and we won that one too. There were 1,300 properties throughout Spain, a lot of them in Madrid, and we paid just over £50 million for them. It took us six or seven years to manage that buy.

Both deals represented a huge commitment on our part to Spain's future. Remember, this is 1980s money. But the two packages included some 100 per cent location sites such as the Torres de Colon in the heart of Madrid, which we refurbished and re-let, then subsequently sold to a major insurance company. The Rumasa and Banesto deals made Heron one of the largest property developers in Spain. At the same time, we more than doubled the value of the deals, which was profit, and that enabled us to cope – at least for a while – with the setback over Pima.

* * *

The American business really screwed us up and we haemorrhaged very severely. I knew I needed to reconstruct Heron. That was a huge task. I also needed to rebuild my reputation. In the wake of Guinness and prison, doing those two things simultaneously became all the more difficult. I can be flippant about that sometimes – I can say, having done it once, I can do it again – but I was staring at what had been the second-largest private company in the UK hanging over the edge. Most people told me I couldn't rebuild it. Many people thought I was crazy for even trying. And there were some people who were hoping I'd simply fall off the edge, never to be seen again.

As a young man, maybe I was aggressive and a bit brash. In my 30s and even into my 40s, I was rockin' 'n' rollin'. I tried not to step on people's toes, although it happened from time to time. I felt if someone didn't like me, so what? I didn't romance politicians and I didn't chase after a title. I got on with my life. But that pissed some people off, even if I didn't really care that it did. So when I ran head first into Guinness and then Heron started sinking, a number of people were happy to see Gerald Ronson down on his knees. It's funny how envy comes into people's psyches. It's as though some people really do not want to see other people succeed. What those people never realised was what made Gerald Ronson in the first place. If I was a mug, I wouldn't have achieved what I had. Those people glossed over that, preferring to waste their time and energy being envious. I didn't have that luxury. I didn't have that time. I needed to spend my energy getting off my knees. I refused to go down for the count.

In September 1991, Alan Goldman ran all the numbers and came to me to say that Pima had been a fatal blow, and that with hundreds of millions of pounds of net worth suddenly disappearing, Heron would eventually go bankrupt. We'd already sold off a lot of properties and we had mortgaged the rest, so our debt was very high in relation to our net worth. Alan said he couldn't see any way we were ever going to be able to raise enough money in the bond markets, the way we had previously, and that there was no conceivable way of rescuing the company.

It wasn't what I wanted to hear. I trusted Alan's reading of the situation, but I still wanted a second opinion. So I rang Alan Wheatley, the chief executive of Price Waterhouse in London. He put his top team onto Heron. It took them three months to go through our books, and they concluded the same thing Alan had – that there was no way Heron could survive. I took it on the chin and it hurt, then did the only thing I could think of doing. I called for the top insolvency people so that we could manage this in an orderly way. The law firm of Allen & Overy sent in their A team. It took them a long time to go through all of our corporate records, which admittedly were complicated, as we had three hundred companies operating in nine countries around the world.

All this time, Heron was still functioning but the accountants and the lawyers had their meters ticking and now we were haemorrhaging legal and accounting fees too. We'd stopped buying properties and were quietly selling some when we could get the right money. But for the most part, the business was static. Our net worth was diminishing and the market was falling away.

After Price Waterhouse and Allen & Overy put together a full report, we went to see our main bankers, who were NatWest and Barclays. For the most part, they were supportive, although in the beginning they were pissed off that we hadn't told them before we called in the accountants and the lawyers. Normally, when banks come in, the first thing they want is all the security that you have. But our advisers told us, whatever pressure they put on you, don't give them security. When another of our banks heard about it, Bank of America, they got very upset. But Americans react differently than the British.

We were operating with a dual holding company structure, one in the UK, one in the US. We also had a number of companies spread over the rest of the world, with different loans and credit. What worried the banks was that we would go into Chapter 11 in the US. That's a legal no-man's-land between solvency and bankruptcy which gives a company a chance to restructure by putting a hold on repaying debt. Another alternative was going into suspension in the Netherlands Antilles, which would have had the same effect of delaying payment of debt to the banks. And the idea of ending up in some foreign country trying to collect money from us terrified the bankers.

Instead, we went through what effectively became the first ever Chapter 11 in the UK. The banks allowed us to stay in control so that we could reorganise and settle our debts without going into bankruptcy. We always had at least £100 million in the bank through the entire process. But no company had ever done this before in the UK. The way we handled this became the model for changing English bankruptcy laws. Today, thanks to us, there is a type of Chapter 11 in the UK.

It took two years, from September 1991 to September 1993, to set up the restructuring. The 15,000 bond holders were the most difficult, because they were desperate. Credit Suisse was one of the big bond sponsors and they wanted us to go bankrupt. If we did, they could write us off and that would be the end of the problem for them. You have to understand the Swiss mentality. It's not their money, it's the clients'. They had a lawyer who did everything he could to stop us from restructuring, to make us disappear.

We weren't at the brink, we were hanging over the edge of it. Heron was going broke. But at the most important creditors' meeting – sitting around an enormous table at the law firm of Lovell White in Holborn, staring down 40 bankers and lawyers looking for their pound of flesh – I wanted them to know that I'd got us into this mess and that I was prepared to get us out of it.

This was the major crunch meeting. There may have been 50 other meetings before now, but this was the one that mattered. And the guys on the other side – the lawyers and bankers representing the bond holders – couldn't look me straight in the eye. I wanted to say to these arseholes, this is costing me a hundred times more than it's costing you, but I didn't. I wanted to say, how come you bankers send in the smart guys when it comes to lending money, but you send in the dumb ones when it comes to collecting it? But I didn't.

Our discussion wasn't going well. I saw only two men at the table on my side. George Cracknell, representing Barclays Bank, who is a very

Milky and Khaia with their children.
At the front are Uncle Tubby and my mother, Sarah.

Me, *circa* 1939

Sarah, Henry and me, *circa* 1939　　　Father and son. Full partners, *circa* 1957.

Dad, Laurence and me

With the man who
mentored me, Marcus Sieff

Life in the early '60s

At an early Heron petrol station with F1 driver
James Hunt and customers

1966 – Gail liked the guy but thought the car was too flash

Our wedding in 1967

Mrs T, me, Gail and Shimon Peres
n Israel at the Henry Ronson
ORT School

Gail and the girls face the press scrum
after the Guinness trial (© *The Sun*)

With the inimitable Golda Meir

A night at the opera: all the royals with the Ronsons (l) and the Maxwells (r) (courtesy of the Royal Opera House)

With Princess Diana

With Prince Charles

Leading from the front
means being on site

The four Heron City sites in Spain
attract 20 million visitors a year

'Don Geraldo' with the King
of Spain and Antonio Eraso,
Heron's director in Spain

Being on a boat is the only situation in my life when I can say,
after two days, I'm relaxed

Dame Gail with Lisa, Amanda, Hayley, Nicole and the 'schlepp-along'
(courtesy of Buckingham Palace)

decent man, and John Melbourne, deputy chief executive of NatWest Bank and a fantastic man. They're mature, experienced bankers and they knew that most of the money that had been lost was mine. The others didn't care about my money or about Heron, they only cared about protecting themselves and doing what they felt was right for their own company.

George and John wanted me to stay on and run the business. But no one else seemed to, especially when my contract was going to cost them £5 million over five years, which included salary, pension and expenses. So these arseholes now start saying that they shouldn't be employing me at all, and they shouldn't be paying me that much money, and that all they really want is to get their own money out of this and move on.

I listened to this – it was like listening to people who want to kill you with a thousand cuts – and I started thinking to myself, I don't need this aggravation. I was thinking to myself, here I am as Mr Muggins saying, I got you into all this difficulty and I'm prepared to sort it all out, and you know what, if you don't want to pay me, don't pay me, just let me get on with it.

I don't know why, but at that moment, I reached into my pocket and grabbed my keys. I blurted out, 'I'm listening to all this and it's like this sign in Times Square, New York . . .'

They looked at me like I'd gone mental.

'. . . and I'm reading that sign, and you know what it's saying? I do not need this shit!'

One of the bankers actually whispered to another banker, 'Did he say shit?'

I said, 'Let me tell you something, gentlemen. You're all very brave, sitting around this table, so brave that you can't even look me in the eye.'

It was a bit theatrical but, by God, did I have their attention.

I said, 'I am prepared to run this business. I got you in this mess, and I'm prepared to get you out of it. Whether you want to pay me the five million that you're so concerned with or you don't, it doesn't matter to me. All I'm telling you is, if you do not choose to employ me or will not work with me, you'll lose another hundred million, because that's how it is. I can put it right. But I am not going to sit here and try to convince you that I can. Either you believe I can or you don't.'

With that, I yanked my keys out of my pocket and slammed them down on the table.

All of a sudden these fuckheads got paralysed.

I said, 'I want to see which one of you is brave enough to pick those keys up. I'm going out to the toilet. When I get back, you can tell me whether you want me to run the business or which one of you is going to run the business.'

Just like that, I got up and walked out.

George Cracknell followed me out and into the toilet. I looked at him and he very quietly said, 'Have you got any cigars on you?'

I replied, 'I always have a cigar on me.'

'Good,' he said 'go out and have a walk round the block, smoke a cigar and cool down. Then come back and we'll have it sorted out.'

I told him, 'I've had enough. I don't need those little fuckers sitting there looking at me like they could kill me. I'm the person who's lost the most money here. More than all of them put together. It's me. And I'll sort it out.'

He said, 'Cool down and go smoke a cigar.'

So I went for a walk round the block.

Alan Goldman caught up with me and said, 'You pushed that a bit far. Were you serious?'

I said, 'Yes. Because enough's enough. They were all happy to have their commission on the bonds when they placed them.'

We went around the block, I finished the cigar and came back inside. As I stepped into the room, before anybody could say anything, George Cracknell got up and announced, 'We've decided that we want you to continue to run the business.'

I looked at Alan and winked. The keys were still on the table. I said 'Good. Do you all agree with that?'

Oh, yes, everyone in the room agreed with that.

I thought, get out of here while you're ahead. I picked the keys up and said, 'I'll leave it to all of you to carry on talking, because I have a business to run.' And I went back to Heron House.

To be frank, none of us thought the restructuring was going to save the company. It was merely going to create order out of chaos so that we could sell assets in a businesslike way to pay down debt.

The ship was taking on water. At that point, I thought, the best I can hope for is to delay the sinking.

CHAPTER 12

·······················

RECONSTRUCTION

The easy way would have been to declare bankruptcy and walk away from everything. Or I could have buried my head in the sand and pretended it wasn't happening. Alan Goldman told me that Heron would go bankrupt and many other businessmen might not have wanted to hear the truth, but that's not my style.

I could have said, I've been badly treated and this embarrassment is too much for me and my family to bear, so the time has come to quit living in England. It wouldn't have been the first time that idea was tossed about. Through all my Guinness shit, people would say to me, what are you doing here? Why not go to live in America? And, don't you want to leave this place and live in Israel? And after I came out of prison, people would say to me, how could you put up with all that crap? Why not start a new life somewhere else?

I'm not sure about starting a new life in America or in Israel, but I could have gone to the south of France. I don't play golf, but I'm sure I could have amused myself with something, because I still had enough money. Maybe I couldn't have lived in great luxury, but I could have lived quite comfortably. I'm basically a modest person. Well, I may not be so modest in all ways, but in terms of my lifestyle, I wouldn't have had a problem with living more modestly. My wife and daughters wouldn't have had any problem with it, either.

But I didn't want to live anywhere else then, and I don't want to live anywhere else now. Leaving the country never entered my mind. I live in England because I'm English and this is the greatest country in the world. I don't even like going anywhere else. I take holidays in exotic places to appease my wife, but I prefer to stay in England, for all the good things it stands for. All right, it sometimes stands for some bad things, but the good far, far outweigh the bad and for me England is home. Good, bad or indifferent, here I am.

Packing up is not what I do. I'm not the sort who runs away from anything. I don't take the easy way out if it's not the right way out.

* * *

Losing money is never easy to swallow, but it goes hand in hand with making money, and if you're not prepared to lose some, you'll never be in a position to make some, at least not over a long run. Making money isn't just a one-way track. You have to speculate to accumulate. Property, for example, goes through cycles of revaluation, exactly the same way all assets do.

The important thing is that when you lose money, you learn from your mistakes. The first time around, we cross-collateralised our assets in the company. That was a $1 billion lesson. More than anything else, that's what nearly cost me my company. Instead of securing each loan with a specific asset, our assets were in the same pot. It meant that lenders could have any or all of the assets spread through all of the companies as repayment for any one debt. With 300 companies in 9 countries around the world, you can imagine what a pig's ear this was.

Today, we don't do that. From 300 companies, we are now less than 50 companies. Not that having fewer is easier, but we don't borrow unsecured. Also, we put our equity in. We finance 25 to 30 per cent of our deals ourselves. And I make sure that the maximum we put up is never more than 10 per cent of our net worth. So if any deal goes wrong, then our downside is just 10 per cent of our net worth. Granted, that's a lot of money, but by limiting our downside, we don't risk losing the entire business.

In my mind, the way out, the most orderly and proper way to wind the company down, was to convert our debt into equity. With new borrowing and new repayment arrangements, we could avoid bankruptcy. So we set off on the long, painful process of doing just that. I asked UBS to find us some equity investors and we started talking to a number of them.

Now, I'm no genius and there were plenty of other people who could have wound things down. A couple of dickheads actually tried to move in on the company. One, from South Africa, thought he could go behind my back, get rid of me and pay Alan Goldman to run the business. Could Alan have systematically broken up the business? Yes. Would he have got the best prices for the properties? Probably not, because he's not a salesman. The other dickhead came indirectly through Merrill Lynch. He wanted to buy the business without the management because he thought he could be the management. I stopped both of them. But I couldn't stop 82 banks, 15,000 bond holders and God knows who else from demanding my head on a platter. As one of those bankers told the press anonymously, coward that he was, 'Heron is a horse with a broken leg. When we saw the cost of fixing the leg, the option of shooting the horse suddenly became much more attractive.'

For me, the death of Heron would have felt like the death of Gerald Ronson.

Everything changed the day when, out of the blue, I received a call from Basil Vasiliou. He'd been a partner in a large brokerage firm, sold out and started his own operation. Basil had helped us in the past, placing debt with investors through some big Swiss bond issues, and those bonds were still trading. Which must have said to Basil that there were people out there who still believed in Heron. On the phone, he suggested one of those people might be Michael Milken.

Back in the 1970s, Mike was a young trader at Drexel Burnham who spotted a huge potential market in seldom-traded non-rated bonds. These were bonds that had an extremely high risk of default. It was very easy to lose your money on these bonds, so they were not for the faint-hearted. To serious money managers, who were only interested in 'investment grade' bonds, this looked like gambling. But the higher the risk, the higher the yield, and if the company somehow managed to come back from the dead, you could make a fortune. A few of these bonds did hit and made millionaires of a lot of people, including Mike and his brother Lowell. But most of these bonds were rubbish, which is how they came to be called 'junk bonds'.

Around the same time that Guinness hit the fan in the UK and Ivan Boesky agreed to a plea bargain on his insider trading violations – the same Ivan Boesky who told the SEC about Guinness and put my name on the table – he also pointed an accusing finger at Michael Milken. A young US attorney in New York named Rudy Giuliani subsequently charged Mike with 98 various criminal acts, which were mainly reporting violations. Mike had his back to the wall, risking many years in prison, so he worked out an agreement which allowed him to plead guilty to six counts and serve around two years. Just as British justice moved the goalposts to send me to prison, the American Justice Department criminalised technical offences to send Mike to prison.

I met him when he was flying high in the mid-1980s and we got on well. He's charming and clever. And I have always liked mixing with people whom I regard as cleverer or smarter than me, because you can learn from people like that. So every time I went to the States – and for those ten years I had businesses there, I went every month – I used to stop by Mike's office in LA for an hour. He wasn't a personal friend, he was a business friend, but we struck up a good rapport and even did a bit of business together through Pima. At one stage, Mike offered to do a $500 million to $600 million bond issue for Heron, but we didn't take him up on it because the rates were something like four or five over base and we didn't have any problems raising liquidity. It wasn't a market for us.

But times had changed and we needed the money. Shortly after my conversation with Basil, I received a call from Mike who said, 'I hear you have a problem.' I explained the situation, especially the trouble we were having with the bond holders. He asked, 'What will it take to sort them out?'

I said, off the top of my head, 'If I had a quarter of a billion dollars I could resolve the problem.'

He promised to get back to me. I didn't think twice about that, as I was in a war zone with my bankers and bond holders and had other things on my mind. But a few days later, he rang to ask, 'How good are the assets?' I told him we had the best. He said, 'OK, goodbye.' I didn't even discuss it with Alan Goldman.

Then Mike rang me again to ask what was going on. Being an open and frank person, I told him I was talking to other people, including Merrill Lynch, a distressed fund and Colony Capital in Texas. Sam Zell, an American real-estate billionaire, had also approached me, as had another big group in New York. I still didn't think Mike was going to get involved until he said, 'This is something we could be interested in.'

I told him, 'We can't deal with this on the phone. You have to send somebody over. I'll take him around London, Paris, Geneva and Madrid. I'll show him the properties. If you get someone in here on a Saturday, I'll have him back on a plane by Monday night.'

Mike is always very polite, never pushes or tries to be clever, which some people do when they know you're in a difficult position. He just promised to ring me back. And an hour later, he did, to say, 'If it's all right with you, I'm sending over Steven Fink. He'll get in early Saturday morning.'

Steven, who was probably around 40 at the time, was Michael's corporate analyst. One of those laid-back Californians, he always struck me as a cold fish with ice water running through his veins. He was tall, in very good shape and never smiled. He looked to me like a hit man from the Mafia. That was then. I've come to know him over the years and now we're friendly. Whenever he's in London, he always comes to the house on Friday night for dinner. He flew overnight from LA, got in at dawn on Saturday, never asked me to meet him at the airport or anything, and just showed up on time at my office. I took him around our main properties in London. He didn't crack a smile. But he asked all the right questions and took a lot of notes on his big yellow pad. The following day, we went to Paris to look at our properties in the centre of the city, then went to Spain and from there went on to Geneva. I showed him that we had the best properties in the best locations.

On Monday night, before he flew back to LA, I asked, 'Do you like what you see?' I think I got a grunt.

Three days later, I received a polite call from Mike. 'Yes, it was interesting what Steven saw . . .' blah, blah, '. . . I'll get back to you.'

Not long after that, we received word that the Milkens were prepared to make a bid for Heron, but in order for them to do that, our investment bank, UBS, needed to know that the money was there. I remember that I was in Paris when I got a call from UBS at around eleven o'clock in the morning to say that Bank of America had notified them they were holding a quarter of a billion dollars to our order. Well, when you get a phone call like that and you're in the position that I was, fielding 100 calls a day to stay alive, it's hard to take it in. My first thought was, maybe this is a joke. Then I started thinking, maybe it isn't. I couldn't call Mike in LA because there's a nine-hour time change between California and France, and even though he got into the office early, I still had to wait until five my time. When he answered, I said, 'I've had a call that the Bank of America is holding a quarter of a billion dollars for the Heron deal.'

Mike answered, as cool as a cucumber, 'Isn't that what you wanted?'

I said, 'Yes.'

And Mike said, 'I'm very happy to be your partner.'

Typical Mike. He always used the word partner, even though I wasn't really a partner in those days, because to save the company I had to give up most of my equity. For the first time in my life, I didn't own my company. I didn't even control the majority of the shares. For all intents and purposes, I became an employee. But the company and my reputation go hand in hand, and that was the most important thing.

He knew, because he knew me, that this would be a very good deal. Mike didn't have to send anyone over to do due diligence because we'd been due-diligenced to death. We'd already spent £70 million between Allen & Overy on the legal side and umpteen other lawyers in every jurisdiction, plus Ernst & Young, who were our own auditors, plus Price Waterhouse. They alone must have cost us £11 million to £12 million. Put all that in today's money, and you don't even want to think about how much these people raped out of the company.

Timing is everything and the timing of this was horrible. We were forced to close down our foreign-exchange currency hedges for technical reasons, and the minute the pound went down and other currencies went up, we lost another £70 million. So before the Milkens showed up, our restructuring cost was already running north of £150 million and we hadn't yet done anything. I can argue that 45 per cent of it was in the Ronson Foundation and the other 55 per cent was my money but, in effect, 100 per cent of it was my money.

Some good friends stood by me, bought bonds and came to the meetings to support me. I also had a good relationship with NatWest Bank – John Melbourne was a fantastic supporter – and Barclays Bank, too. They behaved well. But all the bond holders and all the other banks fought their ground. The Swiss banks especially, those greedy bastards who couldn't wait to grab their commissions when they were selling the bonds, were now moaning, what about our reputation? Well, you only have to look in the papers and read about the debacles of UBS and Credit Suisse and all the rest of them to know what a Swiss banker's reputation is really worth. All they wanted was to grab what they could, hang me upside down and squeeze my balls off. What really bugged them was that, now, they couldn't, because the Milkens had arrived like the cavalry, just in time.

I couldn't negotiate the sale of the creditors' debt to the Milkens, so the creditors appointed SBC Warburg. Everybody wanted their money back and then some, which meant the banks and bond holders were reluctant sellers. They thought they could pocket more by holding on.

To get the deal done, we had to convince 75 per cent of them to agree. Of course, we had the usual bunch of arbitrageurs getting in the way, hoping to screw up the deal for better terms. We also had litigation because one of the bond holders sued us over a property deal in the States. He smelled money, took us to court and lost. But we worked our way through all of that and, as soon as we got the deal done, NatWest and Barclays sponsored a new UK syndicated loan for Heron in the UK. It was the first time that the banks ever syndicated a loan together. That just shows the strength of our relationship with NatWest and Barclays.

The Milkens needed to put their own man on the Heron board and offered up Steven J. Green, who was chairman of two very big companies, Samsonite and Culligan Water. He later served as the United States ambassador to Singapore. He was a nice man, but he was only around for about nine months. The fellow who really handled everything on the technical side was Steven Fink.

Another man working on this with us was Mike's brother and partner, Lowell. Whereas Mike is a corporate big-picture guy, Lowell is a detail guy who has a photographic mind and understands property. After a while, I suggested that Lowell should take over from Green and become chairman. Lowell said he'd like to. And we made Steven Fink deputy chairman.

All these years later, I've never had a row with these people. Sure, there were silly things I could have argued about because, over some issues, they can be petty. They like to leave all their options open to make a decision. Having said that, I get on very well with them. Mind you, I don't see too much of them, because they're in LA and I'm in London, but I talk to Lowell every Friday on the phone to tell him what's going on. I give him the good news and the bad news, I'm totally straightforward and it works. That's my style. I'm an open book. I don't have secrets. And I look after my shareholders' money even better than I look after my own, because I'm not going to sit around the table with them and give them any reason to think I'm an idiot.

When the Milkens and their investors came in, we had a net worth equivalent to all of the debt. Of course, they bought the debt at a 50 per cent discount, betting that by carefully liquidating the assets they would make much more money than they paid. Not having debt problems gave us the opportunity to sell on an orderly basis. And that meant we'd get much better prices for those assets than we would have in a fire sale.

The idea was to liquidate the company over, say, three years, but there was no real timetable. If the board had said to me after 12 months, we'd like you to liquidate the business right now, I would have done that, too. I'd have taken what money I had and what other money I could raise and rolled it back into the game. And I did think about that. It did cross my mind that if they bailed out, if I couldn't follow through on the restructuring with them and the business went bang, I wouldn't have any shortage of people prepared to back me.

Thinking about that now, those backers would have given me more than what the Americans did. But a year after the Americans came in, the business had substantial equity, over and above what it cost, they were making money and I had a promote in the business. The reality was, once they realised the value of our assets, and Steven Green stepped down and Lowell Milken became chairman and he saw that I knew how to manage those assets, the whole ball game changed. Lowell started saying, instead of liquidation, let's build this up. It was understandable from his investors' viewpoint, because seriously rich people don't want to put their money into something only to take it out a year later and say, great, we made a 25 per cent return. Now what? They want to keep investing, which means they're looking to park their money on a long-term basis.

The restructuring just developed from there. As Lowell and I got to know each other, we both felt more comfortable. Together, we decided, let's roll the dice and see what happens. So instead of liquidating the company, we began to develop a much longer-term business plan to build it up. I didn't have to sell everything. I could start buying again. I liked that and so did my seriously rich shareholders.

Mike had put together an interesting group. The Milken Family Trust bought around one-third of the shares. The next big shareholder, Larry Ellison, who is the CEO of Oracle, is probably sitting there with 12 per cent of the company. I don't know him. But after Ellison there was Craig McCaw, who made a fortune in the mobile-phone business, then came up with the idea of laying fibre-optic cable under the city of Seattle and beating the local telephone company at their own game. He's a very bright man, very nice and very unpretentious. He had 8 per cent of the business but when he divorced, part of the settlement was that he turned those shares over to his ex-wife, so she has them today.

Steve Wynn has a small holding. He runs a major hotel and casino empire in Las Vegas and is very smart. He's Mr Smooth. He knows his business inside and out and made a lot of money. I don't think Heron is an important investment for him, I just think that he put some chips in at the beginning because he's a good friend of Mike's, and also maybe because Mike helped him when he was originally building hotels in Vegas. Their relationship goes back a lifetime. I suspect Mike made a phone call to Steve to say, there's this great investment in Heron in London, and Steve wrote out a cheque for £5 million or £10 million. Steve has always been very nice to me, especially the times we've been to Las Vegas. But Las Vegas is not my kind of town. I'm not a gambler.

Rupert Murdoch holds around 4 per cent. I'd known him since the Lew Grade, ACC takeover days, but the Milkens had been friendly with him for years. It goes back to when Rupert fell on difficult times and Mike Milken helped him reconstruct News Corp with bonds and other financial instruments. So Rupert was one of the club. When the Milkens were putting together the bid for Heron, he was on Mike's list. I've bumped into Rupert several times in London over the years, usually at a restaurant, and he's always very friendly. Occasionally, someone from Rupert's office rings me about a property of theirs, like their site at Wapping, and I try to give them the best advice.

Terry Semel, chairman and CEO of Yahoo, also has a small piece. He always struck me as being very pleasant, but I don't know him well.

There are about 10 per cent of the shares floating in the market. The restructuring reduced my shareholding from 100 per cent to just 5 per cent. Other entrepreneurs might have gone out and shot themselves, but at that point money wasn't my motivating factor.

Because all of my shareholders are seriously rich and their interest in Heron is tiny in relation to their personal wealth, they don't pay a lot of attention to us. They get invited to the annual meeting and sometimes they come. They let me get on with running the company. And I must be doing something right, because in 2007 we paid our shareholders an £80 million dividend. At that point, I said to each of them, 'If you want to sell, I'm interested in buying.'

Every one of them said, 'No.'

Not a single one of them bothered to ask, 'How much are you offering?'

* * *

My salary before the restructuring was in the £2 million to £3 million range. My initial deal with the Americans was a salary of about £500,000 plus a share of the profits, my pension plan, my expenses, etc. I could argue that, running this business today, I'm underpaid. But when I negotiated my contract, I didn't hold any aces, except perhaps that I knew how best to maximise the value of our assets. I renegotiated after five years and my salary stayed pretty much the same but my share of the profits increased. My compensation has gone up through other negotiations, but then so have the profits and so has the net worth of the company.

In addition to running the company, I invest alongside Heron, so when Heron puts £50 million into a deal, I will take up, say, 25 per cent of that through one of my private companies. Personally, I'm wealthy enough to afford everything I want. I'm not saying I can afford everything in the world, but I already have just about everything I really want. I'm not someone who shows off with art on the walls or homes all over the world. In fact, I don't have other homes, just the one we live in.

I'm not out to impress anybody with anything. There are few people who have been through what I've been through and come out the other side with their reputations intact. I've been around a long time, and, after what I've survived and after what I've created, I don't feel that I have anything to prove to anyone. I'm not saying that in an arrogant way or to be boastful. But the respect I have in business, the respect I have in the Community, these are things you can't buy. You have to earn them.

With hindsight, my deal with the Milkens wasn't very clever. I gave away too much. Most people would have thought first, what's in it for me? And if there's nothing in it for me, then why am I doing it? But I didn't. My Americans are smart and they understand me. They left me alone to get on with the business and supported me 100 per cent because they knew what was motivating me. It wasn't money. And it certainly wasn't ego. I knew that if we put the business into friendly hands, if we found partners who would support us – just like replanting a bulb in the ground and watering it and nurturing it – then I could rebuild the business and my reputation. That's really what I wanted to do.

Could I have negotiated myself a better deal? Yes. But I decided, first I have to prove what I can do. I am a great believer in this and it applies when I deal with people coming into the business. It's all well and good to say, gimme gimme gimme, but you're in a much stronger position when you're making money. At that point, you can ask for a bigger promote and more equity.

I enjoy doing what I'm doing, the Milkens know I like to do what I do, and they trust me completely. Maybe they also believe that Gerald Ronson's going to walk in the door one of these days with a multibillion-pound deal, and if I do, if I have that deal, they'll be there with me.

* * *

While all this was going on, I had to ask myself, what am I?

I'm not like Michael Milken, a financial visionary. I have developed an investment strategy and I have a focus in real estate, but both have become more simplistic as I've got older. I'm getting rid of baggage. I'm not interested in marginal schemes. I'm not a financial engineer, so I guess the best answer is, I'm a developer. That doesn't mean I can't see a good property investment deal when one comes along. But I've told myself that at this point in life, I'm only going to do things that I want to do, that I enjoy doing and that I do well. Otherwise, what's the point of doing it? I am a creator. I love getting down to the nitty-gritty in everything I build. At times, that irritates the professionals I work with. But that's what I do best and that's what I love doing, so that's what I do. Call me an owner-driver. Thankfully, my partners understand. I have no problem reporting to them and if they have anything to say, they can say it. But you can only have one captain on the bridge. And if the admiral wants to come on the bridge and bring three more captains with him, then what you're going to get is, shall we go north? North-east? Let's go south. South-west?

That's not my style. I don't rule by consensus. I'm prepared to put my head on the block and if I screw up, I'm prepared to put my hands up in the air. But I'm in charge. I don't think of myself as a hired hand and if anybody ever spoke to me as a hired hand, I would be out the door. That doesn't mean to say I'm not a good committee person, because I am good working with people. But at the end of the day, the buck stops at my desk. If I'm running the business and I fuck up, I say so. I don't go and hide. But then, to their credit, my Americans have always been good listeners. I kept saying, 'Stay alive till '95 so we go to heaven in '97.' When 1995 came along, after loads of property companies went bankrupt, the markets changed. Because we were clever or lucky enough to manoeuvre our way through the storm – maybe I should say clever and lucky enough, because you need a bit of both – we had money coming in and could buy undervalued properties.

Clever is good and lucky is good, but, at the same time, you have to keep learning, and I have learned a lot from my Americans. Do they want to win every time? Yes. Do they want to keep their options open on everything they do? The answer is also yes. But that's smart. Even though they are non-executives in the business, and even though I only see them once a quarter, I learn from them every time I see them. Over the years, I've learned to be much more conscious of risk and I've come to understand IRRs, which is the internal rate of return on the investment. It may sound strange and maybe I'm over-egging it for them, but working with Lowell Milken has made me a better businessman.

He'll read this and probably say, I never realised Gerald learned things from me. He might even say, I've also learned things from Gerald. The fact is, he's a very clever man who doesn't really have an ego. I respect him and I have grown to like him. He leaves me alone to manage the business, doesn't second-guess me and has never said no to anything I've put forward. I don't know many other chairmen who are smart enough to do that. It's quite a special relationship, built on trust and loyalty. And trust and loyalty is why I'll carry on. If they were irritating me, if they were second-guessing me, I'd say, fuck it, because I don't need it. But they have stayed loyal and I have delivered everything I ever promised them. Loyalty counts for a lot with me.

Before we reconstructed, I was running a lot of businesses. We had Suzuki, H.R. Owen, my property business, my house-building business Heron Homes and a logistics business, which was transportation. We had National Insurance and Guarantee Corporation, our petrol-retailing business, Media Home Entertainment and a leasing company. In those days, we were turning over £1.5 billion. So when you look at the money we lost – which I don't like talking about, because I lost something like $1 billion of my own money – in the end, they're just numbers. I don't take it lightly, but I don't lose sleep about it, either. All I can say is, I lost it, so I have to get back in the ring and make it again.

Which is what I've been doing. Gerald Ronson and Heron are synonymous and always will be because of what we've gone through in 50 years. I was never a one-hit Johnny. I built my company and my reputation brick by brick. Having done that once, when I lost it, I needed to do it again.

But I wouldn't want to do it again, because it gets harder each time. Having said that, since my partners have been in the business, we have made more than $1 billion.

CHAPTER 13

....

NO ONE EVER SAID IT WAS
GOING TO BE EASY

I am a man driven by success, and I am not ashamed to say that, because there is nothing wrong with making money.

There is nothing wrong with accumulating wealth. If you have money, you can acquire the good things in life, although everybody has their different views as to what they are. I have never been driven solely by money, and I do not think of myself as a greedy person. I knew what I wanted to do from the beginning, which was to prove to my father that I was everything he expected of me, that I could do what he could do and maybe even do it better.

One of the things I appreciate about money, especially having a lot of it, is that it gives me the opportunity to do good things, to help other people, to make a difference, to be charitable. That's very important to me.

Now, there are some people who believe that for a businessman money is the way you keep score. But those are often people who are not in business or do not have any money, because it's not as simple as all that. Money is definitely one factor, but it is not the only factor. You find people in this world who have made a lot of money, have shown themselves to be very caring and very charitable and, in my opinion, those are good people. Then, you find people in this world who have made a lot of money and become total arseholes. Money brings a certain power and in their case power goes straight to their head. They're arrogant and think that just because they're worth a lot of money they're better or more important than everyone else. In many of those instances, with power comes corruption.

Compare them to the many people in this world who are successful in what they do but never get rich. For some of those people, success is measured by fame. Or it's measured by recognition of achievement. Or it comes in the form of the satisfaction they receive from raising a family and giving their kids a better education than they had. You know, from starting their children out in life with more opportunities than they had. Or it's measured in the satisfaction that comes with doing a job really well. Look at all those people who work every day in professions that will never make them rich, like teachers and nurses, people who do very important jobs and get enormous satisfaction from what they do. That's a lot of success.

It is different when you're talking about entrepreneurs, because entrepreneurs are different. They are often single-minded, don't like criticism and have big egos. I happen to be single-minded, but I don't mind criticism and I try to keep my ego under control. Not all entrepreneurs do.

Donald Trump is probably a good example. I like him. His persona is totally different from what comes over on the television, at least I've found that to be the case. He's easy to talk to. Donald created the Trump brand and is a great promoter, a great salesman. He may say he's in the property business, but he's really running a branding company. Somebody else takes the risk. Somebody else does the development. Donald just takes an 8 per cent promote off the top of the sale. It's very clever if you can do it. But I think he's oversold it, because he's letting every Tom, Dick and Harry in Miami and everywhere else sell the brand.

That's not what we're about. We had a meeting with Donald to look at a big residential scheme in London. But we decided that he wouldn't be bringing anything to the table because, with all due respect, the name Trump doesn't have the same clout in London. It's the Heron brand that signifies the quality of the product and adds value to it.

Just as Donald brags about the deals he's done, I am very proud of some of the big deals I have done. And it's the nature of the beast that entrepreneurs judge business deals by how much money they've made. When two entrepreneurs get together, they compare deals, and if one has made more on his deals than the other, then he can say he won. He's got bragging rights. That's especially true if he started with very little. For entrepreneurs who came from nowhere with nothing more than the motivation to create something and the guts to risk everything simply to develop their ideas, bragging rights matter. Now take that a few steps further and look at Henry Ford with his motor car, Edwin Land with his Polaroid camera and Bill Gates with his software. For men like that, it's not just about the money they've made, it's also about how they've changed the world.

Unfortunately, we live in a world today where entrepreneurs and the entrepreneurial spirit are rarer commodities than years ago. I still think

America is the country which generates the greatest entrepreneurs because of its capitalism. There's an old story about the father and son in Britain and the father and son in America, who all see a Rolls-Royce drive by. The father in Britain says to his son, 'Look at that pompous rich bastard. Screw him!' The father in America says to his son, 'If you work hard, some day you can have a car like that, too.'

That's the real difference between America and Britain. America doesn't look down its nose at people who are motivated by success and who are accumulating wealth by trying to make their ideas work. They look up to people who can get rich through hard work and talent. If you're successful in America, the buck is the measurement of your success and money is often what determines how people regard you in that society. And that motivates others to become successful, too. It's not right or wrong, it's just how it is.

* * *

People bring me deals all the time. I probably get offered three or four deals a day. They come through the post or they come in by phone. I give every deal a quick screening test and know right away if any of them are sensible. That's because I have experience and know the country very well. You could ring me up and talk about a property in Grainger Street, Newcastle, or in Atherton or Bolton, and I would know approximately where it is and what it is. You wouldn't have to send me plans, because I could tell you on the phone, yes, I might be interested, or, as is the case 99 times out of 100, thanks but no thanks.

Obviously, I am very particular about the deals we do. I'm a very cautious person and definitely not a gambler. I don't feel like I have anything to prove to anyone, and if that means I do a few less deals because they're marginal, because you need to be a gambler to push out the barriers, then I'll do a few less deals. Do I really want to do 50 deals around the world? No. Do I really want to jump on a plane every day of the week and go to a different place? No. I go to Spain once every month, I go to Stockholm once every two months and I go to France every couple of months because I own assets in those countries, they're valuable and I want to make sure they're being managed properly. Do I want to jump on a plane to do deals in Moscow, Nigeria, Singapore or Beijing? No. I'm past that stage in my life.

I'm not in the business of buying vanilla properties. We're not an institution looking to buy investment assets to fill up a tank. There are plenty of people who can and do make money in property trading, but

I'm not into that. It's not that I mind making a profit out of dealing that way, it's that I'm not an in-and-out flip merchant, because that's a different business. I'm a professional developer. I'm looking for opportunities where we can use our expertise to bring added value. That's key. Because if I can't bring added value to a project, then I'm not interested. I'm not in the 6 to 8 per cent IRR business. I'm in the business of making a minimum return on our equity of 15 per cent. If it's a speculative development, I really want to see 18 to 20 per cent. After assessing the deal itself, and then after assessing the risks, if I can't see that kind of return, I say no. I don't see why we should risk our shareholders' money doing schemes where we are not making that return for the aggravation.

My philosophy is, if I can't produce a premium where I'm going to bring added value, then there's no point in doing the deal. This isn't the way every developer thinks, because not every developer is running a premium business. If he's a public company, as long as his shareholders are getting their 6 to 7 per cent, then he's produced income for them to hedge against inflation and they're probably happy. That's what a big public property company is really all about. But that's not my business. I'm in the property business to make money out of property, which means I have to be opportunistic. We're no longer living in times where low interest, easy money, drives the business. The days of dumb banks lending 95 per cent and 100 per cent on assets are history. If you have no money, forget it. Banks aren't going to lend more than 75 per cent on a prime leased property. You can't get development finance for speculative projects. It will come back four or five years down the road, but it isn't there these days. And a whole raft of people are out of business today.

Heron is different because we have cash and we can afford to fund, say, £250 million a year of new business on a consistent basis. The problem is in finding schemes in the UK that we want to do, because I'm not interested in putting up buildings in New York. I could do that if I wanted to, but I don't. I'd have to add enormous exposure to the company, I don't have the people who can manage all that and it wouldn't have the touch and the feel in the end product.

* * *

Early on in my career, I realised that if you're developing commercial property, the only difference between putting up an office building and redeveloping an entire town centre is the size of the headache. We've done a number of them and our two most successful ones were Cardiff back in the late '70s and Sunderland in the '80s.

The secret of developing a town centre is working with the local authority. That means working with politicians and bureaucrats, most of whom know nothing about property development but insist on telling you that they do, every step along the way. The thing is, you need to get them on side for all sorts of reasons. First, they are most likely to come into the deal as your development partner. If that's the case, they have already compulsorily acquired all the properties and they just hand them over to you. They retain the freehold and you won't make the same margins of profit. These days, that seems to be the only way. If you try to piece it all together yourself so that you wind up owning the freeholds, that's an unbelievably painful route. You also need them on side to grant planning permission and help put in place what are called anchor tenants. Those are the big-name retailers – Marks & Spencer, House of Fraser, etc. – that you need to join in the project so that you can then attract other tenants.

Just to put all this together, you're talking about most probably ten years. Building can then take another three or four. You then need to hold on to the properties until the first review in order to get the uplift. The rents after the fifth year are subject to an upwards review only.

Town centres are great to own as a hedge against inflation, but today they're so complicated and so expensive that you really need to be an institution. Planning permission can be particularly difficult, because as soon as you put your plans on the table, people come out of the woodwork to tell you why they're unacceptable. They use every excuse they can think of to stop you. The plan is going to create traffic problems, it's going to create environmental problems, it's going to create this problem and that problem, and it just goes on and on. All these shops will put some corner store five miles away out of business. People always look at the negatives and tell you the glass is half empty.

Anybody who wants to push the boundaries is going to get a lot of criticism, because people don't like boundaries being pushed. Look at all the objections that came in when George Walker – the ex-boxer – and his partners announced in the early 1970s that they wanted to build Brent Cross, which was the first major shopping centre in the country. It's a great development, but people felt threatened by it. None of their predictions of doom and gloom came true, but because people like to feel safe, they objected to everything George and his partners wanted to do.

It's different in America, where they have enormous amounts of land. But here we don't have the space, so when you're tearing down a town centre, it affects all the small traders, the traffic flows, the bus station, etc. And the objections come piling in. You have to fight transportation issues and car-parking issues. You affect the livelihood of small traders and that becomes political. It doesn't matter that you're buying them out, that you're paying them a lot of compensation. They still object. And on every town council you have to deal with at least three different political parties – Labour, the Conservatives and the Lib Dems – not to mention some independents, who all take different views. So everybody's battling and everybody wants to prove something, and you come along as a London developer and you can count the people on your side on one hand.

That's what we found when we came in to develop Cardiff town centre. The Welsh don't like the English and they like people from London even less, so we were seen as cocky, arrogant and greedy. It took a lot of patience and persistence to change that misconception. This was 1974, and there was only one man who would even consider financing the Cardiff scheme, a bright, capable man named Hugh Jenkins. He is a Welshman who headed up the Coal Board Pension Fund. In those days, the Coal Board was predominantly Welsh, because the mines were in Wales.

I told him I was prepared to develop the town centre, but that it was going to cost £10 million. They financed it. I then had to add a million pounds in 'hurt money', which we would get back as soon as the scheme was completed.

To make the development work, I had to send my property director, Tony Royle, down to Cardiff every week. He was virtually living with the councillors, the planners and the town clerk, waist-deep in all the local politics for years. On top of that, the builder went bankrupt three-quarters of the way through. That company had been owned by Charles Clore. Off their own bat, they brought in McAlpine's to finish building, which added £5 million to the original cost. But they were totally honourable and picked up that bill. That's rare in the property business.

We opened the town centre with Prince Charles, and some time later they gave me the Freedom of the City. They had a dinner in my honour at the castle in Cardiff, where all the good and the great attended. They said they were honouring me for giving them the best shopping centre in the UK. At the time, it was valued at £30 million, which was a lot of money. I eventually sold it back to the Coal Board for a little more than that, making a very good profit. They subsequently did a swap on some properties with Land Securities. They extended it by 50 per cent, and I presented the city with a Steinway grand piano for the concert hall. It cost me £25,000 at the time. You can imagine what it must be worth today. The centre itself is most probably worth more than £100 million.

The development of Sunderland's town centre was equally successful but considerably more painful. My affection for the city went back to the days of that early trip with my dad and Ernie, so when I heard that the Post Office Pension Fund was selling property there, I bought it. Nobody in London was interested because Sunderland seemed too far away, but I knew the city and also knew that Nissan had built a big plant there and was very satisfied with the results. I thought other companies might follow suit, so I jumped in the car, drove up there and bought these properties for £11 million. When the city elders asked me why I had gone to the trouble, I told them the story of how Dad and I first came to Sunderland with Ernie Boyer all those years ago.

The market at the time was in the toilet and the town-centre shopping precinct was tired-looking. There wasn't a lot you could actually do with it, because you had a bus station coming right into the centre. It was also a very messy and complicated deal, because the freehold was owned by Sunderland City Council and they'd built a couple of hundred apartments on top of the shopping centre. There were structural issues, right-of-way issues and services issues. You had one lease for the ground floor but then you had a whole different set of lease-back agreements to the council for the roof level upwards. We also had to keep all the tenants happy while we did the work, which basically meant we kept filling them up with enough brown ale. That didn't run into millions of pounds, but it did run into a few hundred thousand.

We modernised Sunderland town centre and turned it into something really good. It may have taken four years to develop, and I think I kept those properties for nearly ten years. They earned plenty of money in the holding period, showing me most probably 11 per cent while I was borrowing money at around 6 per cent. So there was a 5 per cent spread on the interest in the carry period. I would never have sold those properties, except it was a point in my life when we needed the cash.

I sold the town centre for £38.5 million to the late Peter Hunt, chief executive of Land Securities, on a handshake over lunch. He said he wanted to buy it, we settled on a price and shook hands. When he took the deal back to his people and they saw how complicated this was, they wanted out, but Peter said, 'I agreed the deal with Gerald Ronson, and that's it.' He kept his word like the gentleman he was.

It was the last town centre we developed in the UK. I am, however, building a large centre in Lille, France. It took us almost nine years from when we first bought the site to go through all the aggravation of two mayors, two councils – because Lille and Villeneuve d'Ascq are right next to one another and they're competing economically – two local planning authorities, two different political parties, both of which are socialistic in nature, two economic councils, the regional planning, objectors from everywhere, the construction licence authority, the economic authority, and authorities I never knew existed anywhere else in the world.

Why anybody would want to build today in France, I do not know. Most of the companies we had to deal with are semi-government, institutional organisations, and consents take a lifetime. The trick is you should live that long. Making life more complicated, I don't speak French and 90 per cent of the people I had to deal with, people I had to get into serious negotiations with, didn't speak English. It was a nightmare.

If that wasn't difficult enough, I had to sit on a site for 20 million euros for all that time and finance it, because the banks kept saying to me, you don't have planning permission. Why would I sit on it? Because I am a persistent, determined developer and when I see the opportunity to create something on a great site, I can see what it will look like in my head and I stick with it.

During that time, the scheme only became better, because the location is 100 per cent. It's a very high-profile 20-acre site, which we could pre-let. Once everything was in place, we found we could move quite quickly – 18 months to build it – because the French are efficient builders. But, as I said, just to get to the point of actually putting a shovel in the ground took nine years. That was very painful and, frankly, put an end to my developing town centres. Too many things can come out of the woodwork and bite you. You get to the point where you say, why does anybody want to develop anything? You're fighting everybody and every little arsehole has an opinion. I don't want any more nightmares. That's not unreasonable is it?

* * *

I look at deals differently today than I did when I was younger. When I was in my 30s and 40s, I was only concerned with how much money I was going to make. I'd look at a deal and decide whether or not I was going to do it based on the upside. Today, with the benefit of age and experience, I look at a deal and ask, how much can I lose? I decide whether or not I'm going to do it based on the downside. That probably comes as a surprise to people who don't know the property business – and I'm predominately talking about property development – because so many people equate property with making money.

There are a lot of sites in London that were great buildings when they were built but they're looking tired today. Technology and design have moved on and tenants' requirements have changed. In my view, the life of an office building is no more than probably 20 to 30 years. Whereas before, maybe 20 to 30 years ago, the life of an office building was 100 years and you could convert the building and modernise it. Given technology today, it's not easy to have a building that measures up. If you look at the Empire State Building in New York, it was completed in 1931 and in those days only took about 18 months to build.

Yes, I understand that in England you can't do what they do in the Far East and throw people at it, building twenty-four hours a day, seven days a week. That makes a difference, Here you're only building eight hours a day for five days a week. Because there are so many people who have an input into your plans – like Health and Safety and environmentalists – it takes much longer. And those requirements keep changing. Some of the buildings we did five years ago don't meet the new standards imposed today. Which is why I see office buildings that were put up 20 years ago about to go obsolete. When the 21- or 25-year leases come to an end, those buildings will be rebuilt. They may keep the façades, depending on the planning, because we don't want everything to look like a glass box. But where everything else in the world is going to be recycled, these buildings won't be.

It's very much like the automobile industry. If your car was doing 20 miles to the gallon 10 years ago, that was great. But today, with half the cars on the road running on diesel, you might be dissatisfied if you're only getting 40 or 45 miles per gallon.

Ten years ago, if you moved into prime office space, you might have wanted columns and gigantic floor plates. Today, people want fewer columns, a more environmentally pleasant floor space and faster lifts.

Nothing stands still. You can't be designing things the way you did ten years ago. You design now for the next ten years. But no matter what you do, you can't please everybody. We built 80 Queen Victoria Street in the City, and that building has a green copper façade. It won an Architectural Institute award for the best building that year in the City. It's a good building, even though it cost more than it needed to because of the façade. Half the people who look at it think it's wonderful and the other half think it's awful.

In the end, the best we can do is build quality. We're purists. I know that sounds arrogant, but I want to put the best architecture on the site. I refuse to be associated with second-rate buildings. It's not what we're about at Heron.

Again, without wanting to sound arrogant, because we rate ourselves among the best in the industry, we have to live up to that. We can't get complacent. We have to keep pushing and that requires focus and commitment. Nothing just happens. You have to make it happen. It gets back to passion and focus in what you do.

No one ever said it was going to be easy. And if the people working for me don't share my passion and focus, then they don't work for me for very long. I'm on the job 12 hours a day, my people are on the job 12 hours a day and when I'm paying millions of pounds to professionals, I expect them to do their job. I will accept an excuse once. When I hear it a second time, goodbye. End of story. I recently sacked two major firms on two jobs because I'd had enough. I sat in at meetings, listening to their second-rate people who hadn't done their homework properly and hadn't done their job, even though I was paying them millions in fees – I sacked them because I'm not prepared to listen to excuses.

You may say that that's ruthless. But that's how it has to be. Heron are not easy people to deal with because we do not sit back and take no for an answer. Nor are we prepared to accept second-rate service. We are demanding. But we are good payers and we pay on time, and when you pay good money, you have the right to expect good service. It's just that simple.

If something needs to be done and someone can't do it, all they have to do is put their hands up and say so, and if they need help to get it done, I'll see they get that help. I don't like surprises. If there are problems, I want people to tell me up front and I'll help them solve the problem. I don't expect things to be wrong. I want them dealt with. I won't accept lies. And I won't accept cover-ups. It's the last thing anyone should ever try with me. When things go wrong, I blow up. And when I do, you're facing two smoking barrels. It's not a pleasant experience. But then once I have it off my chest, I don't harbour it. For me, ten minutes later it's forgotten. But the people I get angry at don't forget it, and, hopefully, they won't make that mistake again. I'm not tough because I have nothing better to do. I tell people how I want things done because I know what I'm doing. And if I don't know what I'm doing after 50 years, then forget it.

My focus today is London and Madrid, where I only want to do prime projects. Is that my ego talking? No. I've just reached a point in my career where I don't have to dance at every wedding.

I have £2 billion worth of projects in the pipeline. That will take us to 2014 to finish. At that point, I'll be 75. I'm also looking at opportunities that could take me to 2019, at which point I'll be 80. Please God, if I'm still alive. Whether I'll still have the same enthusiasm at that age, I don't know. I'm sure I won't have the same energy. But I have a very capable management team and hopefully they'll be even more capable by then and they can get on and do it, and maybe I will spend a bit more time on a boat. In the meantime, what we have in Sweden, Spain and France is let and income-producing. These are prime assets and not giving us any sweat. It's just that they're a bit further away than the Marylebone Road.

CHAPTER 14

....

FIRST AND FOREMOST, I AM A PROPERTY MAN

To many people, a building is just a building. Not me. I came out of the old school, where great property developers were always great property enthusiasts.

Passion really does matter. I love getting into the detail, taking a job apart then putting it together. There is nothing I can't do in my business. I can value a property, even though I'm not an accredited valuer. I can build, develop, buy and sell. I couldn't write a lease, because I'm not a lawyer, but I know when I read a lease what the lawyer might have left out. I can't write up a set of accounts, because I'm not an accountant, but I can read them and I know whether they're right or wrong. I'm a jack of all trades, an all-rounder, an enthusiast who can discuss anything and everything about property with anyone.

Property is what I know, what I'm good at. And it's important to know what you're good at, to know what you can and can't do. It's easy to look back after you've tried to do something and know the answer. The difficult thing is to know before you do it. I know I am good at delegating to people I trust, which in my organisation is probably half a dozen. But I don't suffer fools, so if someone comes into a meeting just to occupy a seat, he obviously didn't spot the 'Beware' sign on the door. He will, I assure you, see it fast on his way out.

I also know what I'm not good at, which is a whole long list of things. I'm not good at things I don't understand and I won't sit around bluffing someone into thinking that I do understand, because that's not me. When I don't know, I raise my hands and say, I don't know. But if I don't know and I'm also not interested, then I don't see any purpose getting involved. I can't be hypocritical. I won't go along with things that I don't believe in. I wouldn't make a politician. I'm not good at standing up and making speeches, and anyway I have no desire to be a politician. But I would make a good benevolent dictator.

I see myself as passionate. Others see me as a control freak. But that's not a problem for me. How much of a control freak you have to be if you want to be successful depends on who you talk to. When people say, Gerald Ronson is controlling, I won't disagree. When you are building major projects, somebody has to lead the team. Somebody has to be able to cut through all the bullshit that comes at you every day from agents, planners, builders, suppliers and everyone else you wind up having to deal with. Somebody has to separate fact from fiction in order to maximise what you can actually do with a site. Otherwise, the product can cost you many millions more than necessary.

Money gets wasted in various ways and at various times, especially if you have inflation running over the market. But even in good times, a multitude of mistakes means you're throwing money out the window. You have to control the job properly from day one. That may make me look tough in the eyes of the people who have to run the job, but those opinions don't bother me. A whole bunch of professionals, from planners to contractors to architects, need to earn their money, but they all also need watching. You hire a good firm, but however good the brand is, it's only as good as the man doing the job for you. So the key is to hire the best people, not the brand name over the door. You should also have chemistry with those professionals, especially the architect who is translating what you want to achieve.

It's business. But it's also personal. Unfortunately, my sort of property development is a dying art. After all, there's not a lot of it happening and there aren't a lot of people doing it. The biggest players in the game today are institutions. But institutions don't build great buildings. With institutions, everything is forced through a long, laborious process, and when it finally comes out the other end, the lack of passion shows. Development by committee winds up looking exactly like a development by committee.

Institutions lack imagination. They are primarily interested in producing good dividends for their shareholders, plus a little growth. They can be content with a 5½ to 6 per cent yield. If they wind up getting 6½ to 7 per cent – which means a lot when you're investing £200 million to £300 million – they're really happy. They're not aggressively looking to make a 12 to 15 per cent return on cash, because that's not where they're at. They want to keep their shareholders happy, and if shareholders are beating inflation by a few points, then everyone is pleased. But that's not what we do.

We're looking to make bigger margins through added value and our expertise. We're looking to create iconic buildings, which means you need to make it personal. Great buildings will only be produced by very professional property developers, people who know their business inside out, who understand what they're doing, are creative and working with the best people. Being able to put that together comes with experience. That's one of the big differences between a Premier League developer and those in the lower divisions. The lower-division guys find an investor, hire an architect and then hand the scheme off to some schmuck in the office to look after. They don't have the experience. They don't really know what they're doing. They don't have the passion to make something truly great.

Passion alone isn't enough. You need to think outside the box, to be your own man, to be motivated and focused. A bit of insecurity helps, so that you're always making sure that you have it right. If you have a real passion for your business, know everything about it, eliminate all the bullshit at the front end and spend 24 hours a day keeping it out, then you might succeed.

You can always sell someone a dream, but property is the business of selling reality. The devil is always in the detail. It's about things that most people would find boring – floor heights, finishes, the entrance hall, columns, floor plates, lights. For many people, property is like a car. They don't know how it's made, don't even care how it's made as long as it has four wheels, a roof, seats, the engine starts and away they go. But if you're buying a Ferrari or Porsche, the minute you sit behind the wheel you know it's been built by people who are enthusiasts, people who are concerned with every inch of that great car. When enthusiasts build something, you can feel the difference.

I'm not developing back-office commodity space, I'm building a shop window for a company. It has to reflect the business. It has to be top quality. It's important that everyone who walks into the building says, wow! If it doesn't create that response, why would a major company pay £75 per foot to go there when plenty of office space rents for less? Some developers leave details to their architect. And if all you want is a half-decent office block on the fringe of the M25, you can let your architect get on with it. But a major development is different. What does an architect really know about the tenant who is going to occupy that sort of building? It sounds elementary, but I am often astonished how simple things that make a product special get delegated to people who don't understand what the product is. If you don't put your passion, your heart and soul, into what you're creating, you are never going to create anything memorable.

If you don't deal with the details, you're like someone who designs a car but doesn't drive.

Staying power is also vital, because property is a long-term business. It can take three years to get a project off the ground, then three more years to build it, so you may be looking at six years before you even start making any return on your investment. You can start a major project when the economy's good only to finish at a time when it's bad, and you wind up making no money. No one can be sure what the economy will be like in six months, so how can anyone project six years out? Even if you've got that great location, you could be sitting there with an empty building. Yes, in the long term, the best property will sell. But not everybody can hold on long enough to get the right price.

You need financial muscle to hold on to your project through the good times and bad times, and if you're a public company, that can be a problem. The market is always looking at your share price, looking at what your property values are, and based on those factors, marking your shares up or down. It's different for a privately held business like Heron because, as long as we're making a positive cash flow, we're building long-term capital appreciation for our balance sheet. Some years it grows more than other years. Some years it might not grow at all. But you have to be able to hold on for as long as it takes.

Six years is pretty much the average commercial property. If you're talking about a town-centre development or an iconic building, it can take ten to fourteen years from the initial site acquisition to the arrival of the first tenant. That includes the planning process, which has become truly painful over the years. Planning is one reason why you really have to focus on what you do and where you do it. If you're building in London, you need a good working relationship with the mayor's office, the Greater London Authority, the City of Westminster, various planners and a lot of other people. You have to know them and they have to know that you have integrity – where integrity really means integrity – to deliver the product you're promising.

Someone told me once that at the Harvard School of Business they tell students, if you want to build a business, you're in the right place, but if you just want to get rich, go into real estate. Listening to that, it sounds easy. But most people who come into real estate to get rich get it wrong. They want to buy something today, sell it tomorrow and make their million. Except that's not how the property business works any more. The biggest issue is timing. If you get that wrong, you're going broke. And then, it's not the size of the business which counts, it's the quality of the assets. If you own quality assets, there is strength from the cash flow of the assets and you can get out of trouble even if the market falls on its face. You can always refinance quality assets. It's only a question of what rate you must pay for the money. But if you don't have quality, if all you have is second-rate property, when the market falls – and markets do that – then you're as good as dead. That's what happened in the 1980s and the 1990s, and that's what happened again in 2008, which is why we stopped buying properties in 2006–7. The IRR we were looking to make wasn't there any more.

No matter what, you cannot time the markets. But if you look closely, you can see what they're doing. In 2006–7, it should have been obvious to anyone who knew what to look for that the property business was getting too frothy. It was at its peak and I couldn't see how it could go on. It had to end in tears. All those new kids on the block were jumping into the business, but they didn't have the knowledge and experience to play at that level, which is why they were buyers and we were sellers.

Did we make money because our timing was good? No, it was because we saw people paying prices for things where we couldn't see value. Then, suddenly, in 2008, the world changed. Banks stopped lending, which put pressure on developers building on spec. At the same time, building costs continued to increase. Commodities like steel, aluminium and wood became much more expensive. If building costs increase around 6 per cent per annum, by 2011 that compounds to more than 20 per cent.

I have always believed that cash is king, and I was proved right again this time. When money dried up and banks tidied up on their property lending, a lot of people who borrowed money on property missed out on that little clause in the middle of the contract that said the bank will look at an annual valuation and on that basis borrowers will either have to put in more equity or become forced sellers of the property. Opportunities fell off the back of the truck, so if you were sitting around with cash, there were plenty of good chances to buy with the yields and returns we are looking for. It takes patience, but over the years I've learned how to become a patient man. I'm never unhappy sitting on a pile of cash.

It's funny, but when I have a lot of cash, I don't want to spend it as fast as I might if I didn't have it and had to find the money for every deal I looked at. For me, cash in the bank means I don't have to jump on every bus coming down the street.

Still, despite the frustrations and the aggravation and the bloody noses you get every time you step into this ring, development is the most interesting side of the business. But that's me. The reality of development is that it's tough. Over the longer term, most people drop out because they go bust, or because they almost go bust, or because they realise it's easier to operate as a property investor/trader. There are very few who stay in this game for a lifetime. And I can't really blame them.

Believe me, there are many easier ways to make money.

* * *

Heron was created in 1957 with £150,000 capital realised from the sale of the furniture factory at Harold Hill. Fifteen years later, we were one of the largest privately held companies in Britain and the first British developer audacious enough to head for France. It was 1972, and we launched our invasion of Europe on the most fashionable street in Paris, the Rue de la Paix.

Going into France when we did was, in one sense, like what's happening today with everybody going to Eastern Europe. It's a foreign country, you have to learn from your experiences and those experiences can be painful. On the other hand, going to Paris wasn't like going to Budapest or Bulgaria because France was a mature market and Eastern Europe is still a corrupt place. Some of the countries there are still dangerous to do business in. I've never been hungry enough to put up with that much aggravation. I could always find enough in the UK.

In those days, I knew a young estate agent about my own age called James Croft, who worked for Richard Ellis. Today, Richard Ellis is one of the largest real-estate brokers in the UK and James became one of its senior partners. He was a hard-working, ambitious young man making his way in the world and particularly knowledgeable about Paris. One day back in the 1960s, he told me about a property on the Rue de la Paix. A very upmarket street leading from the Place de l'Opéra to the Place Vendôme, this was the Bond Street of Paris and certainly not a place where you'd expect a London developer to muscle in.

The building itself, 10 Rue de la Paix, had an interesting and colourful history. It had been occupied by the Caron perfume company. Before that it was a motor-car showroom, the Paris headquarters of the champagne company G.H. Mumm and the town house of the Bugatti family. I saw the possibility of turning it into an eight-storey commercial office building, with six levels below ground that could park two hundred cars. But I had to battle for planning consent. It cost £2 million to build, and that was a big number back then. It's a good-looking building, we let it very successfully to a bank and, believe it or not, we still own it. Not only was this the first ever British development in Paris, it was one of the first new developments in the commercial centre of Paris for 50 years.

Later that same year, we announced that we would build another office block in Paris, this time in the Avenue George V. We followed that with a massive development in Montparnasse, which comprised a 1,000-bed hotel, an apartment block, shops, leisure centres and parking for some 3,000 cars. We did it in cooperation with GUS Universal Stores, and it was the largest ever development to be undertaken by a British firm in France. I also built a very big scheme on the Champs-Elysées. For that one, I even received a medal from Monsieur Chirac and the city of Paris. We sold the building for a lot of money but didn't make any profit because a complicated tax structure took away all the profit. Talk about learning a lesson. It was a very expensive medal.

From France, we moved into Switzerland, Belgium, Spain, Portugal and Germany. But developing property in a foreign country is something you do only if you have a lot of experience, because the learning curve is very painful and expensive.

Going into Europe eventually paid off handsomely, but we had a lot to learn and we made many mistakes. We sometimes paid more than we should have paid, spent more on construction than we need have done and we didn't always structure deals as intelligently as was possible. Everything we did in Europe, and everything we do now, is based on two simple principles. First, we only buy the best-quality properties. And second, we work the ground ourselves. The reason this formula works is obvious. Quality will, eventually, win the day.

The thing is, you simply cannot delegate. You have to see for yourself. And whenever my mind turns to the necessity of building up first-hand knowledge, my thoughts turn to Archie Sherman, dead these many years but in his lifetime probably the greatest expert on shop property in the United Kingdom. I met him for the first time maybe 45 years ago, and he gave me some very good advice. He said, 'I know every single high street in the country, and I know every single shop in that high street.' I have worn out a lot of shoe leather in 55 years.

My two favourite places to work are the UK and Spain. I've been in Spain 35 years and find Spain very English-friendly. They've always been friendly with the British, more so than the French or Italians. I get on better with the Spanish than anybody else in Europe. I like them, they're people I can do business with, I've done very good business in Spain, I still do very good business in Spain. I understand the market and the people. I like Madrid, Barcelona and Valencia. So that is my number one continental country, and I spend two days there every month to do business. In 2009, the King of Spain and the Spanish government officially recognised my dedication to the country and awarded me the Spanish Order of Civil Merit, their equivalent of a knighthood. I am humbled by the honour. But my main place to do business is the UK.

A lot of developers and investors see bargains in Eastern Europe. But you not only have to be there yourself once a week or once a fortnight, you need very good people on the ground. People you can trust to know what they're doing. Because this is an away game and the rules can get changed when you're not looking. You also have to be prepared to pay a big price for the privilege of playing that game.

I have paid those prices in France, Spain, Portugal, Germany, Italy, Belgium, Ireland, the States and Scandinavia, and those countries are a far sight better than anything you're going to find in Eastern Europe. The countries there are much too volatile, too high risk. Sure, there are some people who say they have made a lot of money there, but I suspect the only ones making a lot of money there are the locals who get planning on a site and then flip it to the foreigner. I'm not saying that those people who are developing in some of these places aren't going to make money, but it's not what I'm looking to do. I don't want to go to Eastern Europe. I don't wish to go to Russia or the Far East. I have nothing to prove to anyone. I also have the luxury of doing business where I want to. If I'm going to take risks, I'll take them in London, not in some godforsaken place where I don't speak the language, don't know the rules of the game and probably wouldn't be allowed to play by the rules even if I knew them.

A few years ago, I turned down a big development deal in the former USSR. I said no because I knew I'd have to go through a painful learning curve. I couldn't be as good as I am or as clever as I want to be because there is no real property law in these countries. And there is corruption. I knew I would have to deal with people who appear to be very respectable on the surface but are otherwise corrupt, maybe even gangsters.

Most of those people who go abroad because they think it's all very easy come a cropper pretty fast. There's been a boom of people going into Eastern Europe looking for easy money. The banks that opened offices in these places were prepared to lend 90 per cent and in some cases 100 per cent. It looked easy. That is, until they found themselves in the middle of the jungle and they discovered, the hard way, that there are a lot of unpleasant things hiding around every corner.

When you want your consents, when you need your services, whether it be gas, water, electricity, drainage or access roads, the locals hold your life to ransom or blackmail you. Law and order in these places is not the same as British law and order. It's much too messy. I've had too many of these aggravations and those are not experiences I wish to repeat. Call me an old cynic. Perhaps in my younger days I would take chances and be, shall we say, a bit cavalier. Sometimes I made a lot of money, but other times cost me a lot. Forget that game. These days I focus on the markets that I know, because that's where I will make fewer mistakes and hopefully make money. Anything else is a gamble. Gambling is for the needy and greedy. And I am neither. I don't need to gamble, and certainly not with my shareholders' money.

* * *

During Heron's reconstruction, while we were looking at our core business – the development of prime office buildings in major city centres – we started to see patterns changing in the leisure market.

People were looking for an experience. They go out to the cinema or for food or shopping, they're looking for a destination. I kept that somewhere in the back of my mind, until an idea dawned on me when I visited Universal Studios in Los Angeles. I thought to myself, why not create a family entertainment and shopping experience for Europeans? Someplace where you could spend half the day with the family. The parents can do one thing while the children do something else and are safe and secure. I thought to myself, why not combine shopping, leisure and entertainment? And that was the beginning of Heron City.

It's a shopping mall unlike other shopping malls. There are retail stores, but there are also fitness centres, nightclubs, bowling alleys, family entertainment centres, cinemas, cafés and restaurants. It is an outdoor experience and predominantly a night-time business. That means weather is a factor, which means that the concept works best in the sunshine countries where Europeans like to go out in the evening.

It starts with a well-located site that's big enough for a lot of traffic. We estimated that a Heron City needs to have an immediate catchment area of 100,000 to 200,000 people. It needs easy access by road, good parking for 2,000 to 4,000 cars, good landscaping. Each site sits on 20 to 30 acres. You need lighting, because the property has to come alive at night, and water fountains similar to what you see at Las Vegas hotels. It also needs music and street theatre. My daughter Nicole used her television experience to help create something exciting, which we call 'brand experience'.

The first one we built was in Las Rozas, a wealthy suburb south of Madrid. It was successful from day one. Spain lent itself so well to these centres that we built two more, in Valencia and Barcelona, and bought a fourth one in Diversia, Madrid.

It took a lot of work in the early days to lease these properties, because the concept was unconventional. We had to bring on board a prime multiplex cinema operator. Our cinema in Valencia, for instance, has 8,500 seats and 24 screens and is the second-largest cinema in Spain. It pulls in 50,000 visitors a week. The centres are open from 10 a.m. until 2 a.m. and the clubs – like the one in Valencia called Guru, which is four clubs within one and has a capacity of 3,000 people – stay open all night until eight the next morning. Each centre has a Heron City identity – a very strong branding that Lisa and Nicole developed – and we market them on local radio and television. Our four Spanish centres entertain twenty million visitors per annum.

Each Heron City takes two to three years to put together and another five to mature. We do an enormous amount of work getting the concept right, and I don't think there's a major city or town in Europe we haven't visited with a Heron City in mind. But the problem was that from 1997 onwards, land all over the Continent was too overpriced to be profitable. In Italy and France, it wasn't just the price of the land, we couldn't get cinema consents and leisure consents, and local councils insisted we needed all sorts of economic licences. There are so many ifs and buts that it's almost impossible to get the viability to work.

We decided it's not something that would work in England, mainly because of the weather, but we did open a Heron City in Stockholm, which obviously doesn't have Mediterranean weather. We adapted it to Scandinavia. It's indoors, half retail and half leisure, and features slightly different outlets, like home furnishings.

There was a sixth centre, The Quay in Glasgow. It's also known as the Casino on the Clyde. It's not a Heron City, because Heron Cities don't have casinos in them, but here we had a pre-leasing and it's the largest casino in Glasgow. We built it, but we don't run the casino. That's leased to Harrah's. We have since sold the investment on a very good yield. I think we made a £20 million profit on the deal, which cost £60 million. It's not a property that we wanted to keep and hold.

In 2007, we also sold off the Heron City in Barcelona at a good profit, because it was the weakest of our centres and also one of the most aggravating to run.

We do our own management of the centres, which are complicated to run. It's important that the teams we have in place there do detailed inspections, keep the place immaculately clean, keep all systems operational, maintain the landscaping.

The product is unique. But I'm not surprised that nobody in Europe has copied it, because it is difficult to create and maintain. We've had approaches from people in India and Russia who would like us to build Heron Cities there. And in India you could have them outside, because it's hot. We could duplicate in Russia what we have in Stockholm. But I'm not interested in putting up businesses in those countries. It's difficult enough in Sweden, where the locals tend to be narrow-minded and a bit anti-American. It took us five years to turn Stockholm around. It's successful today, but it's been a painful road, and I wouldn't want to expose ourselves to even more aggravation going to Russia or India.

I would love to build ten more in Spain, but it's such a difficult job to build them. We're talking about one million square feet gross, and you have to pay for the land at market price. It's a great concept, but it's just too hard. So we have three Heron Cities in Spain and one in Stockholm. They are most probably worth £400 million. They're cash cows, and I don't visualise selling them.

* * *

Property in the 100 per cent best location will sell or lease even if the economy goes off the boil. And there are times when a development is so good that it creates its own location. Look at the World Trade Center in lower Manhattan. When the Twin Towers were built, that part of New York was not 100 per cent location. But they were so iconic that they created a prime location. It's when you start moving away from a 100 per cent location, or the product itself is not the best, that you run into trouble. At Heron, we're old-fashioned in that we like putting our own cash into a deal. Putting our money in gives us the right to look a banker in the eye and say, we want a better deal on the financing. I may tell him, we're not going to pay you 2 per cent over base, we're only going to pay you 1.25 per cent over. If you're a banker with a client who's put in 25 per cent of his own money, your risk is that much lower. It's why we don't have a problem borrowing money at times when the world seems upside down.

I try to make every deal as simple as possible, which isn't always easy, because we do complicated deals. Many of those deals are made all the more complicated by outside forces. Unlike some other commodities, property is a vital ingredient of the economy. If the capital markets dry up, you don't have availability of cash, which means you're not going to have an active property market. Look what happened in 2008. When you don't have an active property market, you don't have development. No development means no building trade, which means you wind up with unemployment. When you have unemployment, people don't buy houses and companies don't move into new office space. We try to control as much of a deal as we can, but we can't control the economy.

Often, when people think about property and real estate, they quote Mark Twain, who suggested that people should buy land because 'they're not making it any more'. But there is land and there is land. First, it depends on where it is. Then it depends on what you do with it. Having a shop in Bond Street or Oxford Street or Sloane Street in London is one thing – of course, it needs to be the right end of those streets – having a shop in a side street in Wolverhampton is another. Getting it right is never easy, and London has a lot of buildings that show what happens when you get it wrong.

Start with the Dome. It is an abortion that will always be remembered as what happens when you let politicians design things. I think the Government wasted £1 billion, but the whole thing could have been avoided. The Dome is down at the end of nowhere. You can't easily drive there, and you can't easily park there. Location? Forget it.

At one point, Sol Kerzner, who owns the Sun resorts and Paradise Island in the Bahamas, hoped to put a casino in there, but that didn't work out. At least in the early stages, we had the idea of turning it into a Heron City or a sports venue. But everything to do with the Dome got in a knicker twist and, looking back, I'm not sorry.

Centre Point, one of the first skyscrapers in London, is another good example. Built by Harry Hyams, it's a concrete and glass office building at the intersection of Tottenham Court Road and New Oxford Street, right above Tottenham Court Road Tube station. It's 32 storeys high but has small floor plates – only 4,500 to 5,000 square feet – and when it was built, in the mid-1960s, most tenants wanted larger floors.

Besides the fact that the design was considered bad and the location was crappy, Centre Point became highly controversial when Hyams decided he would only rent the place to one client. His price was £1.25 million. When he couldn't find any takers, he left it empty for many years. As it happens, with improvements in Tottenham Court Road and New Oxford Street, it's now better. New development is going on around it, like the Crossrail station that will be built at that end of Tottenham Court Road. So Centre Point will, eventually, be a 100 per cent location. It is already a listed building and regarded as iconic, but it's taken over 40 years to get there.

Then there is 30 St Mary Axe in the heart of the City of London, called the Swiss Re Tower, usually referred to as 'the Gherkin'. It was designed by Lord Foster for the Swiss Re insurance company. I'm not going to knock the design, because it's a matter of taste whether you like it or not. But as a commercial building, it's a disaster.

When it was just three-quarters finished, Swiss Re decided it was costing more money than it should, so they cut back on the internal finishes. Which is why when you go inside it's quite boring. You can see that they decided, we don't need to put marble on the walls, let's just paint and plaster it. That's typical of people who aren't property people. It has a low-level entrance hall, the common parts of the building are poor quality and because of the shape of it, they're losing 45 per cent of the space for circulation – lifts and stairwells and hallways – where normally the most you should lose is 25 per cent. That means instead of 75 per cent prime, useable space, the Gherkin is down to 55 per cent. That's the trade-off for the design.

Maybe it wouldn't have become a white elephant if Swiss Re had been the single owner-occupier. But the board of directors in Zurich didn't know enough about the business to control everything so that they would wind up with an economically sound, high-quality building. Which is exactly what they didn't get. In fact it took five years to fully lease.

The Football Association probably didn't do much better with the new Wembley. The cost and overruns have all been swept under the carpet. It's a great facility, but it should have been designed differently and could have been built for a lot less. If you look at the other 90,000-seat stadiums in the world, you see what works with them and what doesn't work with Wembley. Again, this is what happens when you have people, like the FA, taking charge when they don't know what they're doing.

By contrast, if you compare the new Wembley with Arsenal's new stadium, the Emirates, you see what can happen when someone knows what he's doing. The Emirates Stadium came in on budget and on time. That's because my friend, Danny Fiszman – who is one of the owners of Arsenal – put his heart and soul into the project. He was working there 15 hours a day. He started out knowing nothing about building a stadium, but was smart enough to learn.

* * *

Nine times out of ten, we build on spec, which means that we use our own money. If we need partners, we're not short of people who want to come along with us. But when you build on spec, it's all the more important that you know what you're doing and that you're doing it in 100 per cent prime locations. It's not a game for the faint-hearted.

Take central London. When you're dealing with a small area like the West End or the Square Mile of the City, you have to piece sites together. That means you can need six or seven ownerships in order to get a development going. That takes time, money and a lot of skill. That's the professional property business. And if you can manage that, then you're ahead. Building quality in the West End and the Square Mile gets you premium rent. Even when the market falls on its face, there are enough sophisticated buyers, both in the UK and overseas, who want to own property in locations like that, and if they have to pay another point on the yield, it's not going to make any difference. They're not high-leverage buyers. Property at that end of the market goes to buyers who hold it in their trust for 50 years or maybe even forever.

One of those big projects we're doing in the City of London is The Heron. An island site, it is the only residential development in the City. Making it unique, we're building a 10-storey, world-class facility for the Guildhall School of Music and Drama, with a 38-storey residential tower on top.

The school will include a 625-seat concert hall, a 230-seat theatre and a 110-seat studio theatre. There will be studios for television, radio and rehearsals, plus classrooms for teaching and office space for staff. Above the school, there will be a 'New York lifestyle' building, which is something we don't have over here. The apartments will be finished to West End standards, in addition to having a gym, cinema, a restaurant, roof gardens, club facilities, etc.

It's opposite the Barbican. That was designed in the 1950s and built in the 1960s, and is today a listed building. Which is interesting, because it's a mess of concrete that they can't pull down. The flats there are occupied by professionals who get a good deal out of the City of London, because some of their services are subsidised.

The Heron is a much better building in every way, so it won't be difficult to sell almost 300 apartments. What's more, it will be run like a hotel. There is nothing like it in the City. You find the concept in America. Why hasn't that happened here? Why haven't lots of things been done here? Because nobody wants to take the time, effort and trouble. It's a lot of extra work. Most big properties are built by institutions, not entrepreneurs. The way institutions think is why would you go to all the trouble of adding bells and whistles, when you can sell it anyway without them? They figure, why would we want to drive ourselves mad for X amount of money? The difference between them and me is that I'll put all the bells and whistles on and get X-plus-20 per cent.

We're looking to a niche in the market for business people, with penthouse apartments that are spectacular and would work as a home office. We're also looking for the commuter. There are 350,000 people who work in the City, and many of them have to travel in and travel out from a long way away. They come in for the week, go back to the country for the weekend and can afford a luxurious flat for four nights a week. Because The Heron will have some 130 car parking spaces, they can drive in on Monday, leave the car in the car park, and it's right there when they want to drive home on Friday.

There are also a lot of singles working in the City, especially women, who have to be in a place that's secure, user friendly and with high service facilities.

The site is the last one on that side of the City to be developed. The project went out to a limited tender, we were successful and we're building it in partnership with the City of London.

It will be a beautiful building that mixes the school's needs with those of people who will work and live there. When you cater to a vision, share it with all the authorities who have to approve it and still hold on to all your own ideals and standards of quality, that's when you're talking about a great project. It takes taste and the chequebook to afford it, and a refusal to delegate detail. Top quality does not come cheap. The more design you put into a product, the more it's going to cost. You also have to be able to separate egos from commercial common sense. You have to say, if I build the best, given the location, then I will get a premium to the market. How much that premium is, you never know in the beginning.

But quality will always win in the end.

If the City has never seen anything like The Heron, then Europe has never seen anything like what comes next – a building born out of passion that will change the City of London forever – Heron Tower.

CHAPTER 15

....

CHANGING THE CITY FOREVER

During the summer of 1999, a portfolio of prime properties came onto the market and an agent I've known for many years, Stephen Hubbard, brought it to us. Stephen is deputy chairman of CBRE, the largest real-estate brokers and chartered surveyors in the UK. We've worked together for a long time and I regard Stephen as one of the top advisers in the property business.

The portfolio consisted of seven sites, but there was one we did not want, so we negotiated that out of the deal and paid £208 million. I knew I was paying a premium and could have knocked the price back by £10 million to £15 million, but these were six very prime properties at just under an 8 per cent yield, and I was borrowing money at around 7 per cent, so we could comfortably do the deal. At the time, it was one of the largest deals in the investment market for a long time. Anyway, I had a very strong gut feeling that we could make a lot of money out of this deal, so once we agreed the price, we stuck to it.

The jewel in the crown was the island site on Bishopsgate, in the very heart of the City, just a three-minute walk from Liverpool Street railway station. I think something like 47 million people use Liverpool Street every year, which is more people than use London Heathrow Airport. You can't get a better location than that, and probably won't be able to for the next 100 years. What's more, we were buying at exactly the right time. The Corporation of the City of London and the London Mayor's office were talking about creating a zone where tall buildings would be permitted. This site fell directly into this zone.

At first glance, this looked like a typical opportunistic deal. After all, one of the classic ways you make money in property is to buy a parcel, pick the sites you want and sell off the rest. It's the same thing antique dealers do all the time. But this deal was a double whammy. It was a once in a lifetime chance to create an important tower building in the heart of the City.

To make that happen, we needed to do a lot of things at the same time. There were two old buildings on the site – Bishops House, a nine-storey office block built in 1976, and Kempson House, a fourteen-storey block put up in 1960 and occupied by the law firm Norton Rose. We also had to figure out what we were going to build there, get planning permission and sell off the other properties in the portfolio.

Getting rid of those other properties took a couple of years, but we could afford to take our time and wound up making a very good return on the equity we put into the deal. Looking just at the profit on those other sites, you could say that Bishopsgate cost us very little. But that's an oversimplification and not really how these things are costed because we refinanced Bishopsgate and had to hold onto it for eight years before we could start building. This is where property is a long-term business, not some in-and-out game where you make a quick buck. But when you buy top quality, providing you're prepared to sit on it and sweat, it's worth the time and trouble.

Both buildings on the site had to come down, but before we could demolish them, obviously we had to get the tenants out. So I went to see them to find out what it would take. I try to work well with everybody, but Norton Rose was a hassle because the managing partner of the law firm was like an old-school English headmaster. He didn't take to me, and because he spoke to me like I was a schoolboy, I didn't take to him. I was prepared to offer him a deal, similar to what they do in New York, where you pre-let a building and then give the tenant equity in it, but he just didn't want to know. I had the impression that he was thinking, here comes some smart property boy and I'm going to screw him, because he tried to hold me to ransom.

He said, 'We want £15 million to get out of the lease early.'

I said, 'You're being unreasonable, so thanks but no thanks.'

I reminded him that all his competitors were moving into bigger, more modern premises, while he was stuck here in a miserable, tired, out-of-date building. 'If you want to do a deal with me where you get out, and if we can sort out the dilapidations, which will run into millions of pounds, I may be prepared to look at that.'

But he refused. He wasn't rude, just difficult. He was paying rent and eventually he'd be paying us for the dilapidations, so it didn't really make any difference to me whether we started tearing the place down in a year or in two years. We were getting a good return on the asset and we could wait him out.

When he retired, a more sensible man, Peter Martyr, took over and we got on well. Peter knew the firm needed to move to better premises and did a good deal for office space just south of the river. I was then able to work out a timetable with him for vacant possession, they paid us for the dilapidations and everybody walked away happy.

It's often like that with these deals. They're complicated, aggravating and frustrating if you're dealing with somebody who isn't willing to talk. But once you find someone who is reasonable, you can find a solution. You just need a lot of patience, a lot of expertise, to know your way around the market, and deep pockets.

The building we decided to put on Bishopsgate would prove to be my ultimate test of all those qualities. By the time it's finished, we will have owned the site for more than 12 years. It might take another year or so to fully let it and then five more years before you can have a rent review and start making a real profit.

Talk about patience. Call it 17 years and change.

* * *

Developing a truly iconic building on the Bishopsgate island site meant dealing with a signature architect, and choosing the right one had to be done carefully, because signature architects usually have big egos.

Many of them don't understand, or don't want to know, that there is a difference between an architect and a developer. We're not building dreams, we're building commercial buildings. You can't just say to an architect, go away and design a building. Well, you could, and maybe you would if you were an institution, but when you're an owner-driver, you can't afford to let someone's ego get carried away. I mean, what happens if you tell him you want a really beautiful tall, thin skyscraper and he gives you a building like the Gherkin?

If an architect wants to see his buildings built by us, then those buildings have to be commercial. We are very hands-on at every step along the way. We tell our architect what we want and then he comes back with drawings and it becomes a step-by-step process where we work together. Not all architects like that. Some of them can be very precious. But because I know my business, I don't want to work with a too-precious architect.

That doesn't mean he's only interested in beauty and I'm not. We're both interested in everything about the building. But I am especially interested in the build-ability of a project. I want to know if we can get in an extra floor. I'm looking at the overall net space we have to rent, at the wow factor of the lobby and at the engineering of the foundations. It's easy for an architect to cost you an additional £10 million on the frame, but London isn't in an earthquake zone like San Francisco so it doesn't need to be over-engineered.

I personally get along with the biggest names in British architecture, but I've never done a job with them, possibly because I find them a bit too precious. I don't mean that to be critical of them, but when you're paying for their name and probably only getting one of their people, it could cost me more money than it needs to. I also worry that certain architects over-design because they don't care if it costs the developer more money.

Architects don't usually admit it, but the difference in cost between a signature building and a non-signature building can be £30 to £50 per square foot. That's on the gross area, not the net. Because margins are tight, if you have a prime site and you develop a high-quality signature building, you may need an extra £5 or more per square foot on the rent just to break even. So if the market rent is £50 per square foot and you're needing £55, it will work as long as your building looks and feels better than anything else. But if the people renting it say, it doesn't look or feel better to us, then you have a problem.

So you need to protect your investment from start to finish, and the best way to do that is to begin with a 100 per cent location. It's true that a building can create location, especially if you build big enough and the transportation is there to help you, but that's a much bigger risk.

The best example of that is what Paul Reichmann from Toronto and his managing director George Iacobescu tried to do with Canary Wharf. They were hoping to pull off the same trick in London that they did with Battery Park in New York City. When they first went down to the southern tip of Manhattan, everybody said Battery Park wouldn't work because it wasn't close enough to Wall Street. But getting from Battery Park to Wall Street is easy, and Battery Park created location for itself.

They saw Canary Wharf as the Battery Park of London and put up signature architect buildings there with large floor plates, 40,000 to 60,000 square feet, which is ideal for big back offices of major banks and institutions. They build quality and Canary Wharf is a world-class project. But this time, the critics were right, Canary Wharf was not the City because you couldn't get there from the City.

Which is why Canary Wharf failed to create location. Transportation needed to have been in place from day one, and they were promised that it would be, but it wasn't. It took 20 years for the Tube to arrive there. Before that, all you had was a Mickey Mouse overhead train. And even with the Tube it's still not great today, because the Tube can't really cope with the amount of traffic. Crossrail will be completed around 2017. When it is, they will still be building in Canary Wharf.

Reichmann and Iacobescu build quality and, at the end of the day, quality will out. The market doesn't want compromise. But then, it's actually easier to build million square foot buildings for HSBC or Barclays than it is a half a million square foot building on a very small site that will be let to 20 different tenants.

At Bishopsgate, we didn't need to create location because we already had it. But Bishopsgate is a small site, so we can only offer small floor plates. That means our customers will be using it for their representative offices. The City and Canary Wharf may never physically meet, but when Crossrail finally comes in – and Canary Wharf is making a contribution of about £250 million because they are depending on Crossrail – they'll be two stops away. And where do you come out in the City from that Crossrail station? Right opposite our Bishopsgate site.

* * *

We held a mini-competition for the site, asking several architects to design something. A number of top-flight firms submitted plans, but the one I really liked came from Lee Polisano at Kohn Pedersen Fox. He's an American and president of the firm and has been working in London since 1990. He designed the World Trade Center in Amsterdam, Endesa's headquarters in Madrid and Thames Court in the City of London. Better still, we'd already worked together on the Heron Tower in New York, at 55th Street just off Park Avenue in Midtown Manhattan, and had a good relationship. Lee understood right away the kind of iconic building I was looking for. When we first discussed our ideas for Bishopsgate, he told me that the model we needed to reflect back on was the Seagram Building at 52nd and 53rd streets along Park Avenue in New York.

That building, one of the most famous in the world, was designed by the German architect Mies van der Rohe, working with the American architect Philip Johnson. It is 38 storeys, was completed in 1958 and is considered a modern corporate masterpiece. There is nothing like it anywhere. From its 100 per cent location to its architecture, commerciality and levels of service, it sets a standard that is unique. And it has always commanded a premium rent, no matter how good or how bad the markets are.

London didn't have anything like this, but the time for it had come. London was changing. People were beginning to realise that if the City was going to stay competitive with Wall Street, it needed to offer more than it had been offering. The problem was that tall buildings in the City are controversial. In America, skyscrapers are everywhere. They're symbols of entrepreneurial capitalism. In Europe, skylines are not dominated by money, they're dominated by God and country.

If you stand in the middle of Waterloo Bridge, what you see is the Houses of Parliament to your left and St Paul's Cathedral to your right. Putting up a tall building in the City challenges that by adding capitalism to the view. Yet the Square Mile is at the heart of the nation's economy. There is nothing else like it in the world. Wall Street doesn't write its own policies, and the City does. For more than 1,000 years it's been an economic centre. It's what the City is all about.

But it is not what the historical preservation people are all about. They believe it's OK to have big fat buildings that are ten storeys, and spreading growth outwards is also OK because they don't have to see anything new. But changing the skyline? Definitely not OK.

Luckily for us, the Corporation of the City of London understood the City needed new important buildings, and Ken Livingstone, who was then the Mayor, wanted new, more important buildings in the City, and here we were with a project that could become the most important of all.

Our project, Heron Tower, called for a tall, thin, beautiful building that stood 46 storeys high, was innovative, challenging, green and would become, hopefully, an iconic destination. We researched how buildings work and how people work in them, and recognised that not everybody works in space the same way. To deal with that, Lee developed a 'village concept', which grouped every three floors of the Tower together. That meant we were really building eleven independent little buildings stacked one on top of the other.

Most commercial buildings have a core in the middle where the lifts are, with office space around that. Lee put the core on the side. In other words, the lifts go up and down the entire south side of the building, which means you not only get spectacular views up and down but when you step out of a lift the entire floor is in front of you. Heron Tower is all about setting a new standard, about setting a precedent. We were going to prove that you could have really high-quality modern architecture existing in the same skyline as St Paul's.

We developed the project through regular consultation with the planners at the Corporation of the City of London and the Mayor. It was during this time that I came to know Ken Livingstone well. I found him straight-talking and he always behaved correctly with me. He was never a big favourite of the Jewish community because he was prone to making stupid remarks that made him appear to be anti-Semitic. But I didn't see him that way.

I have spent my whole life fighting anti-Semitism and I always deal with people as I find them. I can smell an anti-Semite from a mile off and never felt that Livingstone fell into that category.

The thing about Ken was that if you asked him for something that didn't fit his bill, the answer was no. But if it did fit his bill, he was cooperative. He believed in towers for London, residential or commercial, and when we showed him what we wanted to do, he got behind it. The new Mayor of London, Boris Johnson, is not pro-tower. But what already has consent has consent, and anyone who's waiting for consent might find themselves tied up for many years. There are calls for residential towers in east London and south London, but if someone is looking to put up a tower in the City, they will have to reduce the height. But that's not my problem, it's theirs.

Our discussions with the Mayor and the City of London planning department were very positive. We had the blessing of the Commission for Architecture and Built Environment, which was established by the Government to comment on the architectural quality of buildings that were looking for planning permission. In fact, Heron Tower was well received by everyone we talked to. On 8 September 2000, we submitted our planning permission application and on 1 February 2001 the Court of Common Council, which is the body in the City of London that judges planners' submissions and proposals, granted us planning permission.

That was when we ran head first into the historic buildings lobby. They have central government's ear through their constituency, like Prince Charles. It's well known that HRH is not pro-tower, that he has his own ideas about architecture, but he didn't come out in any way against Heron Tower. And I don't think it's his business to do so anyway. If he had a point to make, I'm sure he would have made it. I just don't think that's his job. But there are plenty of people who do think it's their job, and English Heritage is one of them. They have a right to object to whatever displeases them. Which is most new things. A public body that manages the 'historic environment' of the nation, they can recommend to central government that a project be called in for investigation. And that's exactly what they did for Heron Tower.

The man who led their charge, Dr Gordon Higgott, an architectural historian, felt that when you looked at the City from Waterloo Bridge, our tower would ruin the view of St Paul's dome. This despite the fact that the Tower is one kilometre away from St Paul's. So John Prescott, who was then Deputy Prime Minister and also Minister for the Environment, announced on 27 February 2001 that the project would be put in front of a public inquiry.

I didn't know Prescott. It suited Tony Blair to have him represent old Labour in the cabinet, to keep the unions at bay, but he always struck me as a bit of a bully, not very bright, and a man who could talk a good game but couldn't play it. Provided he was fed with a couple of Jaguars, a nice home and a good expense account, he would toe the line. Today, he's an ordinary MP up in Hull, an area I know quite well because we have two big petrol stations there. In fact, he uses one of them to buy his petrol.

I don't know what he personally objected to about our plans. Maybe he was just going along with all those people who were objecting. It's what politicians do. When you find yourself confronted by a lot of people who have a strong opinion, open a public inquiry, because it doesn't then matter which way the inquiry decides, you've got yourself off the hook. Politically it was a good time for Prescott to do that. The Labour government was staring at an election and they wanted to be seen to be neutral about tall buildings in the centre of London, even though the Mayor was very supportive. So Prescott stuck his oar in just before the election. Of course, he had the right to do what he did, just as we had the right to go to war against him and English Heritage and everyone else who objected to Heron Tower. But, frankly, I'd rather not have had to do battle, because all it achieved was to throw good money down the drain. It cost the City of London, the Mayor's office, the Government, English Heritage and Heron about £13 million. We could have built a school for that. But that's not how bureaucrats think. No one at English Heritage cared what this cost because it wasn't their money, it was the public's. I cared because out of that £13 million, there was £4.5 million of our money. All of this because some old fuddy-duddies decided the Tower was too tall. Maybe if there was a listed building involved, you'd say to yourself, that makes sense, you know, protecting it. But that wasn't the case here.

The inquiry opened on 23 October 2001 and English Heritage did everything it could to keep us from building the Tower.

Besides that view of the City from Waterloo Bridge, another traditional view is from the terrace at Somerset House. But a row of trees adjacent to Somerset House otherwise blocked the view from there of Heron Tower. So, to prove their point, they paid off the gardener to prune the treetops so that Heron Tower would be visible.

Their tactics were pitiful. One of the directors got on the stand and actually lied. The inspector heading the inquiry caught him out and it was very embarrassing for English Heritage. They relied on a lot of misinformation and primed the press to accuse Lee Polisano of being an American who came to London to destroy the City. Someone actually said that he was planning to do more damage to London than the Nazis ever did. And they fed the press stories about 'convict Gerald Ronson' who was proposing to destroy St Paul's.

English Heritage are not bad people. They just spend their time looking backwards and, in this case, made some bad decisions. Their job is to keep the status quo. Progress is not important to them. Against us, they were also inconsistent and defied logic. Some of the arguments they used to try to stop Heron Tower were the very same arguments they used in support of the Gherkin.

They were joined by the City of Westminster, even though this had nothing to do with them, except that the view of the City from Waterloo Bridge is in Westminster. It didn't make a lot of sense and struck me as another waste of taxpayers' money. There were a few smaller objectors, too. But we were ready for all of them and everything they could throw at us. We pushed the boat way out and provided the inquiry with evidence like they'd never seen before. I told Lee, 'We are going to win this. You can have anything you need, but I want to fight this with dignity. I don't want to stoop to their level. But you need to win.' And Lee went on to set a new standard for how you assess buildings.

English Heritage was saying, if you stand at this point on Waterloo Bridge, you see the building in relation to the dome of St Paul's and it has an impact because you see it next to the figure. That was true. And they said, if you move over here, you see it in relation to another church. The photos they showed were reasonably accurate but not totally, because they were still photos from a certain place that was purposely chosen to show the most harmful impact the building could have. Also, a photo shortens distance, so something two kilometres away looks like it's right on top of something else. That's cheating with depth of field. But that's the way everything was assessed at the time.

Lee decided that was crazy because that's not the way people experience a city. Waterloo Bridge and the terrace at Somerset House were favourite spots, but that was before they opened the Tate Modern. And that view of St Paul's is different. So we came up with a way to show the building in context, the way people would actually see it, and used technologies that had never been used before. Lee built a three-dimensional computer model of the entire City of London and verified it with radar. It was accurate to within six inches. It showed how buildings look not just when you're standing in one place, but when you're moving through the City. When you walk across Waterloo Bridge, when you walk across the Somerset House terrace, when you walk into a building, when you walk out of a building.

I wasn't aware of it because I left it all to Lee, but up to that point the only technology to do what we wanted to do was in the movie industry. Lee used the same software that Hollywood did to make the film *The Matrix* and was able to show the true impact of Heron Tower in a way that had never been done before anywhere in the world.

We had a brilliant QC, Christopher Katkowski, who specialised in planning, and Lee put his entire office on this for a year and a half. They worked round the clock, 30 to 40 people, in two 12-hour shifts. It was so all-consuming that when it was over Lee had no other work. It practically ruined his business.

Lee and Katkowski put together our evidence, and Cahit Atasoy ran the inquiry for us. He joined Heron in 1999 and had already supervised a public inquiry exactly like this, because he'd worked on the Gherkin.

We started with the idea that the best way to see a city is when you cross a bridge, because everything opens up to you. But while you're walking, you don't look at one particular thing, you look at everything. So we showed the inquiry a dynamic video of a person walking along Waterloo Bridge, where we could freeze the frame at every step of the way, so the inspector could actually see the views. Then, instead of handing the inspector tens of thousands of pages of papers, we put everything into a computer and had two guys sitting there projecting whatever the inspector wanted to see onto two giant screens.

The inquiry met every day from 9 a.m. for nearly seven weeks, until 17 December. In February, the planning inspector sent his findings to John Prescott, basically saying, this is a good building and it is not doing the things that English Heritage says it is. He recommended our plans. And on 22 July 2002, Prescott's department officially granted us permission to go ahead with Heron Tower.

The process was painful and costly. We had to deal with so many people with so many different views, none of whom gave a damn about what we were trying to do. They fought us because that's what they do. Being a conservative, traditional people, the British regard skyscrapers as an American phenomenon. But we're building Heron Tower in an area that's been designated for tall buildings. Prescott played a political game and couldn't have cared less how much it cost the taxpayer. But that's all par for the course. If you want to be a trailblazer and push the boundaries, you have to go through this. After Heathrow Terminal 5, ours was the biggest, most expensive public inquiry ever.

* * *

When English Heritage started taking aim at Heron Tower, right when they started objecting and threatening to stop us at any cost, I went to see Ken Livingstone, because I knew if I didn't have his backing, the plan was dead in the water. And he made it quite clear to me that he, and not English Heritage, would be the one to decide what can and cannot be built in London.

I think it might have been the first week he was in power. I showed him the model, discussed it with him, and said, 'If you're prepared to back this, then I will take it all the way.'

He said to me, 'As far as I'm concerned, you can put another ten floors on the building, because I think it's great design in a great location and I'm with you 100 per cent.'

So after Prescott ruled we could build the Tower, I remembered that comment from Livingstone about adding ten storeys. We'd lost two years to the inquiry and costs were going up, and I had to think about what we could add to make the building more viable. This was not a project for the faint of heart, it was very, very expensive, and we needed a little more return. Some people would say that's being greedy, but the reality is that we looked at it carefully, in a very transparent manner.

Lee was already thinking that the Tower looked too squat, that it needed to be taller to work better. The chief city planner agreed. We discussed adding ten storeys, but that didn't look right – it was suddenly too big – so we talked about eight. But that's easier said than done. You can only do so much with a building without putting in more lifts, so whatever space we might have gained with eight or ten storeys would have cost us space throughout the rest of the building. One thing cancelled out the other. But Lee decided we wouldn't need more lifts if we added just six storeys, and any extra building costs would be offset by the extra revenue we'd generate. Six more storeys would put the building on a more equitable basis, so we went back to ask for planning permission to add six storeys. We had to go through a second planning process and there were some objections, but the planners ignored them because they'd already heard them and had overruled them.

Next, we needed a builder who had experience with tall buildings. And there were really only two. There were the Canary Wharf people, who built that project themselves under a contract management basis. And there was Skanska, the second- or third-largest builders in Europe, who had built the Gherkin. We put the job out to tender and wound up hiring Skanska, but on one strict condition. Regardless of reputation, at the end of the day, any construction company is only as good as the people on the job. That's why I insisted they put the same people on Heron Tower as they had on the Gherkin. Anybody can pour concrete, but I wanted experience. Their A team. Most of the same people were still working for Skanska, but some had moved on, which meant if Skanska wanted this job, they'd have to rehire those people. They wanted it and they did.

Once that was done, we faced the usual problem that developers go up against whenever they build in central London, and especially in the City. You never know what you're going to find once you start digging. Bumping into the old city wall of London can stop you building or hold you up for a lot of years. You may have to reposition your pilings and that can add a lot of expense. So we brought archaeologists onto the site to show the planners what was there. We knew that the Bishop's Gate was close by – that was a gate through the actual London Wall – and so was Houndsditch, which is where they used to throw the dead dogs. In the end, we never found the wall. We suspect that when the site was first built on, many years ago, whoever built there destroyed it.

* * *

I am probably more hands-on with this project than I am with any other, because this one is so special.

A lot of people are working to make Heron Tower the best building in the city. We're employing 18 professional firms and all those firms employ hundreds of people. You have builders, subcontractors, plumbers, electricians, heating people and cooling people, etc. There are so many elements that need to be dealt with. I think at the peak there will be 2,000 people working on site. If you then add in the people who are backing up those people, you're talking about a lot of people.

I'm on site one morning a week. I arrive before the work crews get there and usually stay for an hour or so. I walk around and talk to everyone. I meet with my project manager and project director. I see for myself what everyone is doing. I want to see how many piles they've put in the ground. I want to see where they have obstacles. I want to know if there are delays with drawings or subcontractors. I want to see who's there by eight o'clock and who's not, because I'm paying them to start at 8 a.m., not 8.15. People cover for each other. He's had a bellyache. She's missed her train. That kind of crap may go on everywhere, but it goes on much less at a Heron job. Why? Because I can smell when something's not working right. There's nowhere to hide.

It has to be like that, I have to be that hands-on, because there's too much at stake. What we're trying to do is something unique. We're creating a product that must be the best in the marketplace. Every detail must be right. Heron Tower must be the highest quality, from the design, the workmanship and the service to the wow factor.

Lee has created a fabulous work of art, where absolutely everything is thought through. By putting the lifts on the south side, for example, we shield the sun, which means we don't need as much cooling, so the building consumes less energy. We've also put photocells in the glass on the south side, which produces energy for the building, so the project is very high tech and, at the same time, very green.

Most office entrances are marble, with a desk where someone checks your ID or directs you to the lifts. They're all very ordinary. But the minute you step inside the Tower, you will know it's different. There is a triple-height entrance hall with the biggest aquarium in any commercial building in Europe. The tank is 40 feet across, 13 feet deep and 26 feet tall. We found out that there is a Heron Island in the Pacific – it's part of the southern Great Barrier Reef – so we are importing a large number of our tropical fish from there. The aquarium is so big that once a week a diver will have to go in there to help maintain the tank. We're also putting a camera in there that will send images to the lifts.

Speaking of the lifts, they're double-decker. Each lift will service two floors. We're installing a state-of-the-art system called Hall Call, so when you swipe in at the security turnstile, the computer greets you, 'Good morning, Mr Smith,' and tells you, 'Please go to Car D to take you to your floor.' By the time you walk to the lift, it's there waiting for you. There are no buttons to push. You won't wait longer than 25 seconds for a lift anywhere in the building at any time of day.

This is a whole different environment than an ordinary office building. Touch screens will give visitors whatever information they need and there will be a magnificently designed reception desk with young women who speak many different languages. This is an international building, so we will cater to an international clientele.

I insisted from the beginning that we must offer world-class services, so we will also have a full-time concierge, just like in a six-star hotel. He will be there to look after tenants, whether they want shirts done, dinner reservations, plane tickets, flowers sent, whatever. That's what service is about. There will be a light restaurant on the ground floor and a great bar and a great restaurant on the roof, which has phenomenal views. And unlike the Gherkin's restaurant, which is only open to occupiers of the building, our restaurant will have separate lifts and be open to the public. We have designed this to be the number-one office building in the City of London.

Heron Tower is, to date, the biggest and best project we have ever undertaken. I would like to think that some day Heron Tower will be compared to the Seagram Building. Everything is in place for that to happen. It has all the ingredients to become an iconic location, maybe even a destination, a mini-Rockefeller Center. London needs buildings like Heron Tower, and there's no doubt that the property and space surrounding the Tower will improve because of it.

Unlike in America, where they give you four walls, we will fit out the building. Everything will be finished, the ceiling, the walls, all you will have to do when you move in is put in your partitions. Everything will be ready for the decorator to create whatever the tenant wants.

Maintaining the highest standards and quality doesn't stop the day we open the doors, and highly disciplined management doesn't frighten us, because we have the expertise for it. I refer to tenants as customers and know that if you don't look after your customers, they leave. I also know that when you do look after your customers, and your customer loves being in a building like this, he'll pay extra for the privilege. So as soon as the Tower is completed, my asset manager will be walking through the entire building at least once a week, guaranteeing the standard of service and cleanliness. He will be there, seeing for himself that there are no issues with tenants, dealing immediately with whatever needs to be done. Once again, the devil is in the detail.

By the time Heron Tower opens for business, I will be 72. And at that age, I may not be taking on any more long-term major developments. But who knows? I think I will always be looking at deals. No deal is too big, if it is the right deal, because if I know the deal is right – and that's the key – then Heron would take a stake and find investors for the rest. I'd get on a plane and go to America or the Far East and get the financing. Size doesn't frighten me. It's never easy to find deals, because there are other people in the market who are also looking. And if there aren't any deals where we can make money for our shareholders, we won't buy. But just maybe something will come along and it will be too tough to stay away.

I never looked at the Tower and said, this is where I leave my mark, this is my last big development. But then, if it does become my legacy, it's not a bad legacy to have. It will be the best building in the City. It will be a landmark. It will also set a standard for future developers who want to go one better. But that won't be easy. We're setting the bar very high.

Maybe some day my grandchildren will look at it and say, our old granddad did know what he was doing. He had the vision and the balls to create this iconic building.

CHAPTER 16

························

GIVING SOMETHING BACK

I am a Jew. I am a member of a synagogue. I believe in the need to support my Community in this country and the State of Israel. I believe that a Jew should stand up and be counted as a Jew. I also believe that this imposes certain responsibilities. If he is to be respected in the wider community, he must have a sense of responsibility. That includes his obligation to give not only money but also time. Whilst I know plenty of people who give freely without having any religion at all, charity plays a part in every religion. I don't know if I would feel the same way about this if I were not a Jew, but to give and to help other people is a particularly strong feature of what our culture is about.

For true charity there is no payback. The reward is in the deed. Sure, some donors want their charitable deeds to be recognised. They want to be seen, to be thanked, to be honoured. In my view, there's no harm in that. But when charity is anonymous, the reward comes from a sense of duty and is even greater.

In Hebrew, the word for charity is 'tzedekah', which means 'righteousness', in the sense of doing what God would have us do. But Judaism teaches that there is another kind of charity which is just as important. That one is 'loving kindness'. It doesn't matter if someone is rich or poor, we show loving kindness to people who are sick or lonely or depressed.

I believe in the old proverb 'Give a man a fish and you feed him for a day, teach a man to fish and you feed him for a lifetime'. And the seeds of my ideas on charity were sewn in Russia in the year 1880, when a handful of Jews whose talents and expertise made them indispensable to the Tsar and his regime were granted permission to live and prosper in Moscow. Considering how 100 years of anti-Semitism under the tsars had already restricted so many Jews to a life of poverty in the Pale of Settlement, this was truly remarkable.

As these well-to-do Moscow Jews prospered, some of the community leaders realised that they needed to do something to help the mass of impoverished, untrained, jobless Jews who had not been granted such privilege. Believing that along with a livelihood came self-esteem and dignity, the Tsar granted them permission to fund an educational programme to provide practical training for as many of those people as possible, in agriculture and various handicrafts such as mechanics and, especially important for my family, cabinetmaking. Based on the Russian for 'the Society for Trades and Agricultural Labour', the group became known as ORT.

The group prospered in Russia until the First World War, then began expanding into Europe and throughout the Soviet empire. Tens of thousands of Jews were trained and educated by ORT. They continued their work during the early years of the Second World War, but the original group was nearly destroyed by the Holocaust. What saved them was that, by then, other ORT groups had begun work in the rest of Europe and also in North America. When the war ended, ORT moved to help victims of the concentration camps get new skills and, eventually, resettle in Israel.

By the 1950s, Americans had become interested in ORT. Concerned at the time about the Third World, the US was looking for ways to teach people in newly emerging nations the trades and skills they'd need to improve their economies. And they turned to ORT for guidance.

I became interested through my friend Trevor Chinn. In 1979, I went with him to a meeting in Paris where he suggested that I should build a school in the Israeli town of Ashkelon, which is in the western Negev and was made famous in the Bible story about Samson's pillars. He said many children in Israel did not plan to go to college and needed to learn a trade, and that if I built the school through ORT and the Jewish Agency, I could name it after my father. I had the money to build the school and wanted to do it. My own grandfather made his start in Britain because he'd learned a trade as a cabinetmaker. So this was my chance to help people from difficult backgrounds learn a trade. But making it happen was by no means easy, because the Israelis had their ideas about the school, which weren't the same as mine.

For them, building schools starts with the local council. The project then goes through the bureaucracy – which, in Israel, is unbelievable – before it gets to the Ministry of Education. At every step along the way where money is allocated, everyone wants to put their friends in on it. Now, along comes Mr Ronson who insists that nobody is getting a backhander, who insists on checking building specifications, who wants to make sure that the drawings are done properly so that the builder can't hold the project to ransom and demand more money because things have suddenly changed, who wants to make sure these schools are built to last, who wants to make sure jobs go out to tender, who insists that everything comes in on time and is done properly.

As if that isn't enough, this difficult Mr Ronson also insists on controlling the process in an Anglo-Saxon way, not in some Middle Eastern way where everybody has a little bit of the pie because they're in on their political old pal's act. Because the school was going to be funded with my money, I had no intention of tolerating corruption and incompetence. I simply refused to leave this to the Israelis, which is what 99 per cent of people do.

Doing it their way would get the school built later rather than sooner, and then it wouldn't be what it started out to be, because nothing in that part of the world ever turns out to be what you thought it would. That's the way it works in the Middle East. It doesn't mean that we as Anglo-Saxons are more clever than they are. But we are better disciplined, and possibly more focused. We want to know up front what it's going to cost. Too many projects in Israel never get finished at all because they run out of money. Why? Because they didn't check costs right at the beginning. Because you get overcharged. Because they didn't have the drawings done properly. Because they didn't control it. Everything is messy. I don't need that. Not with my money.

By 1981, we had a preliminary design. We also had a budget of $3 million. It took another five years, and another $6 million from the Ronson Foundation before we were ready to proceed. Then, in May 1986, during the first ever visit of a British Prime Minister to Israel, Margaret Thatcher – accompanied by the Prime Minister of Israel, Shimon Peres – visited Ashkelon and laid the foundation stone of the school.

Two years later, we opened the school. When we did, Israel's Minister of Education said that, unlike so many other countries in the world, Israel possessed no natural resources. No oil, no coal, no water power, no gold, no silver. He said, 'Israel's only natural resource is her people. The Israeli people, therefore, must be made into the best-educated people in the world.'

I'd like to think that the Henry Ronson ORT School is a step in that direction.

* * *

My desire to do more and to get others to give more took me closer to the charity worker I have since become. But nobody should venture deep without the advice and guidance of someone of high character and integrity who knows what he's doing. I had the great good fortune to get to know the late Moshe Davis, who was executive director of the office of the then Chief Rabbi, Lord Immanuel Jakobovits.

Moshe was a remarkable man with a great experience of the Community and a wide knowledge of human nature. He was an excellent judge of character, had a strong enough personality to protect the Chief Rabbi from himself and could sense who was really committed to a cause and who was going along for the ride. In 1974, Moshe agreed to become my adviser on charitable works. He sifted through things, put them in perspective, gave them a priority and taught me a lot.

My first foundation began as the Henry Ronson Settlement, but changed its name to the Ronson Foundation. It was chartered in 1967. Because the original deed was too restrictive, we created the Ronson Second Foundation in 1979. Unfortunately, the reconstruction of Heron got in the way of many things we wanted to do and the foundation had to be folded up. It had commitments, a number of charities were counting on us and I didn't want the collapse of Heron to have a fallout effect on them. As it happened, we had just under £4 million, which was enough. Had we not been able to meet our commitments that way, I was ready to reach into my own pocket and deal with any shortfall myself.

Once that money was gone, there was nothing left, which really upset me, because it restricted my ability to support causes I felt strongly about. I could still do it, to some extent, out of my own pocket, but not to the extent that I wanted to. So I decided to dedicate 20 per cent of my time to raise the money I could no longer donate. I actually told people, 'I'm going to be a charity worker.'

It was bizarre that some people said to me, don't you regret all that money you've given away? Because if you hadn't given it away, you'd be sitting on another fortune. But that thought never entered my head. For me, a human being can be judged by the size of his heart.

A lot of other people thought I was mad spending 20 per cent of my time working for charity, because they know that my working day starts when I wake up and doesn't stop until I go to sleep. I don't do eight-hour days. And 20 per cent of a 16-hour day is a lot of time.

No matter, I put the accelerator down and started to raise millions of pounds. I eventually formed the new Gerald Ronson Foundation – it was chartered in October 2005 – and today all of my shares in Heron are bequeathed to it. This will be a major foundation. In the meantime, I'm trying to set an example for other entrepreneurs and other people who have made a lot of money. I want them to think about what they need to do. And now that I am once again in a position to give away substantial money, I'm still spending 20 per cent of my time as a charity worker, raising millions of pounds.

* * *

Because the Henry Ronson ORT School in Israel gave us such a sense of satisfaction, we decided to build more schools in Israel over the next seven years, committing $25 million, to be matched by a similar amount from the Israeli government. The first of those was on Mount Carmel and we built it for the Druze. It is today one of the best schools in the country and the biggest project ever founded in Israel by a Jew for non-Jews.

The Druze are a remarkable people. They are an eleventh-century offshoot sect of Islam who are considered by some scholars to be non-Muslim and by other scholars to be unorthodox Muslims. Because they suffered great persecution right from the beginning, they withdrew to the mountains for safety and remained there for centuries. They were remote, secretive, mysterious, suspicious and always ready to fight to the death against intruders. Today, there are about a million Druze in Syria, Lebanon and Jordan. There are around 70,000 Druze in Israel. You also find small colonies of them in America, Africa and Australia.

In the late 1930s, Druze elders formed a pact with the Zionist leaders, and in 1948, when Israel became a state, they remained and have lived ever since in peaceful coexistence with the local Jews. They inhabit sixteen traditional villages in the Galilee and two villages on Mount Carmel – Isfiya and Daliat el-Carmel.

Druze law charges them to be loyal to the state in which they reside, which is why Druze serve in the Israeli military. Although they have not migrated to the major cities, they have had to abandon their traditional agricultural ways. Yet, compared to other ethnic groups in Israel, the number of Druze going to university has been the lowest. That's one of the reasons why this school was so important, because all children need to have a good education. This school takes them from kindergarten through high school and prepares them to go on to university. I built it because, as far as I'm concerned, these people are being treated as underprivileged citizens.

Once the school was up and running, elders from the Druze community came to me to say that they live in a country where they're treated poorly, and wanted to know how and why, all of a sudden, I came along like the Messiah. I told them not to worry about how and why, I was very glad that I was able to do something for them. They then asked, as a token of their gratitude, if I would become their international ambassador.

Today, if you look in *Who's Who*, I am the only international ambassador the Druze have. That's a title for life. I even have the certificate and gold chain to prove it. Every year, the Druze elders invite me back to the school, but I must confess that I haven't gone back. I should, because everyone tells me it's one of the best-maintained schools in Israel. But I don't go back there for the same reason I never visit any of the schools I build. Because once I've built it, I move on.

I followed that with a second school in Ashkelon. The new Gerald Ronson Foundation is also building a school in the village of Hagalil, on the Lebanese border, which is the poorest area of Israel. That's a big project that will cost $25 million. The foundation put in 10 per cent, the Israeli government put in 30 per cent and some friends are topping up the balance. It is a mixed school, which means that around 20 per cent of the children are Arab. I think it's a good thing that Israeli children and Arab children can go to the same school and, hopefully, create some mutual respect for one another.

In addition to the four schools I've built in Israel, there are five that I have built in the UK. The first was at Bushey in north London. It came about because the late Chief Rabbi, Lord Jakobovits, was a great believer in Jewish education. He wanted to see a new school for Halachic Jewish children. Those are children whose parents were both born Jewish, as were all of their grandparents and great-grandparents before them.

One of the people close to the Chief Rabbi was Stanley Kalms, chairman of Dixons. I've known Stanley for many years and he is a very decent guy. He can be difficult because he is very single-minded, but I like him. He believed strongly in this school, so he and I kicked off the campaign to build it with £1 million each. The overall cost was £10 million and we helped raise most of the rest of the money. When we got to the end, there was still a shortfall of a couple of million pounds. That's when Michael Phillips, Johnny Rubens' son-in-law, stepped in to raise the balance of the money. The school, named after my father, Stanley's father and the Chief Rabbi, is called the Charles Kalms Henry Ronson Immanuel College.

I then went on to build the King Solomon High School in Barkingside. Alan Sugar and I both put up £1 million to start the fund-raising, then subsequently both put in more. Alan has been generous to several projects that I've been involved with, but his primary interest is Jewish Care, and every year he makes a substantial contribution to that. Next, I did the Yesodey Hatorah and the Lubavitch Girls' School in London and added a wing to the new Jewish Free School in Harrow. But the biggest school project I have ever been involved with is the Jewish Community State

School (JCoSS) in Barnet, which will be a cross-communal faith school and take in 1,400 non-Halachic Jewish children.

Under Jewish law, religion is passed through the mother so that a child is Jewish if his or her mother is Jewish. But there are many faith schools that are more strict than that in determining whether a child is Jewish. They insist both parents must be Jewish, or they rule out children with a gentile grandparent. I felt it was important that any child who wants a Jewish education, even if they're half-Jewish, should have that opportunity.

A lot of people in the Community disagree with me, but look what's been happening. There are maybe 250,000 Jews affiliated with the British Jewish community, plus another 100,000 or so who are not affiliated but are Jews. You're talking about 350,000 people. But 30 years ago, there were 500,000 Jews in the UK. That says to me we've lost 150,000 to assimilation. And that's a real problem. The Community has shrunk in the past 30 years and, if we're not careful, 30 years from now we may be down to 200,000.

JCoSS is all-inclusive. It gives people a choice. It is about making people part of the Community whether they're Orthodox, Liberal or Reform. We have to open these doors. The right wing doesn't share my view, and some of them are very vocal about this. But we're living in a country of 60 million people and I'm just as vocal about saying it's important that we don't lose our identity.

The budget for building JCoSS came in at £50 million. We managed to convince the Government to give us 80 per cent. But in order to get the Government's £40 million, I had to raise the remaining £10 million. As with every project I'm involved with, I lead from the front, which means that I am a major donor. So I started the ball rolling with £1 million from my foundation. As I say often, it's easier to be an asker when you're a giver than the other way round.

* * *

Added up, by the time JCoSS is finished, about 10,000 young people will be going to schools I have built. The majority of them are Jewish, but there are children of all different colours and all different denominations.

When I took on the JCoSS project, there were no guarantees that I could raise the rest of the money. There have been times when I've opened an account with a big contribution only to see a project costing £10 million come up short of its goal. When that happens, I reach into my pocket and make up the difference, because I believe that's what we're all supposed to do. But not everybody sees it the same way, and there are people I approach for donations – very rich people – who try to get out of giving by coming up with excuses.

I'm willing to put up with their arrogance for ten minutes, but that's the limit of my patience. After that, I tell them exactly what I think. One fellow who could, without thinking twice, make a very big contribution to JCoSS – in fact, if he really wanted to he could fund it himself – couldn't understand why I was knocking at his door. I reminded him that in a shrinking Community it's very important that we have faith-based schools which will accept children who are not 100 per cent Halachically Jewish. But he kept saying, 'What's everybody driving me mad for? Just because I'm Jewish?'

I asked him, 'Have you ever seen anybody when they're put in a box in the ground? Do they bury them with their money?'

After twisting his arm, reminding him who he is and telling him not to be so stupid, eventually, I got a major donation from him. But I don't understand why it took all that. Sadly, he's not the only one.

I personally feel it's important that we help young people get an education. University, trade school, whatever it is, helping someone get an education means you're also helping them develop self-esteem. It's great if someone wants to be a rocket scientist or a doctor. But we also need plumbers and bricklayers and electricians. We need to make sure that everyone can read and write. That's why I build schools.

But it's not only schools that we support. The Gerald Ronson Foundation gives money to many different causes and, hopefully, will still be giving money away to many more good causes as the years go on. I'd like to think there are no major projects in my Community which are not, in one way or another, connected with the Ronson family, either personally or through the foundation. The tens of millions of pounds I've raised for charity is totally separate from the tens of millions we've given away. The Good Lord's been good to me and my family, and this is my way of giving something back. It's what I do to say thank you.

For the record, the Gerald Ronson Foundation is me. Gail is deputy chairman. Three out of my four daughters – Lisa, Nicole and Hayley – are trustees. So is my joint managing director at Heron, Jonathan Goldstein, who is a lawyer. And my former managing director Alan Goldman, who is an accountant. Jeremy Trent serves as treasurer. My daughter Amanda is peripherally involved, but she doesn't live in the UK.

Some people use their foundation as a tax scam to put money in but never give any money away. That pisses me off. As long as I'm alive, and, I know for a fact, as long as my daughters are alive, my foundation will continue giving to worthy causes. Given the assets I've bequeathed, I'd say the foundation will be worth north of £100 million in years to come.

I have put good professionals in place at the foundation to make certain that my family stays focused once I'm gone. Can I rule from the grave 50 years from now? Of course not. But I've structured things so that when my grandchildren get to the age of 25, they will also come onto the foundation. If they don't want to be involved, that's up to them. But I am leaving them the greatest asset – a way to do good. And that's very important to me.

And if that ethos can remain for the next 50 years, I will have achieved something very important. In fact, it will be the most important achievement of my life. I am leaving my name to my family. And they are the custodians of that through the foundation.

If I could, I'd double or treble what I'm worth, because if I had that much more, then I could double or treble the money the foundation gives away. I'd love to give away £10 million a year. With amounts like that, you can make a difference. I always do what I can. In 1983, when I was told how so many Jews in Russia had suddenly been given permission to go to Israel, we loaded two 747 jumbo jets and flew an exodus mission out of the Soviet Union. More recently, in conjunction with the Holocaust Educational Trust, we have organised day trips to take a planeload of school teachers, non-Jews, to visit the Auschwitz and Birkenau concentration camps in Poland. Those things are easy and I'm trying to do them all the time, either by raising money or funding them through the foundation or by myself.

When you have the kind of money that Bill Gates and Warren Buffet have, it's hard to focus, because you're giving away millions and those causes are global. But with as little as £25 million, I could make an enormous difference to my Community, to people less fortunate. I could touch so many lives, and that would give me a lot of pleasure.

* * *

There are all sorts of reasons why people get involved and all sorts of excuses why people don't. And when you are involved, it's not always smooth sailing, because you have to deal with different personalities. We need people to do the thinking, people to do the asking, people to do the doing. It takes time and a lot of effort to call upon people for favours. If I ask someone to do something, provided they can do it, they usually will. I don't only write letters, I also ring them up. Other people have their own style and not everybody likes my style. Some people say Gerald Ronson is a bull in a china shop who goes right through the front door. But that's how

I am. Not everybody shares my views about fund-raising and giving, but I don't care about that. I'm in the business of getting things done. Occasional bulldozing may not make you popular, but it can get results. The trouble is that there are often big egos sitting at the top of many charities, who block reform. There is a natural resistance to change.

In 2003, a number of my friends and I formed the Jewish Leadership Council (JLC). We felt there was a need to add a dynamic vision to what we have to do in the Community. The Board of Deputies had been around for a long time, as a representative body of the Community to government, but to my mind it is really just a talking shop for 500 people. You have to listen to 500 people who have been elected by their local synagogues up and down the country. How do you get anything done? I have a simple agenda. Let's decide what we have to do, and then do it.

So, Trevor Chinn, Michael Levy, Mick Davis and I brought together the chairmen of 20 respected organisations within the Community to deal with education, security, welfare and the changing face of the Community over the next 20 to 30 years. We invited Henry Grunwald to be our chairman – he was already president of the Board of Deputies – because we felt that was the right thing to do. There was a lot of pressure to derail the JLC because of the politics of the Board of Deputies, but, for better or worse, I will see that the JLC stays on the rails as long as I'm alive, because I believe it is the vehicle that is most representative of the true Community.

We don't distinguish between right or left. There are no egos. There are no rabbis on the Council, because when you want to get things done, you don't want to confuse things. This is not about the talkers, this is about the movers and shakers. But even those people need direction, which is why we have an executive committee. It needs direction, resources, key people, looking at the key professionals that are required over the next 10 to 15 years to give these people focus and a professional career path.

You'd be wrong to think that these things weren't already happening. They weren't happening in a businesslike manner. Everybody had his own little patch. People who were concerned with welfare weren't concerned with education, and people who were concerned with education weren't concerned with security. Of course, everybody is concerned with security when something happens. It's a lot of work, a lot of aggravation, a lot of sitting in meetings listening to a lot of talking, but you have to go through the process. You can't just hit people over the head with a chequebook and wanting what you want done, you have to create understanding and respect. Unless you've been around for a very long time, people don't regard you as a player. When you have been around a long time, they have to respect the fact that you've given your time, your intellect and your money to make things happen.

I also feel it is my responsibility to find the next generation of Community leaders. We started looking at thirty to forty people who we thought had the potential to be the leaders of tomorrow and that's whittled itself down to about eight or ten serious men and women who we are training for that job. We run a young leadership programme, trying to be to some people what Marcus Sieff was to me. Because we need people to take over. But I must say I am disappointed. There are a few very good people in their 30s and 40s, but not enough of them. Instead, I see too many people talking. I don't see the passion, the dedication and the commitment. I don't see people willing to spend the time it takes.

That worries me. I'm worried about who will take over from us. I give 20 per cent of my time working for the Community and have done so for the past 50 years. That's what, ten years of my life? I do it because I feel it's my responsibility. But when I mention the time commitment I've made, and hope that sets an example for them, they moan. They keep telling me, we don't have the time, we start very early in the office and work very late and we have to take Johnny to football and we have to take Sarah to ballet class, which pisses me off profusely. If you have the passion for something, if you have the commitment to do it, you will find the time. Like they say, if you want something done, go to a busy man.

Honestly, if one of these people we're grooming said to me, I want your job, I'd be very happy to hand it over to him.

CHAPTER 17

·······················

ONCE A STREET FIGHTER, ALWAYS A STREET FIGHTER

I was a boy fighting fascists on the streets in London. I know how to look after myself and I don't get intimidated. That doesn't mean to say I was brought up on the streets, because I wasn't, but I know how to handle myself on the streets, and thank God I can, because if I had been brought up wrapped in cotton wool, I would have found life much harder to deal with in later years.

In my early 20s, I was arrested when some hooligans called me a 'Jew bastard' and I fought back. I would never start a fracas, and most of the time the people who were calling me a Jew bastard were bigger and uglier than me. Today, I would probably turn the other cheek, but when I was 21 years of age I didn't walk away, and I ended up getting charged with actual bodily harm (ABH).

It was one night when I was out with two other friends in Highgate, north London. We were minding our own business and six big hooligans started taunting us. They passed us on the street and started making anti-Semitic comments. We were three quiet Jewish boys and they were six arseholes. One thing led to another and they baited us into a fight. I figured that the best way I could even up the odds was to have a lump of wood in my hands. So I looked around and grabbed a nearby stick, and I guess I hit one or two of them with it. When the police showed up, the thugs who started the fight put the blame on us. I had that piece of wood in my hand, the cops perceived it to be a weapon and we were the ones who were charged.

They took us to the police station. We weren't handcuffed and we weren't locked up, but they recorded the incident. I never thought the police would actually charge anyone, but the police in those days were more anti than they were pro. Today, the police are very fair-minded but this was, what, nearly 50 years ago, when cops leaned more to the right than the left. We were eventually charged with ABH, but the judge threw that out, reduced it to a lesser charge and we were bound over to keep the peace for 12 months. Which we did.

If the circumstances were the same and I had to do it again, would I do it that way? The answer is yes. You have to fight fire with fire. You can't over-intellectualise situations. You can't say, there's a fire burning down the road, shall we write to the Local Authority or shall I go down there with a bucket of water? You take action. When bad people are prepared to do bad things, you have to deal with them in whatever way it takes. The elder statesmen of the Community knew about it, they just didn't make a lot of noise. We dealt with the situation.

We had to because very aggressive, extreme right-wing anti-Semitic gangs had been a problem in the UK for a long time. To combat them, a bunch of Jewish soldiers coming home from the war formed the 43 Group and used to go around at night painting anti-fascist signs.

As those men got older, and young men my own age took up the cause, a new group was formed, called the 62 Group. The leader was Cyril Paskin, who had fought in the jungles of Burma during the Second World War. We were like a mini-intelligence organisation to frustrate the fascists and disrupt what we could at their headquarters. We'd order sacks of crazy things which would get sent to particular people, like truckloads of sand. We did everything we could to put them out of business. But the really hardcore individuals, we dealt with physically.

Once, when Cyril heard that some Nazis were coming over from Germany to meet with the British fascists at the Royal Pavilion Hotel in Brighton, we all went down there to put smoke bombs everywhere and completely disrupted the meeting. Cyril was one of those people who always led from the front, and he wound up getting arrested for the Brighton mission. He was sentenced to three years, but his sentence was suspended, so he didn't actually spend time in jail. But the threat of jail didn't stop us. I suppose in those days I leaned to the left. I certainly felt strongly that anti-Semitism was something that simply could not be tolerated in our society. Obviously, I still feel the same way, but I approach it today in a more sophisticated way.

The fascists would meet on Sunday mornings at the top of Brick Lane and, later in the afternoon, in Hyde Park. Cyril and the rest of us in the 62 Group would gather on Sunday mornings not far away. There were a couple of hundred of them, and fifty to seventy of us, and standing in between were a hundred police. To get to the fascists and disrupt their meetings, we'd have to fight our way through the police.

Some time in 1963, we heard that the fascists were going to hold a big rally in Kensington Town Hall and decided we wouldn't stand for it. All their thugs were there, and they had plenty of very tough men, but we also had tough Jewish boys. Even though we were heavily outnumbered – there were a lot more of them than there were of us, so this wasn't so simple – we smashed up their meeting and their leaders and inflicted serious damage. Needless to say, the police didn't like that any more than the fascists did, and two or three of our guys were caught and were severely dealt with by the police.

I became chief fund-raiser for the 62 Group – we needed money not just to run the organisation but to pay fines – so I had some say about how it was run and what we should be doing. By now, however, I was beginning to think that being hooligans to fight hooligans wasn't the smartest way we could fight the enemy. I knew I was dealing with a bunch of loonies, but I was thinking that we needed to beat the enemy by being more sophisticated than them. That meant setting up a new organisation. It had to be more than 200 well-meaning tough boys behaving in an undisciplined fashion. It had to look for long-term solutions and I felt that the greater Jewish community in Britain should fund it. So we set up the Jewish Aid Community of Britain – JACOB for short.

We had some unusual people on the JACOB committee, like Maurice Essex, who was chairman, and Baron Moss. Baron has to be one of the most remarkable men I ever met, a strange mixture, a man of contradictions. He was a Jew, and very proud of it, but he did not practise the faith. He was also an old-time communist but had a successful career in advertising. Both these men were clever, intellectual lefties who refused to serve in the army during the war and became 'Bevan Boys', going down into the mines as conscientious objectors. I used to say to them, 'What's this bollocks that you're a communist when you're driving a Bentley?' I could never work that out.

Their explanation was that they had their own view of communism and, anyway, only the communists were fighting the fascists. I didn't know if they were right or wrong, just that it was all unnecessarily complicated. The fascists were anti-Semites, they hated Jews and were trying to spread their hate for us around the country. You didn't have to be a communist to deal with them.

JACOB would have meetings every week where we developed plans of action – less thuggish, less violent, more intellectual and more devious.

But JACOB wasn't formed to be a charitable organisation, so before long we found that we needed another means of bringing in money to support the fight. Our answer was to create the Group Relations Educational Trust (GRET), which was designed to be a kind of umbrella organisation to coordinate and fund the work we were doing on the ground. In the beginning, we ran up against a lot of suspicious people in government, in politics and in various areas like the police. But we had some heavyweight people on our side to help us. I arranged that Marcus Sieff would be chairman and his cousin Michael Sacher would lend his name to the group, too, which meant we could use M&S as a base. That gave us a lot of creditability with wealthy Jews in the Community. This wasn't Gerald Ronson asking for money – I was, shall we say, the chief executive of GRET – the invitations were coming from Lord Sieff and Michael Sacher, and no one was going to turn them down.

Marcus and Michael supported my efforts, and with their help we built Community involvement. We had to bring new people in and make them understand that this wasn't an extension of the 62 Group. We didn't want to be perceived as a bunch of Jewish hooligans. But as we grew, so did the threats we were facing. At the same time, GRET's activities were narrowly defined by its constitution. Under the bylaws of the Charity Commission, you have to be very careful how these groups use their money. GRET could fund certain activities but not others. And as the threat began to change, we realised that GRET was not set up to face that new and expanding threat, that something new was needed.

* * *

There was a time when aspects of the British class system were anti-Semitic, but in the last 20 years, with so many changes in our society, that's been watered down. The same goes for the City, where the influence of the Americans has been a big help. Before they arrived, there was the old-boy system coming out of some public schools. But that's been watered down, too, and many of the toffee-nosed companies that kept Jews out have been taken over by Americans or Europeans who are more interested in smart people to do the job than the right school tie.

So to some extent, society has changed. Even going back to the Guinness trial, where anti-Semitism was evident, that would not happen today. The viciousness of it was clear in articles published by the national newspapers referring to me as 'a Jewish immigrant's son' – which is not true – and 'a north-west London Jewish businessman'. Why? Because I was rich, self-made and non-Establishment. Because I didn't go to Eton or Harrow and hadn't grown up with public-school politicians. Because I didn't own a newspaper, which meant I didn't have any media protection. Because I had a high-profile image as a Jew. I'm not saying anti-Semitism was the number-one motivator, but put all those things together and you can understand why I was an easy target.

Yes, things have moved on, but we still have plenty of nastiness in our society. Anti-Semitism is called 'the longest hatred' for good reason, and in recent years it has again been stirred up by global events, fears and uncertainties. Anti-Semitic incident levels in the UK are approximately twice as bad now as in the 1990s. In Britain, and in Jewish communities around the world, racist and political violence sees Jews bearing the brunt of hatred over events for which they bear no responsibility, such as Middle East violence or the 9/11 terror attacks.

Since the atrocities in New York and in London, we have all been keenly aware of the threat of terrorism. Those of us who travel, or who work in locations such as the City and Canary Wharf, face a heightened risk. The worst scenario is a large-scale terrorist attack against a Jewish community, mirroring Hezbollah's attack in 1994 against the Jewish Community Centre in Buenos Aires. Or an attack against any Israeli-related target. Since 2001, pro al-Qaeda groups around the world have repeatedly attempted such attacks. While most of them have been foiled by police and security services, they have caused severe loss of life in Istanbul, Kenya, Morocco and Tunisia.

Anti-Semitic rhetoric has changed to fit modern sensibilities, with the word 'Zionist' having largely replaced the word 'Jew' in extremist propaganda. But the objectives remain the same – the desecration of Jewish cemeteries and synagogues and the abuse of Jews in the streets and in their homes. Anti-Semitism is also a social indicator, an early warning sign of tension, extremism and division within our society, and that affects everyone, non-Jews included. The universal lesson of anti-Semitism is clear – it starts against Jews but never ends there.

The problem is further complicated because the left, which used to be supportive of Israel in the early days, now sees Israel as the aggressor and has become pro-Palestinian, which in turn has become pro-Islamic and in many ways is looking to justify Islamic fundamentalism. The extreme right has always been anti-Semitic, but somewhere in between there is latent anti-Semitism, which you find in places you least expect it, such as people you have grown to like and respect. Almost out of the blue you hear them say things like, that's the Jews' fault, because if you didn't have Israel, we wouldn't be paying unbelievable prices for a barrel for oil, or losing soldiers in Iraq. Even though Iraq has nothing to do with Israel, it's easy to throw the Jews in the pot.

Most recently, and possibly most dangerous of all, there is the rise of Muslim fundamentalism being stuffed down people's throats in mosques and in schools.

Put that all together and it's not a very nice society we live in. What's worried me for a long time is that our children haven't been brought up to fight back. When I was growing up, if somebody called you a Jew bastard, you could intellectualise it to a point, but once you got past that point, you looked the arsehole in the eye, said, I'm not taking this crap from anyone, and bang. Today, we want all our children to be lawyers, doctors and bankers. Today, our children only talk the game.

Reading this, you may say, that Gerald Ronson is xenophobic. He wants to punch everybody's lights out. No, I'm not and no, I don't. But if there are people who want to destroy me and my society – and, by the way, most of them want to take down not just Jews but all Westerners – then we need to take them out of our society. We're not going to shoot them, because we don't do that – although these people would think nothing of cutting our throats – so we have to isolate them.

Before we can do that, we have to stand up to these people. We can't afford to turn the other cheek. Personally, I don't have a problem standing up to anyone, because I don't get intimidated. But young people today haven't had the same upbringing I did. Young people in our Community today are weak because they've been mollycoddled, spoilt by all the good things. But there comes a time when they have to put the greater cause before selfish indulgence. They can't hide, they can't pretend to look away, they must never think that, maybe, it will all get better tomorrow.

* * *

As the threat grew, developing beyond local fascist groups to include the rise in global Muslim fundamentalism, those of us in the Community who were leading this fight realised that we needed wider charitable rights to do our work, especially as we were getting involved in political areas. So in 1994, with the help of the police, certain politicians and eminent people in the country, we set up the Community Security Trust (CST), which enables us to really have much broader activities and which receives charitable status.

This is a national organisation today, working with the authorities up and down the country, and held up as an example to every other community around the world as to how a community security organisation should be. With offices in London, Manchester, Liverpool, Leeds and Glasgow, CST is cross-communal, which means we don't have any issues whether you're half-Jewish, fully Jewish, Orthodox, not Orthodox. None of that matters to us.

We cover the whole gambit of security within the Community, including physical security. We run 'streetwise' programmes for 8,000 young people each year to help make them more aware and more secure. We want them to be able to defend themselves, and need them to manage and protect buildings and be capable of dealing with difficult situations. We teach martial arts, boxing and other self-defence skills. We also teach discipline, because when you have over 3,000 volunteers in an organisation, you need structure and discipline. CST looks after more than 1,000 events each year, in addition to protecting 600 synagogues, schools, meeting places and other buildings throughout the country. At the same time, we are active in media relations, as well as community relations. That means we work with the authorities and other ethnic-minority communities, including the Hindu and Sikh communities, and Catholics and Protestants. We also try to build bridges with the Muslim community. We work with anyone and everyone who shares our beliefs, whether they're from the left, the right or the centre of politics, think tanks, journalists, students and moderate British Muslims. Today, thanks to CST, our allies outnumber our enemies.

CST employs 55 full-time professional staff, a big difference from the groups I was involved with 50 years ago. But some of the dangerous people we dealt with then are still around today, except they're smarter and spend a lot of effort pretending not to be dangerous, like the British National Party (BNP). They go under the guise of we love Jews, we love everybody. And instead of openly targeting Jews, they point fingers at Muslims. They're still extreme right wing and the same as they have always been, but they preach hate with the ballot box and that makes them more dangerous than ever.

Every good organisation requires information – if you don't have information you can't stop a situation before it becomes a situation – so CST monitors the activities of the organisations that wish to harm us. We see the biggest threat today coming from the fundamentalists who have openly stated that they intend to destroy our values. And when I say 'our' values, I'm talking about all our values, anybody's values that aren't their values. So we work with the authorities to identify these people and these groups and to track their activities. We call it 'monitoring'. We're not MI5 or MI6. We're not spooks. And we don't indulge in anything that is unlawful. But it is quite amazing how much you can learn if you have people gathering information and monitoring activities, especially with the Internet.

To do that effectively, however, you need people who have been doing it for years, and you need an infrastructure. You can't rely on some clerk who starts work on Monday morning to know what he's looking at or what he should be looking for. We have people who have been doing this work for more than 20 years. They know the names of the people they're looking at, they know the places where these people gather, they know the telltale signs of imminent danger. It's like everything in life – if you've been working at something for 20 years and you know your business, then you know your business.

I must stress very strongly that we do not do things which are in any way illegal. We work 100 per cent within the law. But we have a lot of friends in the media, with the authorities, in government and in opposition. We form and maintain relationships with all the players in the same field and CST makes no secret of the fact that we actively work with everyone we need to, from the Commissioner of the Metropolitan Police – in fact, with police forces across the UK – to the various anti-terrorism units, Interpol and even the FBI.

Forty years ago, we couldn't count on a lot of political support to help us. The Conservatives, for example, were not very friendly towards the Jewish community and some of us felt they were verging on being anti-Semitic. Mrs Thatcher changed that. She was a strong supporter of the Jewish community and things have become better. But anti-Semitism never goes away and, it needs to be said, there are still a few people in the party who seem unsympathetic.

In 2003, after the Archbishop of Canterbury, George Carey, retired from the Church and entered the House of Lords as Lord Carey, he invited two old friends of his to walk him into the House for the ceremony. One of them was my old friend Baron Janner of Braunstone.

Greville Janner is a wonderful man who served as president of the Board of Deputies of British Jews, is founder and president of the Commonwealth Jewish Council, chairman of the Holocaust Educational Trust and the Inter-Parliamentary Council Against Anti-Semitism and a vice president of the World Jewish Congress. He has spent his life trying to better relations between the world's religions, and it was fitting that Lord Carey should ask Greville to walk with him.

But Greville told me that after the ceremony someone from the Tory benches repeated to him a conversation she'd overheard between two members sitting behind her. One of the peers asked, 'Who's that walking with our archbishop?' and the other answered, 'Just some Jew.'

Today, David Cameron has followed Mrs T's example. He is outspoken in the fight against anti-Semitism and racism, and he was guest speaker at a couple of major dinners we held for CST in 2007. I get on with him well and think he's a good man. I got on with William Hague, didn't know Iain Duncan Smith well, never had time for Michael Howard and was not impressed with John Major. I found him too much of a grey-suited-committee type and not a leader.

Understandably, most of the political support we've received over the years has come from those Labour politicians with large Jewish constituencies. And we've had a close working relationship with the Labour government since 1997.

The first time I met Tony Blair was at a private dinner party at a friend's house. He was already Prime Minister, and there were only ten of us sitting round the table. Gail was on his right and I was on his left. He spent the whole evening telling Gail, who was absorbed by this, that he had followed the Guinness trial and that he felt it was very unfair and should never have happened. He didn't have any reason to say it and she couldn't get over it.

I like Gordon Brown because I find him a sincere man who has always been supportive of our Community and a good friend to Israel. To me, that's important. He's a committed family man of the highest values who puts the fight against anti-Semitism at the top of his list. And I'm proud that he and Tony Blair have both been guest speakers at our annual CST dinners.

Those are evenings where 1,200 members of the Community sit down with numerous MPs, senior police officers, civil servants and faith leaders from other communities to hear about issues facing the Jewish community and the response from government. In addition, I have been able to welcome David Blunkett, John Reid and Charles Clarke when they were Home Secretary as guest speakers at CST dinners.

My staff at CST works closely with all three main political parties, ensuring that they understand the issues and concerns that we as British Jews face today in the twenty-first century. And whilst I have no political bias, it's important for me to ensure that CST has a close relationship with the government of the day and also with the opposition. So I have given the Conservative Party the benefit of the doubt and we spend time working with them, too. David Cameron, for instance, was the guest speaker at CST's Manchester dinner in 2006 and again at CST's London dinner in 2008.

At the same time, we have forged strong working relationships with the police. I first met Lord John Stevens, who was head of the Metropolitan Police, through CST and he has been a friend of mine ever since. He's a real man's man, a quality person who has never hesitated when it comes to fighting anti-Semitism. When he left the police, he became a special adviser to both David Cameron and Gordon Brown on terrorist and security matters, and he is still close to CST.

How far we've come in 40 years.

* * *

In many ways, what we're doing with CST in Britain is unique. We only focus on what we have to do in the UK. We don't get involved in anything outside of the UK. At times, we've been asked to look further afield, but we always refuse. Our mission is to do what we think is right for the British Jewish community. I chair the committee that decides what is right for the Community in the UK. Shutters down on all four sides, we don't let anybody interfere.

You don't find anything like CST anywhere else in the world. There are some organisations in other countries in Europe that have the same aims as CST. Although the only other country in Europe where there are a lot of Jews is France. In fact, there are twice as many Jews there as in Britain. But in the French Jewish community there are different factions. There is an organisation in southern France which is independent from the group in Paris. And neither is anywhere near as organised as CST. That's not to say that there shouldn't be a similar organisation in New York, Chicago, LA, to name a few places where there are large Jewish populations. The thing is, it takes years to build and years for the people who manage it to gain the experience. You can't just employ an ex-policeman to set it up. You need people who are integrated, who have been doing it for a long time, who know the potential enemies, who have gained the respect of the police force and different agencies.

On paper, it starts off looking very simple, but it turns out to be very complicated, because you need the depth of infrastructure and have to grow the organisation. If you take England, there's only 250,000 Jews and another 100,000 who are not affiliated. If you look at New York, there are, what, almost two million Jews? Just to set up in New York you might need an organisation almost ten times the size of CST. You need to fund-raise for it – CST costs a lot of money to run – and you need to recruit top people.

The model is there for everyone to see and while the Jewish community in America relies heavily on the police and the state, and while the laws of each state are different – in America they also have armed private security, which we don't in Britain – the New York Jewish community did come to us to ask our advice. They have taken it on board to establish the Secure Community Network, managed by the American Jewish Congress, the Anti-

Defamation League, UJA Federation of New York and the Conference of Presidents – all powerful organisations in their own right.

At CST, we have a budget of £6 million a year, and that will grow over the next five years. I'm hoping that in the years to come we can increase that budget to as much as £10 million a year. After all, it costs a lot of money to support so many different activities and to hire the right people. CST may look like some form of Jewish civil service, but you get what you pay for. I chair CST and want the best people working for us, which means we pay a first-class salary. If a guy was working in the private sector for £100,000 a year, he shouldn't have to work at CST for £40,000 a year. I want the best people doing the job for the Community, because the Community depends on it. And I feel the team at CST are first-class people. They've grown up with the organisation.

They know that I was once a foot soldier out there fighting on the front lines, and that's why I believe the organisation must be fit and tough and that the troops need to be focused. They know that I'm right when I preach that everybody needs to know what they're doing, understand their position and be totally committed.

Yes, I lead from the front, but I think of myself as a team player, because I listen to people. After that, I make up my own mind. Some people involved with CST see me as a bit dictatorial – and because there is so much at stake, maybe I can be – but the Community trusts me. I've been doing this job for a long time. And I've put in place a very competent team of executives, both professional and communal, which is why CST works well. I leave them to get on with what they have to do. If it ain't broke, I don't fix it.

We publicise the fight against anti-Semitism and try to keep the battle on the front pages. We also publish information on our website to keep the public informed. If we come across something the authorities need to know about, we tell them. If we see criminal activity, we alert the police and let them handle it, because that's their job. Not long ago, some information we supplied to the authorities led directly to arrests and prison sentences for some people for up to nine years. If we come across something that needs to be handled in a civil action, we may take care of it in several ways. We may not do it in our name, but we may directly or indirectly finance an action. The important thing is to get the job done, not to put CST on the front pages. There is no ego trip. With most things we do, CST's name isn't there. CST has a finger in a lot of pies, but we keep as low a profile as possible.

CST makes no charge for any of the services it provides. All our funding comes from voluntary donations. I suppose I'm responsible for raising 50 per cent of the money we need. But I'm not about raising £100 or £500. I want £5,000 or £10,000 or £25,000. To get that kind of money from people, you need to have a personal relationship with them. It doesn't fall out the sky. I ring them, take them to lunch and remind them of how important CST's work is. We have fund-raising dinners and when I ring certain people to invite them, they know that I'm going to hit them for money. Maybe they say to me, I don't want to go to a dinner, Gerald, I've been to enough bloody dinners, but they know why I'm phoning and they don't say no to sending a cheque.

You have to put the effort in. If you have the relationship, if you put your energy, time and effort into it, you get ten times more done than if you delegate to an employee of the organisation.

It goes without saying that I spend a lot of time working for CST. I probably dedicate ten hours a week just to CST matters – the structure, the relationships and the funding of the organisation. I'm the executive chairman so decisions don't just get made, they have to be discussed. I'm in constant touch with the chief executive, Richard Benson, who's an extremely capable man. My door is open to anyone involved with CST, which means many people come to discuss different things with me, because CST is not just young people standing outside a synagogue for protection with a radio plug in their ear.

I don't regard CST as a charity, I think of it as a commitment. This is the organisation I spend the most time on outside of my business. It is the organisation I feel most strongly responsible for. To me, it is equally as important as Heron, but in a different way. Where Heron is synonymous in business with Gerald Ronson, this is security and protection of a community by people who are fighting evil.

Once a street fighter, always a street fighter. And I am as proud of CST as I am of Heron.

CHAPTER 18

....

CASH IS KING

Every year, when we release our annual report, we hold a luncheon that has become, I am proud to say, the most important annual luncheon in the UK property business.

I started hosting the event back in the 1970s. The first one, we invited 40 people to the penthouse suite at the Carlton Towers Hotel. As the event grew, we moved it to the Grand Ballroom at the Savoy Hotel. We stayed there for 25 years, until they began a major refurbishment and we had to find someplace else. We tried the Dorchester and, for whatever reason, people seem to prefer that venue. Today we get 450 for lunch.

Of course, it's a PR exercise for Heron, a place where we can announce our annual results and say thank you to the people we've worked with over the past year. But it's also an opportunity for me to see many people I don't get to see on a regular basis. At that first luncheon, we invited only one banker, the man who oversaw our account at Barclays. Today's luncheons are filled with bankers and financial people, in addition to industrialists and property people. We also invite the people I deal with in my charity work, politicians and some people from the media. Relatively speaking, it's not an expensive thing to do. But given the calibre of people who come to the luncheon, we definitely get our money's worth. Of course, we could always do what other companies do and host a cocktail party. But when you have 1,000 people standing around drinking for an hour or two, you can't speak to everyone. This is a much better way for everybody in the room to network.

Throughout the Guinness affair, we continued with the luncheon. I was determined that for Heron, for my charities and especially for me, it would be business as usual. Fortunately, the six months I was away at Ford fell right in between two of the luncheons, so we didn't miss any.

The first luncheon after I came out, in spring 1991, might have been a bit awkward for some people. I could sense that. But other people made it their business to be there. When I stood up to speak, I didn't quite say, I'm back, fellas, it's good to see you, but everybody knew that was what I meant.

Anyone who was invited and didn't come wasn't invited again. I personally looked very carefully at every RSVP card that came back saying, sorry, I'm unavailable, and I didn't just think, oh, well, too bad, because it doesn't work like that. I have a memory like an elephant. I remember the people who have been supportive to Heron and to me, not only during the Guinness affair and after Ford, but later when we did the restructuring of the company. We support the people who have supported us.

At the same time, there were people we didn't invite because not everybody loved us. There were some people who made a lot of money beforehand and didn't feel so friendly afterwards. There were some people who said some unpleasant things about us. And those people weren't invited then and have never been invited since.

As long as I am in business, I will always remember the people who were loyal to us and the people who weren't. The ones who weren't have been cut off. Some of them are today very important people. But I don't want to know. I don't need them. I'm not looking to make new friends or to forgive people who have not been my friends. That's the sort of man I am. Loyalty matters.

* * *

A year later, for the spring 1992 luncheon, when I stood up to give my speech, most of the people in the room knew we were fighting to restructure Heron, and not all of them were sure we could do it. The economy was in freefall and the property market was in the toilet.

I looked at the people in the room and said that what we all needed to do was 'stay alive till '95 and go to heaven in '97'.

What I was reminding them was that bad markets run in cycles and that it would turn good again. The trick was surviving until it did, and it did in 1995. We then had ten very good years. It was so good that I started to believe that maybe 90 per cent of all public companies were overvalued and even suggested that they should sell their assets off and give the profits back to the shareholders. I was saying that they should turn what they owned into cash.

By 2005 or so, I could see that too many people in the business believed that only bad markets run in cycles. They were acting as if the good market would never end. So I used the next few luncheons to warn my guests that the market had gone too far and that the writing was on the wall.

At our luncheon in 2007, I warned that we had seen extraordinary levels of liquidity wash over the world's asset markets. There had been remarkable flows of capital and yields had fallen to a level not seen in over two decades. A big part of the story at that point was hedge funds and property funds. It seemed that just about everybody was starting one. I met a lot of those people and, frankly, I wouldn't have hired some of those start-up fund managers to do my shopping at Tesco's.

Yet they were in charge of massive sums of investors' money. These were fund managers who knew one direction – up. Their analysis and management skills were poor. All they'd ever known was the bull market. Given that, there could only be one ending. I said at that luncheon that we would one day look back and say that the signs were obvious. Sadly, for the new kids on the block my words were written in invisible ink.

By the 2008 luncheon, anyone who had believed that property was a fast track to riches was learning some very harsh lessons. I said, 'We are currently sailing in a force 9 storm in the middle of the Atlantic, but we all know that ultimately storms subside, and it is those of us with sound foundations and long-term vision who will survive the storm and come out stronger and wiser the other side.'

I'd been through three recessions in my lifetime, so I felt that I knew what I was talking about. Of course, I had no way of knowing that in October 2008 the entire world economy would sink in that storm and we would be faced with the worst global economic crisis since the Great Depression. The cheap, cheap money era was over. The era of borrowing 100 per cent or 95 per cent from banks was dead and buried. For many people, there was going to be a lot of pain.

At Heron's 2009 luncheon, with the world in the midst of an economic crisis the likes of which we hadn't seen since 1929, I called for a return to the basics. 'Good old-fashioned property investment values, where proper equity is put in. Back to deals showing positive cash flow and to conservative leverage.'

I said that quality, well-run businesses with experienced managers will survive even the toughest of environments. But I warned, 'You can't push a bus uphill if the brake is on. Property is a long-term business and that has never been more true than today.'

I said that what we need now is 'to return to a work ethic of honesty, integrity and leadership. Leading from the front is what it takes.'

For Heron, the difference between pre-crash and post-crash is that I'd learned to prepare for the worst. The market was substantially overheated, banks were lending money to people without doing what I would call 'serious' due diligence, so we at Heron began selling into that market and building up our hard-cash reserves. When the crisis came that autumn, we were sitting on something north of £200 million.

Sure, when the sun is shining everyone thinks of property as the golden egg. But you just had to look at the market in 2006 and 2007 to see that there was no way, even with the big merry-go-round of cheap money, you could make deals work. When developers came to the banks looking for cheap money, the bankers should have been asking, how much are you putting into the deal? They shouldn't have been lending more than 75 per cent of the actual cost. But all their discipline went out the window. They were rushing to get the money out so they could claim their big bonuses. It was greed, greed, greed.

On top of that, you had all those property funds coming into the marketplace. Now, anyone can set up a fund if you speak nicely to people and say please and thank you. Whether you were raising money from foreigners or institutions, the first thing you had to do was make sure to get your 20 per cent promote up front. Very nice business if you can get it. Then draw yourself a nice salary of £500,000 or £750,000. That was how the game was played. Except that now, all those funds have to be given mouth-to-mouth resuscitation because they're 25 per cent under water. Naturally, the managers of the funds are still getting paid their money, or they've taken big bonuses fast and got out so they're still smiling even if they're unemployed.

There's a price to pay for that kind of thinking. And if the bankers and developers and fund managers had bothered to look back to recent history, they would have known what it was going to cost them. Property is a long-term proposition, so you need cash flow coming off of the property to keep your head above water. That means that during the good times you can't afford to be in denial. You have to understand that one day the market will turn against you. Therefore, if you put money in the bank when you have it, you should be OK. If not, if you think you can walk on water, if you overreach yourself, then you only have yourself to blame for winding up in bad financial shape.

In 1991, when Heron was hanging over the edge of the cliff, what I realised was that for every £10 we made, we needed to put 50p or £1 in the biscuit tin.

Which gets me back to my unshakeable belief that cash is king.

There's a cushion that sits on one of the couches in my office that has that embroidered across the front of it. Everybody who comes into my office notices it, but I'm not sure how many people believe it. I'm afraid it's one of those lessons people learn the hard way. In fact, most people don't normally learn this lesson until they're in their 50s. That's when they wake up and say to themselves, I don't want to be here when I'm 65 or 70. That's when they understand that, after working all their life, the last thing they want is to be walking the streets with no soles on their shoes. That's when they understand that you can lose in life.

A little bit of reserve in your back pocket, maybe 10 to 15 per cent of your earnings, can be enough. My advice is put it in the bank. Don't buy shares, just leave it in the bank, where it might earn 4 per cent or 5 per cent, it doesn't make any difference. What you're doing is buying security so that if it all went bang tomorrow, you'd have enough money to live well with your family for the rest of your life.

That's how I look at life. It doesn't mean other people look at it the same way. Some people have a lot more reserve, others have less. Think of it like driving a car on a motorway. You don't wait until the gauge is down and the red light comes on to say the tank is empty.

* * *

It's by doing that you gain experience. In my lifetime, I've been in, most probably, 20 different businesses. But the only businesses I'm in today are the ones I understand – property investment and development. I'm not a financial engineer, so I'm talking about purist investment, not financial engineering. Yes, I understand money and I understand running petrol stations. Do I need to do any more than that at my age? The answer is no. That's why I'm not into owning a software division or a football club. I'm not in any ego business and I'm not in any high-tech business. I'm not interested in any business I don't understand and I'm not interested in the ego bit. I am a detail person. I'm hands-on. I want to know what's going on. I may be criticised as a control freak – control, yes, freak, no – but I recognise what my strengths are.

When I hire someone to work for me, I expect them to play to their strengths as well. We try to find out what those strengths are and do it in a fairly unique way. For the past 20 years or so, whenever we hire senior people, we use a graphologist named Anna Koren to analyse their handwriting. It's amazing what she can tell about someone after they scribble four lines with a ballpoint pen. She comes back to us with a six-page report detailing everything from high blood pressure to emotional issues. Don't ask me how. It's an art form.

But it's not foolproof, because not everybody knows what their strengths are, and some people pretend to be strong in certain areas to cover up for the fact that they're really weak. The problem is that sometimes you don't know the truth until it's too late.

Yes, the people you pay not to make mistakes can make mistakes. That's only human. But when a mistake happens, and people who are being paid a lot of money to get a job done simply shrug their shoulders and say, oh well, I get very angry. Do they mean by, oh well, that it's not a problem because it's not their money? Except it is a problem, because it's my money, my company's money, my shareholders' money.

It's unbelievable. I would be very embarrassed if something went wrong in a company that I'm responsible for. The buck stops on my desk. I could never look at my shareholders and say, oh, well, it wasn't me who made this mistake that's cost us X-million pounds.

Unfortunately, that's the nature of so much business these days. Look at the excuses of the CEOs in the City and on Wall Street whose huge financial institutions have suddenly gone broke, greedy and sometimes dishonest idiots who have lost £10 billion in some financial services company. Their business takes a dive and their shareholders lose fortunes, and nobody throws them out. It's not us, they say, it's the economy. Or if they do leave, they walk away with a huge golden handshake, a reward for losing so much money. It wasn't my fault, everybody else lost money too, we tried to lose less.

Come on. When you get professional managers who say, everybody else is losing money too, you have to say to yourself, what's going on in the world? You have to say to yourself, didn't these fucking morons know what they were doing? Fortunately, I've got it right for the last few years and if I'd have got it wrong, I might be having a different conversation! But, I mean, if that was me, God forbid, I don't know what I would do. Probably shoot myself.

There's a good North Country expression, 'There's nowt so queer as folk.'

In business, when you don't see the wood for the trees, you fail.

* * *

I am, sometimes, referred to in the property business as a 'guru' – and a few other names besides – but I don't have a crystal ball, I can't see into the future and maybe the only reason people refer to me that way is because I've been around a lot longer than most other people in this business. Because experience counts, I am always being asked by friends, and friends of friends, to speak to their sons and daughters who might be thinking about going into the property business. I'm always willing to mentor young people, to talk to them and give them my advice, because I think that's important, but it never ceases to amaze me how often they don't want to hear the truth.

I probably get one young person a week coming into the office. I explain how I started in business and almost right away I see their eyes turning around in their heads because they don't believe me when I say I was 14½ years of age. For them, it sounds a little bit like running away and joining the Foreign Legion. Then I ask them why they want to get into property – you know, what interests you? – and almost all of them tell me what interests them is making a zillion pounds by the time they're 25. Of course, that's not going to happen, and they don't especially like it when I tell them it's not going to happen. Those get-rich-quick days are gone. The world has changed and so has the property business.

I tell them it's very different today than it used to be and if all you want is to make money, go work for an estate agent. Learn that side of the business, specialise in a specific area, understand the values and understand what it costs to improve a property because, if the market is there, you can make money buying old houses and doing them up. At least, that used to work until that market dried up. House prices and building costs went through the roof and buying to let became a non-game. Some day it will come back, because that's what markets do, but no one knows when.

So I take them through that scenario, which tends to bore a lot of them because they want to jump right in, buy something, fix it up, turn it over and put all that money in their pocket. It doesn't dawn on them that they don't know what they're doing, won't know what they're buying and probably don't have the money for it anyway.

Then there are those who want to do bigger schemes. I tell them, go to work for one of the major agents to see if it's the development side of the business that really interests you or if it's the commercial side. I even try to point them in the direction of where to apply. A few years later, one or two of these young people might stop by to say they took my advice and want me to know that they've done well. I like that. But most of them who come in for advice, I never see or hear from again.

Most of them are three-quarters bright, but they confuse working hard in the property business with making easy money in investment banking. They've read about people in the City getting £1 million, £2 million, £5 million a year and that's what they want. I understand how young people can want that. I just don't necessarily take them too seriously, because you say one thing at 18 or 22 and wind up thinking very differently at 30. What they don't understand when they're just starting out is how money, greed, is the wrong motivation.

It's very hard for younger people today to know what direction they should be taking. I tell them that I don't have the answers and that I can't give them a road map that says do this, this and this and you will succeed. But what I say to help get them going in the right direction is that if you learn your business, if you know your business, if you work hard at it, if you have a passion for it and if you really want to succeed, then sooner or later your persistence will pay off. How much money you'll make, nobody knows. But if you're passionate about what you do, then what you're doing is not about money.

I also tell them that development is a supply and demand business. Where you had oversupply in many sectors in 2008, that's going to take three or four years to absorb before demand takes over again. By then, building costs will have gone up and who knows what the pound will be worth against other currencies, which changes the cost of materials. So you're fighting inflation. My bet is that the next wave of development will most probably have to be done with pre-let properties, because the banks won't lend the money and costs will be too expensive. So looking out from 2009–10, there could be five years of misery.

That's why when young men and women who thought they wanted to go into the property business came to see me in 2008, I told them, you may want to do something else and look at property again in 2015. That would give them the time to become a lawyer, to understand property law, to understand tax, to understand accountancy and maybe go to work for an estate agent and become a professional manager.

I painted a very bleak picture. And some of them were smart enough to believe me. But most of them didn't. I could see their eyes glazing over because my version of the real world didn't match their version of some romanticised world.

It doesn't matter to me how well educated they are – Oxford, Cambridge, Harvard – I want to see passion, I want to see what drives them, I want to see the spark that gets them up at dawn every morning and keeps them working till late at night. Instead, with only a few exceptions, I see young people who don't want to make sacrifices or never thought they'd have to. But achieving success in business is no different to getting anything else in life. You have to focus your mind on what you want and then go after it. If you don't know what you're talking about or haven't done your homework properly, then you're not going to last long. If you're not prepared to take the pain, you're going to get knocked down and you won't get back up.

I warn them, if you step into the ring, you are going to get a black eye and a bloody nose and you are going to get knocked down, so be prepared for that because if you are going to stay in the ring, then you have to pick yourself up and you have to keep punching.

But they don't like hearing that.

And they especially don't like hearing me say, if you think you're going to make a million in five years, forget it.

EPILOGUE

Some people imagined that when I came out of prison, the world would look at me like a leper. They urged me to go and live abroad. They said, you've been badly dealt with by the system. It's so embarrassing. Why stay and have to face that music?

But there was no embarrassment. There was no music to face. We're a very strong family, so I had that backup, and I knew I could always make a living. I had money, we wouldn't starve, but then I don't live expensively. The plane and the boat went, because I don't believe in keeping up appearances. If you've lost money in business, you have to be prepared to eat humble pie and if that means the material things go, so be it. They can always be replaced.

I stayed and tried to rebuild my world and some of those same people now wanted to know, you're not broke – why are you trying to do it again?

It was as if they were challenging me. Did I think I was going to be as successful as I had been? Actually, I never thought I couldn't be. Maybe it's because I don't sit around counting my chips – how much money have I made today, how much money am I going to be able to make – I just get on with it.

A few others said, you're not a young man any more. It's not going to be as easy this time.

When I heard that, I thought back to a dinner I attended at No. 10 that Mrs Thatcher gave for Dr Armand Hammer and his wife.

Hammer was an American entrepreneur who had originally trained as a doctor. He stopped practising medicine right after medical school, but he loved being called Dr Hammer. He was CEO of the Occidental Petroleum Corporation, an art collector and a philanthropist. He lived and worked in Russia in the 1920s and because of that, during the Cold War, he was probably the only private American citizen who could talk directly to the Soviet leadership. Hammer sat next to Mrs T and I was close enough to watch him. He was slim and certainly didn't look his age, which was well past 85. His wife, who must have been in her early 80s, got on well with Gail, which didn't surprise me, because Gail gets on with everybody. So I sat there and watched him, and I always reflect back on that when people say to me, I don't know how you do it, or, why bother at your age? Hammer was a man who did so many fantastic things during his life – a lot of them he didn't even start to do until he was in his 60s – and here he was pushing 90, and he still had all his marbles and he was still in the ring.

Me too.

And it is very flattering when people outside my business recognise that. In 2009, Northumbria University awarded me an honorary doctorate of civil laws. Not bad for a kid who quit school at 14½.

When I leave home at seven in the morning and don't come back until eight thirty at night, I sometimes think for a man my age that isn't too clever. As you get older, you're supposed to slow down a bit. Well, I'm not slowing down. I'm working twice as hard as many people half my age.

Maybe people think I'm mad, but I look forward to going into my office every morning. When I was younger, I used to go out every night of the week and I don't do that any more. We don't go out on Friday nights and we try not to go out on Saturday nights, but most weeks Gail and I are out four nights because we have social, charity and business obligations. I admit that I do get a bit tired in the evenings. That's why, if we're going to see friends, I like to do that at Sunday lunchtime. I'm more alert. When I get tired I get irritable and I'm not the best of company, especially since I can't smoke a cigar wherever I want to, like after dinner with a glass of wine, which aggravates me.

I also get tired travelling, especially if it means sleeping in a strange bed. I don't sleep well in hotels, I keep waking up, and that catches up to me the next day. Some people I know nap in their office, but I can't do that because I need a proper bed to sleep in. I can't sleep in a chair. Maybe I could on a comfortable couch, but then I'd need a pillow. And then the phone is going to start ringing, and I can't stop the phone from ringing by telling people, don't call me, I'm sleeping.

Gail is always saying to me, 'Take the day off. What are you going to do this Saturday, going around to look at 12 petrol stations, that you couldn't do next Saturday? Is anything going to be any different?'

As it happens, Gail is perfectly right. But it's discipline and I'm very disciplined. That's how I am. Anyway, if I didn't enjoy it, I wouldn't be doing it.

I know that I can't go on forever, nothing lasts forever, but I'm not planning my retirement. What would I do? I can't go sit on a beach somewhere or play golf forever. That's not me. I think once you retire you switch off, and you are switched off because you're no longer in the ring, you're a spectator. I enjoy being in the ring. Do I still think I am capable in doing what I'm doing? Yes. Do I still have that passion, do I still have that drive, that motivation and desire to double and treble the size of Heron? The answer is yes, I do. My life is what my life is, so I won't retire.

Gail likes to tell me, 'Your problem is that you peaked too early.' Frankly, I'd like to think that I haven't peaked yet. I certainly haven't lost any zest for business. I definitely have a lot of steam left in me. The only thing is that now I don't want to be adventurous. My life is simple and I want to keep it that way. I don't want to go through any more learning curves. Ten years from now, I may not still be doing the day-to-day chief executive's job, but I plan on doing something until they put me in a box.

Of course, I think about the future of Heron. Lisa won't take over from me because that isn't what Lisa wants to do. And that's not what I would like Lisa to do. She does an excellent job as marketing director, but her responsibility, long term, will be to manage the family office. I have put very good men in place to look after Heron and know that the business will be in good hands. I'm not staying around just in case, I'm staying around because I want to. I could leave today and do anything I want, but what I want is to keep on doing what I'm doing.

I can't think of anything that I haven't done that I'd like to do. If there was something, I'd do it. I am wealthy enough to afford everything that I want, which is not the same as saying I can afford everything in the world, but then, I think I already have everything I want. I'm not interested in impressing people. I have nothing to prove to anyone. I'm not saying this to be arrogant or boastful, but there are very few people who have been through what I've been through and come out the other side with their reputation intact. Did I survive because I'm tough? In a lot of people's eyes, yes. I believe in respect, power, position. But you have to earn these things. You may be worth £1 billion and live in the biggest house and drive the biggest car and throw your weight around, and, sure, people will be nice to you because they want your money, but that doesn't mean they respect you.

There's no denying that I have made mistakes in my life. But everybody makes mistakes. I believed in certain people I should never have believed in. I got involved with things that weren't my business. Some people still say that the mistakes I made were driven by greed, but that's just not true, because there was no personal gain. Maybe, because of the excitement of the game, I didn't see that the people I was dealing with were dishonest. But that's life. I don't linger on mistakes, I learn from them.

At the same time, the Good Lord looked after me and gave me the strength to come through those mistakes. He gave my family the strength to come through them, too. Nobody should be so arrogant as to think they're some sort of genius and did it all by themselves. It's the Good Lord who blesses us with ability. And as the Good Lord has given me the ability to make money, there isn't anything I can't find time to do if I believe it needs to be done to help my Community as well as the wider community, to give back to good causes, to help the underprivileged. That's the responsibility that comes along with his blessings.

But when I look back on my life, I know that my greatest blessings are my wife, my four daughters and my six grandchildren. Family gives me my stability. So many good things have happened to me that they far outweigh the bad things. Having my family makes me understand, every day, how lucky I am. And I wouldn't mind being remembered as someone who was very grateful for having been so lucky.

That may sound simplistic, but I really do think of myself as a simple man.

Then again, if someone a long time from now looks at Heron Tower and says, Gerald Ronson built this, that would please me. I don't see myself as artistic, but I suppose I must have some sort of artistic streak to be able to create what I've created. And I wouldn't mind being remembered as a builder, a property man who created iconic buildings.

If someone a long time from now makes a success out of his or her life and says, Gerald Ronson helped me when I needed help, that would please me too.

If someone a long time from now happens to mention my name, I'd like it a lot if they said, he was a good man. And I wouldn't argue if they also said, with Gerald Ronson, what you saw was what you got.

INDEX

267